JOYCE KILMER'S
ANTHOLOGY OF
CATHOLIC POETS

Joyce Kilmer's
ANTHOLOGY OF
Catholic
Poets

With a New Supplement by

JAMES EDWARD TOBIN

Liveright Publishing Corporation

NEW YORK

Library of Congress Catalog Card No. 55=6322

ABOUT THE EDITORS:

JOYCE KILMER (1886–1918), born in New Brunswick, N. J., educated at Rutgers and Columbia Universities, was in turn teacher of Latin at Morristown High School, editor of a trade journal, book salesman, free-lance journalist, writer of articles for *Harper's Magazine* and the New York *Times,* poetry editor of the *Literary Digest,* and soldier. He enlisted a few days after the outbreak of World War I, went to France as a sergeant with the Rainbow Division, and was killed in action in the Battle of the Marne. Thus, in his thirty-first year, he ended a career which had gained friends and followers across the country through his criticism and lectures, and especially through his poetry volumes: *Summer of Love, Trees,* and *Main Street.* He also edited a selection of Hilaire Belloc's verse, and the present collection of Catholic poets, under the title *Dreams and Images;* several essays appeared in *The Circus;* his complete poetry and prose were later issued with a warm and illuminating memoir by Robert Cortes Holliday.

JAMES EDWARD TOBIN, a graduate of Boston College, has also studied at Harvard, Fordham, and New York Universities, and now teaches at Queens College, N. Y. He is a member of the Editorial Boards of the Catholic Book Club and of the Fathers of the Church and is a Director of the Catholic Poetry Society. His books include *The Happy Crusaders, Eighteenth Century English Literature, Ardent Marigolds,* an edition of Thomas F. Woodlock's *Thinking It Over,* and several textbooks and reading lists. His poems have appeared in *America,* Baltimore *Sun,* Boston *Transcript, Commonweal,* New York *Herald-Tribune, Spirit, Thought,* and in eight anthologies.

Introduction

This is not a collection of devotional poems. It is not an attempt to rival Orby Shipley's admirable *Carmina Mariana* or any other similar anthology. What I have tried to do is to bring together the poems in English that I like best that were written by Catholics since the middle of the Nineteenth Century. There are in this book poems religious in theme; there are also love-songs and war-songs. But I think that it may be called a book of Catholic poems. For a Catholic is not a Catholic only when he prays; he is a Catholic in all the thoughts and actions of his life. And when a Catholic attempts to reflect in words some of the Beauty of which as a poet he is conscious, he cannot be far from prayer and adoration.

The Church has never been without her great poets. And in the Nineteenth Century there was a splendid renascence of Catholic poetry written in English. It had already begun when Francis Thompson wrote his Essay on Shelley, in which he longed for the by-gone days when poetry was "the lesser sister and helpmate of the Church; the minister to the mind, as the Church to the soul." The members of the Pre-Raphaelite Brotherhood were not Catholics, but their movement was related to the renascence of Catholic poetry—it was an attempt to restore to art and letters some of the glory of the days before what is called the Reformation. Coventry Patmore carried the theories of the Pre-Raphaelite Brotherhood to their logical conclusion, as Newman did those of the Tractarians. Coventry Patmore became a Catholic, and found in his Faith his inspiration and his theme. And his disciple Francis Thompson, born to the Faith which Patmore reached by way of the divine adventure of conversion, with art even greater than that of his master, made of the language of Protestant England an instrument of Catholic adoration.

A few of the poets represented in this book were not yet Catholics when they wrote the poems I have quoted. But I do not think that anyone will find fault with me for including Newman and Hawker among the Catholic poets. I am very sorry that the limitations of space have made me exclude many poems dear to me, many poems that are part of the world's literary heritage. There should be many Catholic anthologies.

The poet sees things hidden from other men, but he sees them only in dreams. A poet is (by the very origin of the word) a maker, but a maker of images, not a creator of life. This is a book of reflections of the Beauty which mortal eyes can see only in reflection, a book of dreams of that Truth which one day we shall waking understand. A book of images it is, too, containing representations carved by those who worked by the aid of memory, the strange memory of men living in Faith.

JOYCE KILMER

August, 1917
165th Regiment, Camp Mills,
Mineola, New York

Preface to the New Edition (1955)

When Joyce Kilmer published his anthology in 1917 he was something of a discoverer, a pioneer. England could look back on several names; Ireland had lost too many young voices in 1916; America could count few Catholic poets beyond Louise Imogen Guiney, Maurice Francis Egan, T. A. Daly, and Fr. Charles L. O'Donnell. If any one figure caused conversation, set a stage, blew on a pile of green twigs to start a fire, it was Kilmer. His poems, his essays, even the dramatic brevity of his career all had their effect. Most of all, it was his enthusiasm. He was memorized and memorialized; literary societies borrowed his name; the torch he held up in a once almost empty room flared brightly and boldly. More and more came to fill the halls, to coal other hearths.

Because he had been enthusiastic, people read the writers he championed; because his poems were successful and appealing, many came to write poems and more came to read them. There were, of course, other factors. For one thing, a score of Catholic magazines have willingly and eagerly fostered poetry during the past forty years. Two in particular have maintained exceptionally high standards: *America* and *Commonweal*. Also in this period the Catholic Poetry Society of America was born, whose own magazine devoted exclusively to the interests of poetry, *Spirit*, has offered a continuingly effective medium to exciting creations. Further, a tradition of reading has been brought to larger numbers because two more generations of formally educated Catholics have come to recognize the cultural advantages which can be theirs and which were not at hand for many of their less financially fortunate elders in the first part of the century. Whatever the single cause—if there is one—poetry has flourished. More than 75 of the poets in the present *Supplement* have published individual volumes and 30 can boast of more than one.

When Joyce Kilmer looked at the pile of poems he had to forego for lack of space (a painful task which disturbs all anthologists, including the present one), he sighed with honest regret. He even added: "There should be many Catholic anthologies." And since his day there have been: gatherings of contemporaries by William A. Braithwaite and Maurice Leahy; campus compilations from Boston College, Fordham, Georgetown, Marquette, Marywood, Mundelein, Notre Dame, St. Joseph's, Brooklyn (and there must have been others); and, particularly, Theodore Maynard's *Modern Catholic Verse,* Fr. Francis X. Talbot's *America Book of Verse,* and the three anthologies of the Catholic Poetry Society: *From the Four*

Winds, Drink from the Rock, and *From One Word.* All have served to do more than introduce new names.

The present volume brings together old names and new. No omissions from or additions to Kilmer's original selections have been made in reprinting the first unit; here are his friends and favorites as he noted them in 1917. In 1926 and again in 1937, supplements were added by the late Shaemas O'Sheel; these drew on the work of 65 additional poets. From these two supplements certain poems by Joseph Campbell, Francis Carlin, James J. Daly, James L. Duff, Aline and Joyce Kilmer, Mary Kolars, Francis Ledwidge, and Sister M. Madeleva have been retained. The present *Supplement* contains 279 poems by 164 poets. Of Joyce Kilmer's poets, 56 were men (including 18 priests) and 30 were women (including 4 nuns); additions include 93 men (28 priests) and 71 women (42 nuns); in all, 175 Americans, 41 English, and 29 Irish poets.

While the number of readers has increased with the years, the variety of subject matter which has appealed to them and to their poets is the same as ever. The present-day poet who is a Catholic is as aware of the seasons and the out-of-doors, of people as individuals and as voices of idealism, of ambitions and desires, of courtship and marriage, of birth and death and eternity, of friendship and history and places, as any other. He can be aware of time, and comment on television, the seismograph, the hydrogen bomb as familiarly as on the north star, a coat of mail, or the catacombs. He is, quite naturally, concerned as often with things of the spirit—with God and His purposes and His friends. He thus finds timelessness more important than the now. Hence, there is little evidence in these pages of "modern" philosophical outlooks: no crudeness, blasphemy, corruption, cynicism, despair. The modern idiom is present, both in the tight analysis of ideas and the taut handling of emotions; yet there are also lines which are simple, or amusing, or homely, or commonplace—for there are as many kinds of readers as there are of poets.

Such a variety of readers, ever growing (in all senses), should individually find at least a dozen poems to suit their "taste"; perhaps even a second dozen; perhaps more. But, even if there are only a score of favorites for each reader, an audience has been served—served, not created; there is a difference between the generations of readers. Better yet, the audience can serve itself, can taste the delights set before it, may even be teased into wanting more of the company of the hosts who are gathered here, ready to sing their songs. If such is the result, then poetry will continue to mature, the adventure of reading will bring ever greater reward, and those who reflect upon what they have read will come to better appreciate both the maker of poems and the Maker of poets.

JAMES EDWARD TOBIN

Simons; Sr. Claude of Jesus, S.N.J.M.; Sr. M. Athanasius, B.V.M.; Sr. M. Catherine, O.S.U.; Sr. M. Catherine, S.C.; Sr. M. Estelle, O.P.; Sr. M. Gilbert; Sr. M. of the Visitation; Sr. M. Stephanie, O.M.; Sr. Rita Agnes; R. Sullivan; S. W. Taylor; Rev. G. Toelle, O. Carm.; Rev. J. P. Walsh, S.J.; and J. H. Wildman.

A. M. Sullivan, for "Seismograph" from *Stars and Atoms Have No Size,* published, 1946, by E. P. Dutton & Co., copyright transferred to author; and for other selections, from *Incident in Silver,* published by The Declan X. McMullen Company, Inc., copyright, 1950, by A. M. Sullivan.

Thought, Fordham University Quarterly, for "If Stones Can Dream" by Rev. D. Berrigan, S.J.; "Dostoievsky" by Rev. D. J. Honan; "Image Imagination" by E. Sewell; "This Sharpening Tension" by Sr. M. St. Virginia, B.V.M.; and "Conversation in Clichés" by J. E. Tobin.

Today, Chicago, Ill., for "Academy" by Sr. M. Jeremy, O.P.

A. P. Watt & Son, London, and Dorothy E. Collins, executrix of the Chesterton estate, for "Lepanto," and "Music," and "The Ballade of Suicide," from *The Collected Poems of G. K. Chesterton,* published by Methuen & Company, Ltd.; and for "The Grave of Arthur," published by Faber and Faber, Ltd.

Bond Wheelwright Company, for selection from *The Mystery of Hamlet* by Percy MacKaye.

And to the great number of poets and editors who so graciously facilitated the above selection.

ACKNOWLEDGMENTS For advice and assistance in collecting and arranging these poems, I am grateful to many friends, especially to Mr. T. R. Smith, Miss Caroline Giltinan and Mr. John Bunker. The publishers, editors and authors who have kindly consented to let me use copyright material are numerous and I assure them of my deep sense of obligation. In particular I desire to thank the following publishers for their generous permission to use all that I required from their lists: Charles Scribner's Sons, John Lane Company, Small, Maynard Company, P. J. Kenedy Sons, Frederick A. Stokes Company, *The Catholic World,* Houghton Mifflin Company, The Encyclopaedia Press, Henry Holt & Company, The Devin-Adair Company, Little, Brown & Company, The Macmillan Company, Elkin Mathews, *The Ave Maria,* Laurence Gomme, and Wilfrid Meynell.

1917   J. K.

Grateful acknowledgment for permission to use some of the supplementary material included in this anthology is also made to the following publishers and publications: D. Appleton & Company; Harcourt, Brace & Company; Jonathan Cape, Ltd.; Burns, Oates, & Washbourne; *Commonweal;* and *Spirit.* "I Shall Not Be Afraid" is from *Selected Poems* by Aline Kilmer and "Olim Meminisse Juvabit" is from *Candles That Burn* by Aline Kilmer, and both are used by permission of Doubleday and Company.

1926, 1937   S. O'S.

CONTENTS

15

16

17

18

19

21

22

23

24

25

29

30

31

32

33

JOYCE KILMER'S
ANTHOLOGY OF
CATHOLIC POETS

TO

REV. JAMES J. DALY, S. J.

HILAIRE BELLOC

Our Lord and Our Lady

They warned Our Lady for the Child
    That was Our blessed Lord,
And she took Him into the desert wild,
    Over the camel's ford.

And a long song she sang to Him
    And a short story told:
And she wrapped Him in a woollen cloak
    To keep Him from the cold.

But when Our Lord was grown a man
    The rich they dragged Him down,
And they crucified Him in Golgotha,
    Out and beyond the Town.

They crucified Him on Calvary,
    Upon an April day;
And because He had been her little Son
    She followed Him all the way.

Our Lady stood beside the Cross,
    A little space apart,
And when she heard Our Lord cry out
    A sword went through her heart.

They laid Our Lord in a marble tomb,
    Dead, in a winding sheet.
But Our Lady stands above the world
    With the white moon at her feet.

To the Balliol Men Still in Africa

Years ago when I was at Balliol,
    Balliol men—and I was one—
Swam together in winter rivers,
    Wrestled together under the sun.
And still in the heart of us, Balliol, Balliol,
    Loved already, but hardly known,
Welded us each of us into the others:
    Called a levy and chose her own.

Here is a House that armours a man
    With the eyes of a boy and the heart of a ranger,
And a laughing way in the teeth of the world
    And a holy hunger and thirst for danger:
Balliol made me, Balliol fed me,
    Whatever I had she gave me again:
And the best of Balliol loved and led me,
    God be with you, Balliol men.

I have said it before, and I say it again,
    There was treason done, and a false word spoken,
And England under the dregs of men,
    And bribes about, and a treaty broken:
But angry, lonely, hating it still,
    I wished to be there in spite of the wrong.
My heart was heavy for Cumnor Hill
    And the hammer of galloping all day long.

Galloping outward into the weather,
    Hands a-ready and battle in all:
Words together and wine together
    And song together in Balliol Hall.
Rare and single! Noble and few! . . .
    Oh! they have wasted you over the sea!
The only brothers ever I knew,
    The men that laughed and quarrelled with me.

Balliol made me, Balliol fed me,
    Whatever I had she gave me again;
And the best of Balliol loved and led me,
    God be with you, Balliol men.

The South Country

When I am living in the Midlands
    That are sodden and unkind,
I light my lamp in the evening:
    My work is left behind;
And the great hills of the South Country
    Come back into my mind.

The great hills of the South Country
    They stand along the sea;
And it's there walking in the high woods
    That I could wish to be,
And the men that were boys when I was a boy
    Walking along with me.

The men that live in North England
  I saw them for a day:
Their hearts are set upon the waste fells,
  Their skies are fast and grey;
From their castle-walls a man may see;
  The mountains far away.

The men that live in West England
  They see the Severn strong,
A-rolling on rough water brown,
  Light aspen leaves along.
They have the secret of the Rocks,
  And the oldest kind of song.

But the men that live in the South Country
  Are the kindest and most wise,
They get their laughter from the loud surf,
  And the faith in their happy eyes
Comes surely from our Sister the Spring
  When over the sea she flies;
The violets suddenly bloom at her feet,
  She blesses us with surprise.

I never get between the pines
  But I smell the Sussex air;
Nor I never come on a belt of sand
  But my home is there.
And along the sky line of Downs
  So noble and so bare.

A lost thing could I never find,
  Nor a broken thing mend:
And I fear I shall be all alone
  When I get towards the end.
Who will there be to comfort me
  Or who will be my friend?

I will gather and carefully make my friends
  Of the men of the Sussex Weald,
They watch the stars from silent folds,
  They stiffly plough the field.
By them and the God of the South Country
  My poor soul shall be healed.

If I ever become a rich man,
  Or if ever I grow to be old,
I will build a house with deep thatch
  To shelter me from the cold,

And there shall the Sussex songs be sung
  And the story of Sussex told.

I will hold my house in the high wood
  Within a walk of the sea,
And the men that were boys when I was a boy
  Shall sit and drink with me.

The Early Morning

The Moon on the one hand, the Dawn on the other:
The Moon is my Sister, the Dawn is my Brother,
The Moon on my left and the Dawn on my right:
My Brother, good morning; my Sister, good night.

The Prophet Lost in the Hills at Evening

Strong God which made the topmost stars
  To circulate and keep their course,
Remember me; whom all the bars
  Of sense and dreadful fate enforce.

Above me in your heights and tall,
  Impassable the summits freeze,
Below the haunted waters call
  Impassable beyond the trees.

I hunger and I have no bread.
  My gourd is empty of the wine.
Surely the footsteps of the dead
  Are shuffling softly close to mine!

It darkens. I have lost the ford.
  There is a change on all things made.
The rocks have evil faces, Lord,
  And I am awfully afraid.

Remember me! the voids of Hell
  Expand enormous all around.
Strong friend of souls, Emmanuel,
  Redeem me from accursed ground.

The long descent of wasted days,
  To these at last have led me down;

Remember that I filled with praise
The meaningless and doubtful ways
That lead to an eternal town.

I challenged and I kept the Faith,
The bleeding path alone I trod;
It darkens. Stands about my wraith,
And harbour me—almighty God!

The Birds

When Jesus Christ was four years old,
The angels brought Him toys of gold,
Which no man ever had bought or sold.

And yet with these He would not play.
He made Him small fowl out of clay,
And blessed them till they flew away:
Tu creasti Domine.

Jesus Christ, Thou child so wise,
Bless mine hands and fill mine eyes,
And bring my soul to Paradise.

Courtesy

Of Courtesy, it is much less
Than Courage of Heart or Holiness,
Yet in my walks it seems to me
That the Grace of God is in Courtesy.

On Monks I did in Storrington fall,
They took me straight into their hall;
I saw three pictures on a wall,
And Courtesy was in them all.

The first the Annunciation;
The second the Visitation;
The third the Consolation,
Of God that was Our Lady's Son.

The first was of Saint Gabriel;
On wings a-flame from Heaven he fell;
And as he went upon one knee
He shone with Heavenly Courtesy.

Our Lady out of Nazareth rode—
It was her month of heavy load;
Yet was her face both great and kind,
For Courtesy was in her mind.

The third it was our little Lord,
Whom all the Kings in arms adored;
He was so small you could not see
His large intent of Courtesy.

Our Lord, that was Our Lady's Son,
Go bless you, people, one by one;
My rhyme is written, my work is done.

Noel

On a winter's night long time ago
    (*The bells ring loud and the bells ring low*),
When high howled wind, and down fell snow
    (Carillon, Carilla).
Saint Joseph he and Notre Dame,
Riding on an ass, full weary came
From Nazareth into Bethlehem.
    And the small child Jesus smile on you.

And Bethlehem inn they stood before
    (*The bells ring less and the bells ring more*),
The landlord bade them begone from his door
    (Carillon, Carilla).
"Poor folk" (says he), "must lie where they may,
For the Duke of Jewry comes this way,
With all his train on a Christmas Day."
    And the small child Jesus smile on you.

Poor folk that may my carol hear
    (*The bells ring single and the bells ring clear*),
See! God's one child had hardest cheer!
    (Carillon, Carilla).
Men grown hard on a Christmas morn;
The dumb beast by and a babe forlorn.
It was very, very cold when our Lord was born.
    And the small child Jesus smile on you.

Now these were Jews as Jews may be
    (*The bells ring merry and the bells ring free*).
But Christian men in a band are we
    (Carillon, Carilla).

Empty we go, and ill be-dight,
Singing Noel on a Winter's night.
Give us to sup by the warm firelight,
    And the small child Jesus smile on you.

ROBERT HUGH BENSON

After a Retreat

What hast thou learnt today?
Hast thou sounded awful mysteries,
Hast pierced the veilèd skies,
Climbed to the feet of God,
Trodden where saints have trod,
Fathomed the heights above?
        Nay,
This only have I learnt, that God is love.

What hast thou heard today?
Hast heard the angel-trumpets cry,
And rippling harps reply;
Heard from the throne of flame
Whence God incarnate came
Some thund'rous message roll?
        Nay,
This have I heard, His voice within my soul.

What hast thou felt today?
The pinions of the angel-guide
That standeth at thy side
In rapturous ardours beat,
Glowing, from head to feet,
In ecstasy divine?
        Nay,
This only have I felt, Christ's hand in mine.

The Teresian Contemplative

She moves in tumult; round her lies
    The silence of the world of grace;
The twilight of our mysteries
    Shines like high noonday on her face;
Our piteous guesses, dim with fears,
She touches, handles, sees, and hears.

In her all longings mix and meet;
    Dumb souls through her are eloquent;
She feels the world beneath her feet
    Thrill in a passionate intent;
Through her our tides of feeling roll
And find their God within her soul.

Her faith the awful face of God
    Brightens and binds with utter light;
Her footsteps fall where late He trod;
    She sinks in roaring voids of night;
Cries to her Lord in black despair,
And knows, yet knows not, He is there.

A willing sacrifice she takes
    The burden of our fall within;
Holy she stands; while on her breaks
    The lightning of the wrath of sin;
She drinks her Saviour's cup of pain,
And, one with Jesus, thirsts again.

WILFRID SCAWEN BLUNT

How Shall I Build

How shall I build my temple to the Lord,
Unworthy I, who am thus foul of heart?
How shall I worship who no traitor word
Know but of love to play a suppliant's part?
How shall I pray, whose soul is as a mart,
For thoughts unclean, whose tongue is as a sword
Even for those it loves, to wound and smart?
Behold how little I can help Thee, Lord.

The Temple I would build should be all white,
Each stone the record of a blameless day;
The souls that entered there should walk in light,
Clothed in high chastity and wisely gay.
Lord, here is darkness. Yet this heart unwise,
Bruised in Thy service, take in sacrifice.

46

Song

O fly not, Pleasure, pleasant-hearted Pleasure;
 Fold me thy wings, I prithee, yet and stay:
  For my heart no measure
  Knows, or other treasure
 To buy a garland for my love today.

And thou, too, Sorrow, tender-hearted Sorrow,
 Thou gray-eyed mourner, fly not yet away:
  For I fain would borrow
  Thy sad weeds tomorrow,
 To make a mourning for love's yesterday.

The voice of Pity, Time's divine dear Pity,
 Moved me to tears: I dared not say them nay,
  But passed forth from the city,
  Making thus my ditty
 Of fair love lost forever and a day.

The Desolate City

Dark to me is the earth. Dark to me are the heavens.
 Where is she that I loved, the woman with eyes like stars?
Desolate are the streets. Desolate is the city,
 A city taken by storm, where none are left but the slain.

Sadly I rose at dawn, undid the latch of my shutters,
 Thinking to let in light, but I only let in love.
Birds in the boughs were awake; I listen'd to their chaunting;
 Each one sang to his love; only I was alone.

This, I said in my heart, is the hour of life and pleasure.
 Now each creature on earth has his joy, and lives in the sun,
Each in another's eyes finds light, the light of compassion,
 This is the moment of pity, this is the moment of love.

Speak, O desolate city! Speak, O silence in sadness!
 Where is she that loved in my strength, that spoke to my
  soul?
Where are those passionate eyes that appealed.to my eyes in
  passion?
 Where is the mouth that kiss'd me, the breast that I laid to
  my own?

Speak, thou soul of my soul, for rage in my heart is kindled.
 Tell me, where didst thou flee in the day of destruction and
  fear?

47

See, my arms enfold thee, enfolding thus all heaven,
See, my desire is fulfilled in thee, for it fills the earth.

Thus in my grief I lamented. Then turned I from the window,
Turn'd to the stair, and the open door, and the empty street,
Crying aloud in my grief, for there was none to chide me,
None to mock my weakness, none to behold my tears.

Groping I went, as blind. I sought her house, my beloved's.
There I stopp'd at the silent door, and listen'd and tried the
latch.
Love, I cried, dost thou slumber? This is no hour for slumber,
This is the hour of love, and love I bring in my hand.

I knew the house with its windows barr'd, and its leafless fig-
tree,
Climbing round by the doorstep, the only one in the street;
I knew where my hope had climbed to its goal and there en-
circled,
All those desolate walls once held, my beloved's heart.

There in my grief she consoled me. She loved when I loved not.
She put her hand in my hand, and set her lips to my lips.
She told me all her pain and show'd me all her trouble.
I, like a fool, scarce heard, hardly return'd her kiss.

Love, thy eyes were like torches. They changed as I beheld
them.
Love, thy lips were like gems, the seal thou settest on my
life.
Love, if I loved not then, behold this hour thy vengeance;
This is the fruit of thy love and thee, the unwise grown wise.

Weeping strangled my voice. I call'd out, but none answered;
Blindly the windows gazed back at me, dumbly the door;
She whom I love, who loved me, look'd not on my yearning,
Gave me no more her hands to kiss, show'd me no more her
soul.

Therefore the earth is dark to me, the sunlight blackness,
Therefore I go in tears and alone, by night and day;
Therefore I find my love in heaven, no light, no beauty,
A heaven taken by storm, where none are left but the slain!

TERESA BRAYTON

A Christmas Song

O Lord, as You lay so soft and white,
    A Babe in a manger stall,
With the big star flashing across the night,
    Did you know and pity us all?
Did the wee hands, close as a rosebud curled,
    With the call of their mission ache,
To be out and saving a weary world
    For Your merciful Father's sake?

Did You hear the cries of the groping blind,
    The woe of the leper's prayer,
The surging sorrow of all mankind,
    As You lay by Your Mother there?
Beyond the shepherds, low bending down,
    The long, long road did You see
That led from peaceful Bethlehem town
    To the summit of Calvary?

The world grown weary of wasting strife,
    Had called for the Christ to rise;
For sin had poisoned the springs of life
    And only the dead were wise.
But, wrapped in a dream of scornful pride,
    Too high were its eyes to see
A Child, foredoomed to be crucified,
    On a peasant Mother's knee.

But, while the heavens with glad acclaim
    Sang out the tale of Your birth,
A mystic echo of comfort came
    To the desolate souls of earth.
For the thrill of a slowly turning tide
    Was felt in that grey daybreak,
As if God, the Father, had sanctified
    All sorrow for One Man's sake.

O Child of the Promise! Lord of Love!
    O Master of all the earth!
While the angels are singing their songs above,
    We bring our gifts to Your birth.
Just the blind man's cry, and the lame man's pace,
    And the leper's pitiful call;
On these, over infinite fields of space,
    Look down, for You know them all.

49

NANCY CAMPBELL

Like One I Know

Little Christ was good, and lay
Sleeping, smiling in the hay;
Never made the cows round eyes
Open wider at His cries;
Never when the night was dim,
Startled guardian Seraphim,
Who above Him in the beams
Kept their watch round His white dreams;
Let the rustling brown mice creep
Undisturbed about His sleep.
Yet if it had not been so—
Had He been like one I know,
Fought with little fumbling hands,
Kicked inside His swaddling bands,
Puckered wilful crimsoning face—
Mary Mother, full of grace,
At that little naughty thing,
Still had been a-worshipping.

ETHNA CARBERY

Mea Culpa

Be pitiful, my God!
    No hard-won gifts I bring—
But empty, pleading hands
    To Thee at evening.

Spring came, white-browed and young,
    I, too, was young with Spring.
There was a blue, blue heaven
    Above a skylark's wing.

Youth is the time for joy,
    I cried, it is not meet
To mount the heights of toil
    With child-soft feet.

When Summer walked the land
    In Passion's red arrayed,

Under green sweeping boughs
    My couch I made.

The noon-tide heat was sore,
    I slept the Summer through;
An angel waked me—"Thou
    Hast work to do."

I rose and saw the sheaves
    Upstanding in a row;
The reapers sang Thy praise
    While passing to and fro.

My hands were soft with ease,
    Long were the Autumn hours;
I left the ripened sheaves
    For poppy-flowers.

But lo! now Winter glooms,
    And gray is in my hair,
Whither has flown the world
    I found so fair?

My patient God, forgive!
    Praying Thy pardon sweet
I lay a lonely heart
    Before Thy feet.

In Tir-na'n-Og

                In Tir-na'n-Og,
                In Tir-na'n-Og,
Summer and spring go hand in hand, and in the radiant
        weather
Brown autumn leaves and winter snow come floating down
        together.

                In Tir-na'n-Og,
                In Tir-na'n-Og,
The sagans sway this way and that, the twisted fern uncloses,
The quicken-berry hides its red above the tender roses.

                In Tir-na'n-Og,
                In Tir-na'n-Og,
The blackbird lilts, the robin chirps, the linnet wearies never,
They pipe to dancing feet of *Sidhe* and thus shall pipe forever.

In Tir-na'n-Og,
In Tir-na'n-Og,
All in a drift of apple blooms my true love there is roaming,
He will not come although I pray from dawning until gloaming.

In Tir-na'n-Og,
In Tir-na'n-Og,
The *Sidhe* desired by Heart's Delight, they lured him from my keeping,
He stepped within a fairy ring while all the world was sleeping.

In Tir-na'n-Og,
In Tir-na'n-Og,
He hath forgotten hill and glen where misty shadows gather,
The bleating of the mountain sheep, the cabin of his father.

In Tir-na'n-Og,
In Tir-na'n-Og,
He wanders in a happy dream thro' scented golden hours,
He flutes, to woo a fairy love, knee deep in fairy flowers.

In Tir-na'n-Og,
In Tir-na'n-Og,
No memory hath he of my face, no sorrow for my sorrow,
My flax is spun, my wheel is hushed, and so I wait the morrow.

PATRICK J. CARROLL, C.S.C.

St. Patrick's Treasure

Called son by many lands,
Thou art a father unto one.
Of all these mothers claiming thee,
By honored titles naming thee,
We ask: Where is thy priceless birthright gone?

That blessed faith of thine,
They mothering thee have sold.
But she, thy daughter dutiful,
Has kept thy treasure beautiful
Through many sorrows in her heart of gold.

Lady Day in Ireland

Through the long August day, mantled blue with a sky of Our
  Lady,
  They are there at the well from the dawn till the sea birds
    go home;
And the trees bending down with broad leaves offer spots that
    are shady,
  Where the heart is at rest, sighing prayers till the shadows
    are come.

The brown beads and the crucifix pass in procession through
    fingers
  That are pale as the snow or are hardened from labor and
    pain.
In each *Ave* they whisper the deep Celtic tenderness lingers,
  Like a sweet phrase in song that is echoed and echoed again.

Marching down the white road with the sun in the noon of his
    splendor
  Are the children, with joy in the blue of their innocent eyes;
In their hearts is a song, breaking forth into words that are
    tender,
  Unto her with the gold of the stars and the blue of the skies.

In the still summer air there's a chorus of minstrelsy breaking,
  There are flashes of gold with a flutter and waving of wings:
Mary's birds are they, come with the dawn, all the green woods
    forsaking,
  Every heart in them breaking for love with the message it
    brings.

Through the calm August day, with Our Lady's blue sky far
    above them,
And beyond the grey mountains where slumbers the Irish
    green sea,
There they speak to her, weep while they pray to her, beg her
    to love them,
Till beyond the bright stars where their home and their
    treasure shall be.

D. A. CASEY

The Spouse of Christ

He came to her from out eternal years,
A smile upon His lips, a tender smile
That, somehow, spoke of partings and of tears.

'Twas eventide, and silence brooded low
On earth and sky—the hour when haunting fears
Of mystery pursue us as we go.

Strange, mystic shadows filled the temple dim,
But on the Golden Door the ruby glow
Spoke orisons more sweet than vesper hymn.

No human accents voiced His gentle call,
No crashing thunderbolts did wait on Him,
As when of old He deigned to summon Saul.

But heart did speak to heart, an unseen chord
In Love's own scale did sweetly rise and fall;
Nor questioned she, but meekly answered "Lord!"

Tonight some household counts a vacant chair,
But far on high Christ portions the reward,
A hundredfold for each poor human care.

PADRAIC COLUM

Christ the Comrade

Christ, by Thine own darkened hour
Live within my heart and brain!
Let my hands not slip the rein.

Ah, how long ago it is
Since a comrade rode with me!
Now a moment let me see

Thyself, lonely in the dark,
Perfect, without wound or mark!

54

An Old Woman of the Roads

Oh, to have a little house!
To own the hearth and stool and all!
The heaped-up sods upon the fire,
The pile of turf against the wall!

To have a clock with weights and chains,
And pendulum swinging up and down!
A dresser filled with shining delph,
Speckled and white and blue and brown!

I could be busy all the day
Clearing and sweeping hearth and floor,
And fixing on their shelf again
My white and blue and speckled store.

I could be quiet there at night
Beside the fire and by myself,
Sure of a bed, and loth to leave
The ticking clock and shining delph!

Och! but I'm weary of mist and dark,
And roads where there's never a house or bush,
And tired I am of bog and road,
And the crying wind and the lonesome hush!

And I am praying to God on high,
And I am praying Him night and day,
For a little house—a house of my own—
Out of the wind's and the rain's way.

KATHERINE ELEANOR CONWAY

The Heaviest Cross of All

I've borne full many a sorrow, I've suffered many a loss—
But now, with a strange, new anguish, I carry this last dread
        cross;
For of this be sure, my dearest, whatever thy life befall,
The cross that our own hands fashion is the heaviest cross of
        all.

Heavy and hard I made it in the days of my fair strong youth,
Veiling mine eyes from the blessed light, and closing my heart
        to truth.

55

Pity me, Lord, whose mercy passeth my wildest thought,
For I never dreamed of the bitter end of the work my hands
    had wrought!

In the sweet morn's flush and fragrance I wandered o'er dewy
    meadows,
And I hid from the fervid noontide glow in the cool green
    woodland shadows;
And I never recked, as I sang aloud in my wilful, selfish glee,
Of the mighty woe that was drawing nigh to darken the world
    for me.

But it came at last, my dearest—what need to tell thee how?
Mayst never know of the wild, wild woe that my heart is bear-
    ing now!
Over my summer's glory crept a damp and chilling shade,
And I staggered under the heavy cross that my sinful hands
    had made.

I go where the shadows deepen, and the end seems far off
    yet—
God keep thee safe from the sharing of this woeful late regret!
For of this be sure, my dearest, whatever thy life befall,
The crosses we make for ourselves, alas! are the heaviest ones
    of all.

Saturninus

He might have won the highest guerdon that heaven to earth
    can give,
For whoso falleth for justice—dying, he yet shall live.

He might have left us his memory to flame as a beacon light,
When clouds of the false world's raising shut the stars of
    heaven from sight.

He might have left us his name to ring in our triumph song
When we stand, as we'll stand at tomorrow's dawn, by the
    grave of a world-old wrong.

For he gave thee, O mother of valiant sons, thou fair, and sore
    oppressed,
The love of his youth and his manhood's choice—first-fruits
    of his life, and best.

Thine were throb of his heart and thought of his brain and toil
    of his strong right hand;
For thee he braved scorn and reviling, and loss of gold and
    land,

56

Threat and lure and false-hearted friend, and blight of a
    broken word—
Terrors of night and delay of light—prison and rack and
    sword.

For thee he bade death defiance—till the heavens opened wide,
And his face grew bright with reflex of light from the face of
    the Crucified.

And his crown was in sight and his palm in reach and his
    glory all but won,
And then—he failed—God help us! with the worst of dying
    done.

Only to die on the treacherous down by the hands of the
    tempters spread—
Nay, nay—make way for the strangers! we have no right in
    the dead.

But oh, for the beacon quenched, that we dreamed would
    kindle and flame!
And oh, for the standard smirched and shamed, and the name
    we dare not name!

Over the lonesome grave the shadows gather fast;
Only the mother, like God, forgives, and comforts her heart
    with the past.

ELEANOR ROGERS COX

Dreaming of Cities Dead

Dreaming of cities dead,
Of bright queens vanished,
Of kings whose names were but as seed wind-blown
E'en when white Patrick's voice shook Tara's throne,
My way along the great world-street I tread,
And keep the rites of Beauty lost, alone.

Cairns level with the dust—
Names dim with Time's dull rust—
Afar they sleep on many a wind-swept hill,
The beautiful, the strong of heart and will—
On whose pale dreams no sunrise joy shall burst,
No harper's song shall pierce with battle-thrill.

57

Long from their purpled heights,
Their reign of high delights,
The queens have wended down Death's mildewed stair,
Leaving a scent of lilies on the air,
To gladden Earth through all her days and nights,
That once she cherished anything so fair.

Death of Cuchulain

Silent are the singers in the purple halls of Emain,
  Silent all the harp-strings untouched of any hand,
Wan as twilight roses the radiant, royal women,
  Black unto the hearthstone the erstwhile flaming brand.

Inward far from ocean the storm's white birds are flying,
  Darting, like dim wraith flames across the falling night.
Winds like a *caoine* through quickened groves are sighing,
  On no lip is laughter, in no heart delight.

For thitherwards witch-wafted athwart the sundering spaces,
  Lo, a word doom-freighted unto Conchubar has come,
Whispering of one who in far-off, hostile places
  Strikes a last defending blow for king and home.

And the king pacing lone in his place of high decision,
  Gazing with rapt eyes on that far-flung battle-plain,
Through the red rains rising beholds with startled vision
  Sight such as man's eye shall not see again.

For one there is dying, of his foes at last outnumbered,
  One whose soul a sword was, shaped by God's own hand,
One who guarded Ulaidh when all her knighthood slumbered,
  Prone beneath the curse laid of old upon the land.

And dying so, alone, of all mortal aid forsaken,
  Dead his peerless war steeds, dead his charioteer,
Yet the high splendor of his spirit all unshaken,
  Shines morning-bright through the death-mists drawing near.

And radiant round his brow yet the hero-flame is gleaming,
  And firm yet his footstep upon the reddened sod,
As with sword uplifted towards the day's last beaming,
  Forth goes the spirit of Cuchulain unto God.

Leaving to his land and the Celtic race forever
  That which shall not fail them throughout the fading years,
Heritage of faith unchanged, of fear-undimmed endeavor,
  And a quenchless laughter ringing down the edge of hostile
    spears.

Gods and Heroes of the Gael

Forth in shining phalanx marching from the shrouding mists
of time,
    Bright the sunlight on their foreheads, bright upon their
golden mail,
Lords of beauty, lords of valor, lords of Earth's unconquered
prime,
    Come the gods, the kings, the heroes of the Gael.

Lugh, the splendor of whose shining lit the forest and the fen,
    He whose smile at first illuming all the shadow-haunted
space
Of the vast, primeval ranges, death-engirdled, shunned of men,
    Over virgin seas to Erin led our race.

Mananaan, great lord of Ocean—he whose fair domain outspread
    Wheresoever tides foam-flowered to the moon's high man-
date move,
Aengus, clothed in youth immortal, on immortal ardors fed,
    Who of old in golden Brugh reigned lord of Love.

And his name a knightly pennon on the ramparts of the world,
    And his fame a fire unfailing on Time's utmost purple
height,
Erin's peerless gage of courage to the vaunting ages hurled—
    Sunward evermore Cuchulain holds his flight.

They are coming with the silver speech of Erin on their lips;
    The speech that once of all the mighty Celtic race made kin,
They are coming with the laughter that has known no age-
eclipse,
    They are coming with the songs beloved of Finn.

Yea, with gifts regenerating to all men of women born—
    Flame of courage that shall fade not, flame of truth that
shall not fail,
To the music of a thousand harps they're marching through
the morn,
    Deathless gods and kings and heroes of the Gael!

At Benediction

Joy, beauty, awe, supremest worship blending
In one long breath of perfect ecstasy,
Song from our hearts to God's own Heart ascending,
The mortal merged in immortality.

59

There, veiled beneath that sacramental whiteness,
The wonder that all wonders doth transcend,
The Word that kindled chaos into brightness,
Our Lord, our God, our origin, our end.

Light, light, a sea of light, unshored, supernal,
Is all about our finite being spread,
Deep, soundless waves of harmonies eternal
Their balm celestial on our spirits shed.
O Source of Life! O Fount of waters living!
O Love, to whom all powers of mind and soul,
We give, and find again within the giving,
Of Thee renewed, made consecrate and whole.

OLIVE CUSTANCE

Primrose Hill

Wild heart in me that frets and grieves,
Imprisoned here against your will . . .
Sad heart that dreams of rainbow wings . . .
See! I have found some golden things!
The poplar trees on Primrose Hill
With all their shining play of leaves . . .
And London like a silver bride,
That will not put her veil aside!

Proud London like a painted queen,
Whose crown is heavy on her head . . .
City of sorrow and desire,
Under a sky of opal fire,
Amber and amethyst and red . . .
And how divine the day has been!
For every dawn God builds again
This world of beauty and of pain . . .

Wild heart that hungers for delight,
Imprisoned here against your will;
Sad heart, so eager to be gay!
Loving earth's lovely things . . . the play
Of wind and leaves on Primrose Hill . . .
Or London dreaming of the night . . .
Adventurous heart, on beauty bent,
That only Heaven could quite content!

Twilight

Spirit of Twilight, through your folded wings
    I catch a glimpse of your averted face,
And rapturous on a sudden, my soul sings
    "Is not this common earth a holy place?"

Spirit of Twilight, you are like a song
    That sleeps, and waits a singer—like a hymn
That God finds lovely and keeps near Him long,
    Till it is choired by aureoled cherubim.

Spirit of Twilight, in the golden gloom
    Of dreamland dim I sought you, and I found
A woman sitting in a silent room
    Full of white flowers that moved and made no sound.

These white flowers were the thoughts you bring to all,
    And the room's name is Mystery where you sit,
Woman whom we call Twilight, when night's pall
    You lift across our Earth to cover it.

THOMAS AUGUSTINE DALY

To a Thrush

      Sing clear, O! throstle,
        Thou golden-tongued apostle
And little brown-frocked brother
    Of the loved Assisian!
Sing courage to the mother,
    Sing strength into the man,
For they, who in another May
    Trod Hope's scant wine from grapes of pain,
Have tasted in thy song today
    The bitter-sweet red lees again.
To them in whose sad May-time thou
Sang'st comfort from thy maple bough,
    To tinge the presaged dole with sweet,
O! prophet then, be prophet now
      And paraclete!

That fateful May! The pregnant vernal night
    Was throbbing with the first faint pangs of day,

The while with ordered urge toward life and light,
    Earth-atoms countless groped their destined way;
        And one full-winged to fret
        Its tender oubliette,
The warding mother-heart above it woke,
    Darkling she lay in doubt, then, sudden wise,
Whispered her husband's drowsy ear and broke
    The estranging seal of slumber from his eyes:
    "My hour is nigh: arise!"

Already, when, with arms for comfort linked,
    The lovers at an eastward window stood,
The rosy day, in cloudy swaddlings, blinked
    Through misty green new-fledged in Wister Wood.
        Breathless upon this birth
        The still-entranced earth
Seemed brooding, motionless in windless space.
    Then rose thy priestly chant, O! holy bird!
And heaven and earth were quickened with its grace;
    To tears two wedded souls were moved who heard,
    And one, unborn, was stirred!

O! Comforter, enough that from thy green
    Hid tabernacle in the wood's recess
To those care-haunted lovers thou, unseen,
    Should'st send thy flame-tipped song to cheer and bless.
        Enough for them to hear
        And feel thy presence near;
And yet when he, regardful of her ease,
    Had led her back by brightening hall and stair
To her own chamber's quietude and peace,
    One maple-bowered window shook with rare,
    Sweet song—and thou wert there!

Hunter of souls! the loving chase so nigh
    Those spirits twain had never come before.
They saw the sacred flame within thine eye;
    To them the maple's depths quick glory wore,
        As though God's hand had lit
        His altar-fire in it,
And made a fane, of virgin verdure pleached,
    Wherefrom thou might'st in numbers musical
Expound the age-sweet words thy Francis preached
    To thee and thine, of God's benignant thrall
    That broodeth over all.

And they, athirst for comfort, sipped thy song,
    But drank not yet thy deeper homily.

Not yet, but when parturient pangs grew strong,
   And from its cell the young soul struggled free—
      A new joy, trailing grief,
      A little crumpled leaf,
Blighted before it burgeoned from the stem—
   Thou, as the fabled robin to the rood,
Wert minister of charity to them;
   And from the shadows of sad parenthood
   They heard and understood.

Makes God one soul a lure for snaring three?
   Ah! surely; so this nursling of the nest,
This teen-touched joy, ere birth anoint of thee,
   Yet bears thy chrismal music in her breast.
      Five Mays have come and sped
      Above her sunny head,
And still the happy song abides in her.
   For though on maimèd limbs the body creeps,
It doth a spirit house whose pinions stir
   Familiarly the far cerulean steeps
   Where God his mansion keeps.

      So come, O! throstle,
      Thou golden-tongued apostle
   And little brown-frocked brother
   Of the loved Assisian!
Sing courage to the mother,
   Sing strength into the man,
That she who in another May
   Came out of heaven, trailing care,
May never know that sometimes gray
   Earth's roof is and its cupboards bare.
To them in whose sad May-time thou
Sang'st comfort and thy maple bough,
   To tinge the presaged dole with sweet,
O! prophet then, be prophet now
      And paraclete!

To a Robin

I heard thee, joyous votary,
   Pour forth thy heart in one
Sweet simple strain of melody
   To greet the rising sun,
When he across the morning's verge his first faint flare had
      flung

And found the crimson of thy breast the whisp'ring leaves
    among,
        In thine own tree
        Which sheltered thee,
  Thy mate, thy nest, thy young.

I marked thee, sorrow's votary,
    When in the noon of day
Young vandals stormed thy sacred tree
    And bore thine all away;
The notes of grief that rent thy breast touched kindred chords
    in mine,
For memories of other days, though slumbering still confine
        In mine own heart
        The bitter smart
  Of sorrow such as thine.

I hear thee now, sweet votary,
    Beside thy ruined nest,
Lift up thy flood of melody
    Against the crimsoned west,
Forgetful of all else in this, thy one sweet joyous strain.
I thank thee for this ecstasy of my remembered pain;
        Thou liftest up
        My sorrow's cup
  To sweeten it again.

To a Plain Sweetheart

I love thee, dear, for what thou art,
    Nor would I wish thee otherwise,
For when thy lashes lift apart
    I read, deep-mirrored in thine eyes,
The glory of a modest heart.

Wert thou as fair as thou art good,
    It were not given to any man,
With daring eyes of flesh and blood,
    To look thee in the face and scan
The splendor of thy womanhood.

The Poet

The truest poet is not one
Whose golden fancies fuse and run
To moulded phrases, crusted o'er
With flashing gems of metaphor;

Whose art, responsive to his will,
Makes voluble the thoughts that fill
The cultured windings of his brain,
Yet takes no soundings of the pain,
The joy, the yearnings of the heart
Untrammeled by the bonds of art.
O! poet truer far than he
Is such a one as you may be,
When in the quiet night you keep
Mute vigil on the marge of sleep.

If then, with beating heart, you mark
God's nearer presence in the dark,
And musing on the wondrous ways
Of Him who numbers all your days,
Pay tribute to Him with your tears
For joys, for sorrows, hopes and fears
Which He has blessed and given to you,
You are the poet, great and true.
For there are songs within the heart
Whose perfect melody no art
Can teach the tongue of man to phrase.
These are the songs His poets raise,
When in the night they keep
Mute vigil on the marge of sleep.

October

Come, forsake your city street!
Come to God's own fields and meet
   October.
Not the lean, unkempt and brown
Counterfeit that haunts the town,
Pointing, like a thing of gloom,
At dead summer in her tomb;
Reading in each fallen leaf
Nothing but regret and grief.
Come out, where, beneath the blue,
You may frolic with the true
   October.

Call his name and mark the sound,
Opulent and full and round:
   "October."
Come, and gather from his hand
Lavish largesse of the land;
Read in his prophetic eyes,
Clear as skies of paradise,

65

Not of summer days that died,
But of summer fructified!
Hear, O soul, his message sweet.
Come to God's own fields and meet
      October.

AUBREY DE VERE

Sorrow

Count each affliction, whether light or grave,
God's messenger sent down to thee; do thou
With courtesy receive him; rise and bow;
And, ere his shadow pass thy threshold, crave
Permission first His heavenly feet to lave;
Then lay before Him all thou hast; allow
No cloud or passion to usurp thy brow,
Or mar thy hospitality; no wave
Of mortal tumult to obliterate
Thy soul's marmoreal calmness. Grief should be
Like joy, majestic, equable, sedate;
Confirming, cleansing, raising, making free;
Strong to consume small troubles; to commend
Great thoughts, grave thoughts, thoughts lasting to the end.

Human Life

Sad is our youth, for it is ever going,
Crumbling away beneath our very feet;
Sad is our life, for onward it is flowing,
In current unperceived because so fleet;
Sad are our hopes, for they were sweet in sowing,
But tares, self-sown, have overtopped the wheat;
Sad are our joys, for they were sweet in blowing;
And still, O still, their dying breath is sweet;
And sweet is youth, although it hath bereft us
Of that which made our childhood sweeter still;
And sweeter our life's decline, for it hath left us
A nearer Good to cure an older Ill;
And sweet are all things, when we learn to prize them
Not for their sake, but His who grants them or denies them.

Cardinal Manning

I learn'd his greatness first at Lavington:
The moon had early sought her bed of brine,
But we discours'd till now each starry sign
Had sunk: our theme was one and one alone:
"Two minds supreme," he said, "our earth has known;
One sang in science; one served God in song;
Aquinas—Dante." Slowly in me grew strong
A thought, "These two great minds in him are one;
'Lord, what shall this man do?'" Later at Rome
Beside the dust of Peter and of Paul
Eight hundred mitred sires of Christendom
In Council sat. I mark'd him 'mid them all;
I thought of that long night in years gone by
And cried, "At last my question meets reply."

Song

Seek not the tree of silkiest bark
    And balmiest bud,
To carve her name while yet 'tis dark
    Upon the wood!
The world is full of noble tasks
    And wreaths hard won:
Each work demands strong hearts, strong hands,
    Till day is done.

Sing not that violet-veined skin,
    That cheek's pale roses,
The lily of that form wherein
    Her soul reposes!
Forth to the fight, true man! true knight!
    The clash of arms
Shall more prevail than whisper'd tale,
    To win her charms.

The Warrior for the True, the Right,
    Fights in Love's name;
The love that lures thee from that flight
    Lures thee to shame:
That love which lifts the heart, yet leaves
    The spirit free,—
That love, or none, is fit for one
    Man-shap'd like thee.

67

JAMES B. DOLLARD

The Sons of Patrick

Into the mists of the pagan island
    Bearing God's message great Patrick came;
The Druid altars on plain and highland
    Fell at the sound of his mighty name!

Swift was the conquest—with hearts upswelling
    The Faith they took, and to God they swore:
That precious spark from their bosoms' dwelling,
    Man's guile or torture should snatch no more.

And ever since, while the wide world wonders,
    This steadfast people their strength reveal,
As Time Earth's kingdoms and empires sunders,
    They stand by Patrick in ranks of steel!

The nations mock them, like Christ's tormentors;
    "Descend," they cry, "from your cross of shame;
Abjure the Faith—see the road that enters
    The groves of pleasure and wealth and fame!"

Like those that passed where the Cross rose dimly
    Their wise beards wagging—"What fools!" they say;
But the Sons of Patrick make answer grimly:
    "Our God we've chosen—the price we'll pay.

"Ever about us the foes' commotion,
    The anguished sweat on our brows ne'er dry;
Our martyr's bones strew the land and ocean,
    Lone deserts echo our exiles' cry.

"Unto our hearts is earth's pride forbidden,
    Unto our hands is its gold denied;
We do not question the Purpose hidden—
    Let Him who fashioned our souls decide!

"Yet though once more to us choice were given,
    And the long aeons were backward rolled,
We'd walk again before Earth and Heaven
    The blood-stained pathway we walked of old!"

The Soul of Karnaghan Buidhe

It was the soul of Karnaghan Buidhe
  Left his lips with a groan.
Like arrowy lightning bolt released
  It sprang to the Judgment throne.

Spoke the Judge: "For as many years
  As the numbered drops of the sea
I grant you heaven—but thenceforth hell,
  Your bitter lot shall be."

Prayed the soul of Karnaghan Buidhe
  (*The trembling soul of Karnaghan Buidhe*)
"Dear Lord, who died on Calvary,
  Too brief that span of heaven for me."

Then spoke the Lord: "For as many years
  As numbered sands on the shore,
The joys of heaven. I give—but thence
  You'll see my face no more."

Pleaded the soul of Karnaghan Buidhe
  (*The shuddering soul of Karnaghan Buidhe*)
"Blessed Lord who died on the shameful tree,
  Too brief that span of heaven for me."

Once more the Judge: "The blades of grass
  That earth-winds ever blew
A year of heaven I'll count for each
  Till hell shall yawn for you."

Prayed the soul of Karnaghan Buidhe
  (*The anguished soul of Karnaghan Buidhe*)
"Kind Lord, who died in agony,
  Too brief that spell of heaven for me.

"But this I ask, O Christ—a year
  Of hell for each of these:
The blades of grass, the grains of sand,
  The drops that make the seas!
And after this, sweet Lord, with Thee
  In heaven for all eternity!"

Spoke the Judge, and His smile of love
Gladdened the waiting choir above:
"Sin and sorrow forever past,
Heaven I grant you, first and last!"

69

Song of the Little Villages

The pleasant little villages that grace the Irish glynns
Down among the wheatfields—up amid the whins,
The little white-walled villages crowding close together,
Clinging to the Old Sod in spite of wind and weather:
    Ballytarsney, Ballymore, Ballyboden, Boyle,
    Ballingarry, Ballymagorry by the Banks of Foyle,
    Ballylaneen, Ballyporeen, Bansha, Ballysadare,
    Ballybrack, Ballinalack, Barna, Ballyclare.

The cozy little villages that shelter from the mist,
Where the great West Walls by ocean spray are kissed;
The happy little villages that cuddle in the sun
When blackberries ripen and the harvest work is done.
    Corrymeela, Croaghnakeela, Clogher, Cahirciveen,
    Cappaharoe, Carrigaloe, Cashel and Coosheen,
    Castlefinn, Carrigtohill, Crumlin, Clara, Clane,
    Carrigaholt, Carrigaline, Cloghjordan and Coolrain.

The dreamy little villages, where by the fires at night,
Old Sanachies with ghostly tale the boldest hearts affright;
The crooning of the wind-blast is the wailing banshee's cry,
And when the silver hazels stir they say the fairies sigh,
    Kilfenora, Kilfinnane, Kinnity, Killylea,
    Kilmoganny, Kiltamagh, Kilronan and Kilrea,
    Killashandra, Kilmacow, Killiney, Killashee,
    Killenaule, Killmyshall, Killorglin and Killeagh.

Leave the little villages, o'er the black sea go,
Learn the stranger's welcome, learn the exile's woe,
Leave the little villages, but think not to forget,
Afar they'll rise before your eyes to rack your bosoms yet.
    Moneymore, Moneygall, Monivea and Moyne,
    Mullinahone, Mullinavatt, Mullagh and Mooncoin,
    Shanagolden, Shanballymore, Stranorlar and Slane,
    Toberaheena, Toomyvara, Tempo and Strabane.

On the Southern Llanos—north where strange light gleams,
Many a yearning exile sees them in his dreams;
Dying voices murmur (passed all pain and care),
"Lo, the little villages, God has heard our prayer."
    Lisdoonvarna, Lissadil, Lisdargan, Lisnaskea,
    Portglenone, Portarlington, Portumna, Portmagee,
    Clondalkin and Clongowan, Cloondara and Clonae,
    God bless the little villages and guard them night and day!

D. J. DONAHOE

The Angelic Chorus

At midnight from the zenith burst a light
  More radiant and more beautiful than dawn,
  And the meek shepherds on the shadowy lawn
Gazed upward in mute wonder on the sight;
The stars sank back in pallor, and the skies
Trembled responsive to rich harmonies.

And lo! an angel spake, "Be not afraid!
  I bear glad tidings; for this happy morn
  A Saviour and a King to man is born;
He sleepeth in a manger lowly laid."
Then rolled along the heavens the glad refrain;
"Glory to God on high and peace to men!"

Soon from the skies the streaming light was gone,
  And Night and Silence rested on the hill;
  But the mute shepherds, looking upward still,
Could hear the heavenly echoes rolling on.
So evermore the listening world can hear
The Angelic Chorus ringing sweet and clear.

ELEANOR C. DONNELLY

Ladye Chapel at Eden Hall

Close to the Sacred Heart, it nestles fair—
A marble poem; an aesthetic dream
Of sculptured beauty, fit to be the theme
Of angel fancies; a Madonna-prayer
Uttered in stone. Round columns light as air,
And fretted cornice, Sharon's Rose is wreathed—
The passion-flower, the thorn-girt lily rare,
The palm, the wheat, the grapes in vine-leaves sheathed.

Tenderly bright, from mullioned windows glow
Our Lady's chaplet-mysteries. Behold,
Her maiden statue in that shrine of snow,
Looks upward to the skies of blue and gold;
Content that in the crypt, beneath her shining feet,
The holy ones repose in dreamless slumber sweet.

71

Mary Immaculate

"Pure as the snow," we say. Ah! never flake
    Fell through the air
    One-tenth as fair
As Mary's soul was made for Christ's dear sake.
    Virgin Immaculate,
The whitest whiteness of the Alpine snows,
Beside thy stainless spirit, dusky grows.

"Pure as the stars." Ah! never lovely night
    Wore in its diadem
    So pure a gem
As that which fills the ages with its light.
    Virgin Immaculate,
The peerless splendors of thy soul by far
Outshine the glow of heaven's serenest star.

ELEANOR DOWNING

The Pilgrim

Behind me lies the mistress of the East,
    Golden in evening, fairy dome on dome
    Poised and irised like the far-flung foam
    Lashed on the ribs of some forsaken coast.
    Wicked and lovely temptress, fruitless boast
Of all that man may build and little be,
Mart of the world's base passions, where thy feast
Of shame was spread, thy sin encompassed me,
    Where all desires and all dreams were rife
    With lust of flesh and eye and pride of life,
    Lo! I have reft thy carnal mastery—
    I have gone forth and shut the gates of thee.

Before me lies the desert and the night,
    White star and gold above a pathless waste,
    Blue shade and gray to where the world effaced
    Flings shadows loose on the lap of God.
    Briars and dust upon my brow, unshod,
In pilgrim weeds athwart a vineless land,
My feet shall pass and mark the path aright,
For lo! Thy staff and rod are in my hand;
    And with the light Thy city shall unfurl
    Its golden oriflames and tents of pearl—
    Dead Babylon, thy gilden clasp I flee;
    Jerusalem, lift up thy gates to me!

On the Feast of the Assumption

"Mary, uplifted to our sight
In cloudy vesture stainless-white,
Why are thine eyes like stars alight,
  Twin flames of charity?"
"Mine eyes are on His glorious face
That shone not on earth's darkened place,
But clothed and crowned me with grace—
  The God who fathered me!"

"Mary, against the sinless glow
Of angel pinions white as snow,
Why are thy fair lips parted so
  In ecstasy of love?"
"My lips are parted to His breath
Who breathed on me in Nazareth
And gave me life to live in death—
  My Spouse, the spotless Dove!"

"Mary, whose eager feet would spurn
The very clouds, whose pale hands yearn
Toward rifted Heaven that fires burn
  Where once was fixed the sword?"
"The fires I felt when His child head
Lay on this mother's heart that bled,
And when it lay there stark and dead—
  My little Child, my Lord!"

Mary

A garden like a chalice-cup,
  With bloom of almond white and pink,
  And starred hibiscus to the brink,
From which sweet waters bubble up.
A garden walled with ilex-trees
  And topped with blue, white clouds between
  Save where the glossed leaves' twinkling green
Is stirred by some soft-footed breeze
A place apart, a watered glade,
  Where sin and sorrow have not been,
  And earth's complaint grows hushed within
Its greening aisles of sacred shade.

The circling arms, the flower face,
  Such were they to the Child soft-pressed,
  Who drew all sweetness from the breast
Of her whom angels crowned with grace.

A night of storm and wailing stress,
   A coast that cradles to the shock
   Of waves that lap the pitted rock,
And winds that shriek their wrathfulness;
A night of all wild things unpent,
   Strange voices and strange shapes that beat
   To chill the heart and snare the feet.
And through the tempest, beacon-bent
To shelter from the driving damp
   Bespeaking warmth and sweet repose
   Within its sanctuary close,
The welcome of a red shrine-lamp.

So unto Him who, weary, pressed
   Through the fierce storm of wrath and hate,
   Shone Mary's love, a chapel-gate
Where He might enter Him and rest.

.A desert filled with shining sand,
   And still as death the skies that bend
   Where to horizon without end
The rounding distances expand.
A desert white with burning heat
   And parched silence without stir,
   And at its heart a voyager,
Where Death and daggered noonday meet;
And Thirst that grips him by the throat;
   When from the distance wreathing blue,
   No mirage, but a dream come true,
Crowned palm-tree and pale waters float.

To Christ upon the rood, when dim
   Fell on His brow the Shade accurst,
   So Mary slaked His burning thirst
With her white soul held up to Him.

ERNEST DOWSON

Extreme Unction

Upon the eyes, the lips, the feet,
   On all the passages of sense,
The atoning oil is spread with sweet
   Renewal of lost innocence.

The feet, that lately ran so fast
    To meet desire, are soothly sealed;
The eyes, that were so often cast
    On vanity, are touched and healed.

From troublous sights and sounds set free
    In such a twilight hour of breath,
Shall one retrace his life, or see,
    Through shadows, the true face of death?

Vials of mercy! Sacring oils!
    I know not where nor when I come,
Nor through what wanderings and toils,
    To crave of you Viaticum.

Yet, when the walls of flesh grow weak,
    In such an hour, it well may be,
Through mist and darkness, light will break,
    And each anointed sense will see.

Benedictio Domini

Without, the sullen noises of the street!
    The voice of London, inarticulate,
Hoarse and blaspheming, surges in to meet
    The silent blessing of the Immaculate.

Dark is the church, and dim the worshippers,
    Hushed with bowed heads as though by some old spell,
While through the incense-laden air there stirs
    The admonition of a silver bell.

Dark is the church, save where the altar stands,
    Dressed like a bride, illustrious with light,
Where one old priest exalts with tremulous hands
    The one true solace of man's fallen plight.

Strange silence here: without, the sounding street
    Heralds the world's swift passage to the fire;
O Benediction, perfect and complete!
    When shall men cease to suffer and desire?

Carthusians

Through what long heaviness, assayed in what strange fire,
Have these white monks been brought into the way of **peace,**
Despising the world's wisdom and the world's desire,
Which from the body of this death bring no release?

Within their austere walls no voices penetrate;
A sacred silence only, as of death, obtains;
Nothing finds entry here of loud or passionate;
This quiet is the exceeding profit of their pain.

From many lands they came, in divers fiery ways;
Each knew at last the vanity of earthly joys;
And one was crowned with thorns, and one was crowned **with**
    bays.
And each was tired at last of the world's foolish noise.

It was not theirs with Dominic to preach God's holy **wrath,**
They were too stern to bear sweet Francis' gentle sway;
Theirs was a higher calling and a steeper path,
To dwell alone with Christ, to meditate and pray.

A cloistered company, they are companionless,
None knoweth here the secret of his brother's heart:
They are but come together for more loneliness,
Whose bond is solitude and silence all their part.

O beatific life! Who is there shall gainsay,
Your great refusal's victory, your little loss,
Deserting vanity for the more perfect way,
The sweetest service of the most dolorous Cross.

Ye shall prevail at last! Surely ye shall prevail!
Your silence and your austerity shall win at last:
Desire and Mirth, the world's ephemeral lights shall fail,
The sweet star of your queen is never overcast.

We fling up flowers and laugh, we laugh across the wine;
With wine we dull our souls and careful strains of art;
Our cups are polished skulls round which the roses twine:
None dares to look at Death who leers and lurks apart.

Move on, white company, whom that has not sufficed!
Our viols cease, our wine is death, our roses fail:
Pray for our heedlessness, O dwellers with the Christ!
Though the world fall apart, surely ye shall prevail.

AUGUSTA THEODOSIA DRANE

Maris Stella

Mary, beautiful and bright
    Velut Maris Stella,
Brighter than the morning light,
    Parens et Puella,
I cry to thee, look down on me;
Ladye, pray thy Son for me,
    Tam pia,
That thy child may come to thee,
    Maria.

Sad the earth was and forlorn,
    Eva peccatrice,
Until Christ our Lord was born
    De te Genitrice;
Gabriel's *"Ave"* chased away
Darksome night, and brought the day,
    Salutis;
Thou the Fount whence waters play,
    Virtutis.

Ladye, Flower of living thing,
    Rosa sine spina;
Mother of Jesus, heaven's King,
    Gratia divina;
'Tis thou in all dost bear the prize,
Ladye, Queen of Paradise,
    Electa,
Maiden meek and Mother wise,
    Effecta.

In care thou counsellest the best,
    Felix fecundata;
To the weary thou are rest,
    Mater honorata;
Plead in thy love to Him who gave
His precious Blood the world to save
    In cruce,
That we our home with Him may have
    In luce.

Well knows he, that he is thy Son,
    Ventre quem portasti;
All thou dost ask Him, then, is won,
    Partum quem lactasti;

77

So pitiful He is and kind,
By Him the road to bliss we find
    Superni;
He doth the gates of darkness bind
    Inferni.

MICHAEL EARLS, S.J.

An Autumn Rose-Tree

It seemed too late for roses
    When I walked abroad today,
October stood in silence,
    By the hedges all the way:
Yet did I hear a singing,
    And I saw a red rose-tree:
In fields so gray with autumn
    How could song or roses be?

Oh, it was never maple
    Nor the dogwood's coat afire,
No sage with scarlet banners,
    Nor the poppy's vested choir:
The breeze that may be music
    When the summer lawns are fair
Will have no heart for singing
    In the autumn's mournful air.

As I went up the roadway,
    Under cold and lonely skies,
A song I heard, a rose-tree
    Waved to me in glad surprise:
A red cloak and a ribbon,
    (Round the braided hair of jet)
And redder cheeks than roses
    Of a little Margaret.

Now God is good in autumn,
    He can name the birds that sing,
He loves the hearts of children
    More than flowery fields of spring:
And when the years of winter
    Gray with Margaret will be,
God will find her love still blossom
    Like a red rose-tree.

To a Carmelite Postulant

Oh, the banks of May are fair,
  Charm of sound and sight,
Breath of heaven fills the air,
  To the world's delight.

Far more wondrous is a bower,
  Fairer than the May,
Love-of-God it wears in flower,
  Blooming night and day.

Love-of-God within the heart
  Multicolored grows,
Now a lily's counterpart,
  Now the blood-red rose.

Come the sun or chilling rain,
  Come the drought or dew,
Crocus health or violet pain,
  Love-of-God is true.

Hard may be the mountain-side,
  Soft the valley sod,
Yet will fragrance sure abide
  With the Love-of-God.

Where the grace of Heaven leads,
  There it makes a home,
Hills a hundred and the meads
  Will its pathway roam.

Carmel by the western sea
  Holds your blessed bower:
Love-of-God eternally
  Keep your heart a-flower.

HELEN PARRY EDEN

A Purpose of Amendment

He who mangold-patch doth hoe,
Sweating beneath a sturdy sun,
Clearing each weed-disguised row
Till daylight and the task be done,

79

Standeth to view his labour's scene—
Where now, within the hedge-row's girth,
The little plant's untrammeled green
Stripes the brown fabric of the earth.

So when the absolution's said
Behind the grille, and I may go,
And all the flowers of sin are dead,
And all the stems of sin laid low,

And I am come to Mary's shrine
To lay my hopes within her hand—
Ah, in how fair and green a line
The seedling resolutions stand.

The Confessional

My Sorrow diligent would sweep
That dingy room infest
With dust (thereby I mean my soul)
Because she hath a Guest
Who doth require that self-same room
Be garnished for His rest.

And Sorrow (who had washed His feet
Where He before had been)
Took the long broom of Memory
And swept the corners clean,
Till in the midst of the fair floor
The sum of dust was seen.

It lay there, settled by her tears,
That fell the while she swept—
Light fluffs of grey and earthly dregs;
And over these she wept,
For all were come since last her Guest
Within the room had slept.

And, for nor broom nor tears had power
To lift the clods of ill,
She called one servant of her Guest
Who came with right good will,
For, by his sweet Lord's bidding, he
Waiteth on Sorrow still;

So, seeing she had done her part
As far as in her lay
And had intent to keep the place

More cleanly from that day,
Did with his Master's dust-pan come
And take the dust away.

She thanked him, and Him who sent
Such succour, and she spread
Fair sheets of Thankfulness and Love
Upon her Master's bed,
Then on the new-scoured threshold stood
And listened for His tread.

*An Elegy, for Father Anselm, of the Order of
    Reformed Cistercians*

You to whose soul a death propitious brings
Its Heaven, who attain a windless bourn
Of sanctity beyond all sufferings,
It is not ours to mourn;

For you, to whom the earth could nothing give,
Who knew no hint of our inspired pride,
You could not very well be said to live
Until the day you died.

'Tis upon us—father and kindly friend,
Holy and cheerful host—the unbidden guest
You welcomed and the souls you would amend,
The weight of sorrow rests.

From Sarum in the mesh of her five streams,
Her idle belfries and her glittering vanes,
We are clomb to where the cloud-race dusks and gleams
On turf of upland plains.

Southward the road through juniper and briar
Clambers the down, untrodden and unworn
Save where some flock pitted the chalky mire
With little feet at dawn.

Twice in a week the hooded carrier's lamp,
Flashing on wayside flints and grasses, spills
Its misty radiance where the dews lie damp
Among the untended hills;

Here lies the hamlet ringed with grassy mound
And brambled barrow where, superbly dead,
The dust of pagans turned to holy ground
Beneath your humble tread.

Here we descend at drooping dusk the side
Of the stony down beneath the planted ring
Of beeches where you showed with pastoral pride
The folded lambs in spring;

Here pull at eve the self-same bell that hastened
Your rough-shod feet behind the hollow door—
Yet never see you stand, the chain unfastened,
Your lantern on the floor.

Others will spread the board now you are gone
Here where you smiled and gave your guests to eat,
Learning your menial kingliness from One
Who washed His servant's feet;

Along the slumbering corridors betimes
Others will knock and other footsteps pass
Down the wet lane e'er the thin shivering chimes
Toll for the early Mass.

Yet in the chapel's self no sorrows sing
In the strange priest's voice, nor any dolour grips
The heart because it is not you who bring
Your Master to its lips.

Here let us leave the things you would not have—
Vain grief and sorrow useless to be shown—
"God's gift and the Community's I gave
And nothing of my own,"

You would have said, self-deemed of no more worth
Then that green hands that guard a poppy's grace—
Blows the eternal flower and back to earth
Tumbles the withered case.

Nay, but our Lord hath made renouncement vain,
Himself into those humble hands let fall,
Guerdon of willing poverty and pain,
The greatest gift of all;

To you and all who in that life austere
Mid fields remote your harsher labours ply
Singing His praise, girt round from year to year
With sheep-bells and the sky—

This, that to you is larger audience given
Where prayer and praise with sighing pinions shod
Piercing the starry ante-rooms of Heaven
Sway the designs of God:

82

And now yourself, standing where late hath stood
The echo of your voice, are prayer and praise—
O sweet reward and unsurpassing good
For that small gift of days.

Yourself, who now have heard such summoning
And seen such burning clarities alight
As broke the vigilant shepherds' drowsy ring
On the predestined night,

Who made such haste as theirs who rose and trod
To Bethlehem the dew-encumbered grass,
Trustful to see the showing forth of God
And the Word come to pass;

With how much more than home-spun Israelites'
Poor hungry glimpse of Godhead are you blest
Whom Mary shows for more than mortal nights
The Jewel on her breast.

Yet, as one kneeling churl might chance to think
Of the wan herd behind their wattled bars,
Moving unshepherded with bells that clink
And stir beneath the stars,

And, for the thought's space wishing he were back,
Pray to that Sum of Sweetness for his sheep—
"Take them, O Thou that dost supply our lack,
Into Thy hands to keep."

So you who in His presence move and live
Recall, amid your glad celestial cares,
Your chosen office, to your children give
The charity of prayers.

Sorrow

Of Sorrow, 'tis as Saints have said—
That his ill-savoured lamp shall shed
A light to Heaven, when, blown about
By the world's vain and windy rout,
The candles of delight burn out.

Then usher Sorrow to thy board,
Give him such fare as may afford
Thy single habitation—best

To meet him half-way in his quest,
The importunate and sad-eyed guest.

Yet somewhat should he give who took
My hospitality, for look,
His is no random vagrancy;
Beneath his rags what hints there be
Of a celestial livery.

Sweet Sorrow, play a grateful part,
Break me the marble of my heart
And of its fragments pave a street
Where, to my bliss, myself may meet
One hastening with piercèd feet.

FATHER EDMUND, C.P.

Our Lady's Death

And didst thou die, dear Mother of our Life?
Sin had no part in thee; then how should death?
Methinks, if aught the great tradition saith
Could wake in loving hearts a moment's strife
(I said—my own with her new image rife),
'Twere this. And yet 'tis certain, next to faith
Thou didst lie down to render up thy breath:
Though after the seventh sword, no meaner knife
Could pierce that bosom. No, nor did: no sting
Of pain was there; but only joy. The love,
So long thy life ecstatic, and restrained
From setting free thy soul, now gave it wing;
Thy body, soon to reign with it above,
Radiant and fragrant, as in trance, remained.

MAURICE FRANCIS EGAN

Maurice de Guerin

The old wine filled him, and he saw, with eyes
Anoint of Nature, fauns and dryads fair
Unseen by others; to him maidenhair
And waxen lilacs, and those birds that rise
A-sudden from tall reeds at slight surprise,

84

Brought charmed thoughts; and in earth everywhere
He, like sad Jaques, found a music rare
As that of Syrinx to old Grecians wise.
A pagan heart, a Christian soul had he,
He followed Christ, yet for dead Pan he sighed,
Til earth and heaven met within his breast;
As if Theocritus in Sicily
Had come upon the Figure crucified
And lost his gods in deep, Christ-given rest.

The Old Violin

Though tuneless, stringless, it lies there in dust,
    Like some great thought on a forgotten page;
The soul of music cannot fade or rust,—
    The voice within it stronger grows with age;
Its strings and bow are only trifling things—
    A master-touch!—its sweet soul wakes and sings.

Vigil of the Immaculate Conception

A sword of silver cuts the fields asunder—
    A silver sword tonight, a lake in June—
And plains of snow reflect, the maples under,
    The silver arrows of a wintry noon.

The trees are white with moonlight and with ice-pearls;
    The trees are white, like ghosts we see in dreams;
The air is still: there are no moaning wind-whirls;
    And one sees silence in the quivering beams.

December night, December night, how warming
    Is all thy coldness to the Christian soul:
Thy very peace at each true heart is storming
    In potent waves of love that surging roll.

December night, December night, how glowing
    Thy frozen rains upon our warm hearts lie:
Our God upon this vigil is bestowing
    A thousand graces from the silver sky.

O moon, O symbol of our Lady's whiteness;
    O snow, O symbol of our Lady's heart;
O night, chaste night, bejewelled with argent brightness,
    How sweet, how bright, how loving, kind thou art.

O miracle: tomorrow and tomorrow,
    In tender reverence shall no praise abate;
For from all seasons shall we new jewels borrow
    To deck the Mother born Immaculate.

He Made Us Free

As flame streams upward, so my longing thought
        Flies up with Thee,
Thou God and Saviour who hast truly wrought
Life out of death, and to us, loving, brought
A fresh, new world; and in Thy sweet chains caught,
        And made us free!

As hyacinths make way from out the dark,
        My soul awakes,
As thought of Thee, like sap beneath the bark;
As little violets in field and park
Rise to the trilling thrush and meadow-lark,
        New hope it takes.

As thou goest upward through the nameless space
        We call the sky,
Like jonquil perfume softly falls Thy grace;
It seems to touch and brighten every place;
Fresh flowers crown our wan and weary race,
        O Thou on high.

Hadst Thou not risen, there would be no more joy
        Upon earth's sod;
Life would still be with us a wound or toy,
A cloud without the sun—O Babe, O Boy,
A Man of Mother pure, with no alloy,
        O risen God!

Thou, God and King, didst "mingle in the game,"
        (Cease, all fears; cease!)
For love of us—not to give Virgil's fame
Or Croesus' wealth, not to make well the lame,
Or save the sinner from deserved shame,
        But for sweet Peace!

For peace, for joy—not that the slave might lie
        In luxury,
Not that all woe from us should always fly,
Or golden crops with Syrian roses vie
In every field; but in Thy peace to die
        And rise—be free!

FREDERICK WILLIAM FABER

The Grandeurs of Mary

What is this grandeur I see up in heaven,
    A splendour that looks like a splendour divine?
What creature so near the Creator is throned?
    O Mary, those marvellous glories are thine.

But who would have thought that a creature could live
    With the fires of the Godhead so awfully nigh?
Oh, who could have dreamed, mighty Mother of God,
    That ever God's power could have raised thee so high?

What name can we give to a queenship so grand?
    What thought can we think of a glory like this?
Saints and angels lie far in the distance, remote
    From the golden excess of thine unmated bliss.

Thy person, thy soul, thy most beautiful form,
    Thine office, thy name, thy most singular grace—
God hath made for them, Mother, a world by itself,
    A shrine all alone, a most worshipful place.

Mid the blaze of those fires, eternal, unmade,
    Thy Maker unspeakably makes thee his own;
The arms of the Three Uncreated, outstretched,
    Round the Word's mortal Mother in rapture are thrown.

Thy sinless conception, thy jubilant birth,
    Thy crib and thy cross, thine assumption and crown,
They have raised thee on high to the right hand of Him
    Whom the spells of thy love to thy bosom drew down.

I am blind with thy glory; in all God's wide world
    I find nothing like thee for glory and power:
I can hardly believe that thou grewest on earth,
    In the green fields of Juda, a scarce-noticed flower.

And is it not really eternal, divine?
    Is it human, created, a glorified heart,
So like God, and not God? Ah, Maker of men,
    We bless thee for being the God that thou art.

O Mary, what ravishing pageants I see,
    What wonders and works centre round thee in heaven,
What creations of grace fall like light from thy hands,
    What creator-like powers to thy prudence are given.

What vast jurisdiction, what numberless realms,
　　What profusion of dread and unlimited power,
What holy supremacies, awful domains,
　　The Word's mighty Mother enjoys for her dower.

What grand ministrations of pity and strength,
　　What endless processions of beautiful light,
What incredible marvels of motherly love,
　　What queenly resplendence of empire and right.

What sounds as of seas flowing all round thy throne,
　　What flashings of fire from thy burning abode,
What thunders of glory, what tempests of power,
　　What calms, like the calms in the Bosom of God.

Inexhaustible wonder; the treasures of God
　　Seem to multiply under thy marvellous hand;
And the power of thy Son seems to gain and to grow,
　　When He deigns to obey thy maternal command.

Ten thousand magnificent greatnesses blend
　　Their vast oceans of light, at the foot of thy throne;
Ten thousand unspeakable majesties grace
　　The royalty vested in Mary alone.

But look, what a wonder there is up in God:
　　One love, like a special perfection, we see;
And the chief of thy grandeurs, great Mother, is there—
　　In the love the Eternal Himself has for thee.

The Right Must Win

Oh, it is hard to work for God,
　　To rise and take His part
Upon this battlefield of earth,
　　And not sometimes lose heart.

He hides Himself so wondrously,
　　As though there were no God;
He is least seen when all the powers
　　Of ill are most abroad.

Or He deserts us at the hour
　　The fight is all but lost;
And seems to leave us to ourselves
　　Just when we need Him most.

Ill masters good; good seems to change
    To ill with greatest ease;
And, worst of all, the good with good
    Is at cross-purposes.

Ah! God is other than we think;
    His ways are far above,
Far beyond reason's height, and reached
    Only by child-like love.

Workman of God! Oh, lose not heart,
    But learn what God is like;
And in the darkest battlefield
    Thou shalt know where to strike.

Thrice blessed is he to whom is given
    The instinct that can tell
That God is on the field when He
    Is most invisible.

Blessed, too, is he who can divine
    Where real right doth lie,
And dares to take the side that seems
    Wrong to man's blindfold eye.

For right is right, since God is God;
    And right the day must win;
To doubt would be disloyalty,
    To falter would be sin.

JOHN FITZPATRICK

Mater Dolorosa

She stands, within the shadow, at the foot
Of the high tree she planted: thirty-three
Full years have sped, and such has grown to be
The stem that burgeoned forth from Jesse's root.
Spring swiftly passed and panted in pursuit
The eager summer; now she stands to see
The only fruit-time of her only tree:
And all the world is waiting for the Fruit.
Now is faith's sad fruition: this one hour
Of gathered expectation wears the crown
Of the long grief with which the years were rife;
As in her lap—a sudden autumn shower—
The earthquake with his trembling hand shakes down
The red, ripe Fruitage of the Tree of Life.

ALICE FURLONG

Yuletide

In a stable bare,
Lo, the great Ones are.
Strew the Ivy and the Myrtle
Round about the Virgin's kirtle!

Ass and oxen mild
Breathe soft upon the Child!
Blow the scent of bygone summer
On your breath to the New-comer!

Be ye well content
To be straitly pent
Backwards in the rocky chamber
From the angel's wings of amber!

Rapt the seraphs sit,
With godly faces lit
In a radiance shining solely
From the Christ-child, meek and holy.

High they chant and clear
Of the lovely cheer,
Ring down the new evangels
Of the mystic, midnight angels.

Faring with good will
From the misty hill,
Every shepherd sacrificeth
To the prophet that ariseth.

Joseph, Mary's spouse,
Prince of David's House,
Bendeth low in adorations
To the Ruler of the Nations.

Who doth sweetly rest
On his Mother's breast,
Lord of the lightnings and the thunders!
Mary's heart keeps all these wonders.

FRANCIS A. GAFFNEY, O.P.

Our Lady of the Rosary

Lepanto marks the spot of victory,
O'er crescent cruel and strong, by forces weak,
Of hallowed cross; of which, "if sign you seek,"
'Tis not of man but a Divinity.
The white-robed Pius Fifth the Rosary
Uplifted like the rod of Moses, meek;
Whilst Ottomans on Christians wrath would wreak
And, as of old, engulfed them in the sea.

O Lady of the Rosary, today
Thy clients all beseech thee, hear their prayer,
And beg the Christ who raging storms did quell,
Bid warring nations cease their bloody fray;
His power and thine honor, we declare,
O Thou All-Fair, thou Joy of Israel.

EDWARD F. GARESCHÉ, S.J.

At the Leap of the Waters

How the swift river runs bright to its doom,
   Placid and shining and smooth-flowing by,
Blue with the gleam of the heavenly room,
   Smiling and calm with the smile of the sky!
Ah, but the plunge! and the shock and the roar,
   The spray of vast waters that hurl to the deep,
The churn of its foam, as the measureless pour
   Of that wide-brimming torrent leaps sheer from the steep!
Look ye; it reaches small fingers of spray
   To clutch at the brink, as unwilling to go
Through the perilous air, and be fretted away
   In the tumult of vapor that boileth below.
List ye! the voice of the huge undertone
   That murmurs in pain from the cataract's breast,
Where the bruised, shattered waters perpetual moan
   And wander and toss in a weary unrest.
Feel ye the breath of the cool-spraying mist,
   Cloudy and gray from the depths of its pain;
Not as when sunbeams the waters have kissed,
   Rising in vapor to gather in rain,
But fiercely and madly flung forth on the air,

91

A shroud for this river that leaps to its death,
A veil o'er the throes of the cataract there,
    And rolling and rent with its agonized breath!
Wild torrent! God put thee to thunder His name!
    With the roar of thy waters to call to the sky
Of His might, who hath set thee forever the same,
    To topple in foam to the gulfs from on high.
Loud hymn of the lake-lands! from shore unto shore,
    Still clamor His praises who called thee to be,
Till the ears of the nations are tuned to thy roar,
    And they hear the vast message He trusted to thee.

Niagara

God, in His ages past the dawn of days,
Writ one white line of praise,
Which now, in this great stress and hour of need,
I bend my soul to read.
I break the sullen bonds of wearying time,
And with one leap sublime,
Force my astounded soul go back and stand
In the primeval land!

The tresses of the ancient flood are kissed
With virginal, white mist.
The same soft, thunderous sound
Thrills the wild woods around,
But oh the vast and mighty peace that broods
On these green solitudes,
Where the great land, with one tremendous tone,
Litanies to God, alone!

Tongue of the continent! Thou whose hymning shakes
The bosom of the lakes!
O sacrificial torrent, keen and bright,
Hurled from thy glorious height!
Thou sacerdotal presence, clothed in power,
At once the victim and the white-robed priest,
Whose praise throughout these ages hath not ceased,
Whose altar steams with incense every hour!
Lo, in all days, from thy white waters, rise
The savors of perpetual sacrifice!
I see pale prophecy of Christ's dear blood!—
The transubstantiation of thy flood!

Oh the wild wonder of the vast emotion
Of the perturbèd wave,

92

That cries and wanders like the fearful ocean,
Seeking, with none to save!
In their wide agony the rapids roam,
A world of waves, an universe of pain!
The vexed, tumultous clamor of their foam
Crying to God with agonized refrain,
Where the sad rocks their quivering summits hide
In the loud anguish of the refluent tide.

Yet, with a willingness that leaps to sorrow
Swift run the ragged surges to the height,
And from their pain is born a pure delight—
The fear today, the snowy peace tomorrow!—
Cleaving like darts their swift and silvery way
With sudden gleams, and barbs of glittering spray,
They hurry to the brink, and swift are lost
In that stupendous leap, that infinite holocaust!

Oh Christ-like glory of the praying water
That leaps forever to its mystic death!
And from the anguish of that sobbing slaughter
Lifts the clear glory of the torrent's breath,
Where like a paean of rapturous victory calls
The solemn jubilation of the falls!

O alabastrine priest—thy splendor spraying
More lasting than the immemorial hills!
O monument of waves, O undecaying
While God's right hand thy flowing chalice fills!
Under the transient world's astonished eyes
Thou offerest abiding sacrifice!

In the pale morning, when the rising sun
Flatters thy pouring flood with slanting beams,
Most reverent thy duteous waters run,
And hymn to God with all their thousand streams.
And in the blazing majesty of noon,
Still lifts thy wave its sacrificial tune,
And spills, like jewels of some eastern story,
Its bright, impetuous avalanche of glory!

And in the stilly spaces of the night,
While heaven wonders with its wakeful stars,
Thou prayest still, beneath the solemn light,
In booming tones that reach to heaven's bars,
Keeping thy vigils, while the angelic moon
Walks on thy perilous verge with glorious shoon,
Chanting from foam and spray without encease
Thy yearning immemorial prayer for peace!

93

CAROLINE GILTINAN

Communion

Mother Mary, thee I see
Bringing Him, thy Babe, to me.
Thou dost say, with trusting smile:
"Hold Him, dear, a little while."
Mother Mary, pity me,
For He struggles to be free!
My heart, my arms—He finds defiled:
I am unworthy of thy Child.
Mary, Mother, charity!
Bring thy Baby back to me!

GERALD GRIFFIN

The Nightingale

As the mute nightingale in closest groves
Lies hid at noon, but when day's piercing eye
Is locked in night, with full heart beating high
Poureth her plain-song o'er the light she loves;

So, Virgin ever-pure and ever-blest,
Moon of religion, from whose radiant face
Reflected streams the light of heavenly grace
On broken hearts, by contrite thoughts oppressed:

So, Mary, they who justly feel the weight
Of Heaven's offended Majesty, implore
Thy reconciling aid with suppliant knee:
Of sinful man, O sinless Advocate,

To thee they turn, nor Him they less adore;
'Tis still His light they love, less dreadful seen in thee.

LOUISE IMOGEN GUINEY

The Wild Ride

I hear in my heart, I hear in its ominous pulses
All day, on the road, the hoofs of invisible horses,
All night, from their stalls, the importunate pawing and
    neighing.

Let cowards and laggards fall back! but alert to the saddle,
Weatherworn and abreast, go men of our galloping legion,
With a stirrup-cup each to the lily of women that loves him.

The trail is through dolor and dread, over crags and morasses;
There are shapes by the way, there are things that appal or
    entice us:
What odds? We are Knights of the Grail, we are vowed to the
    riding.

Thought's self is a vanishing wing, and joy is a cobweb,
And friendship a flower in the dust, and glory a sunbeam:
Not here is our prize, nor, alas! after these our pursuing.

A dipping of plumes, a tear, a shake of the bridle,
A passing salute to this world and her pitiful beauty:
We hurry with never a word in the track of our fathers.

I hear in my heart, I hear in its ominous pulses
All day, on the road, the hoofs of invisible horses,
All night, from their stalls, the importunate pawing and
    neighing.

We spur to a land of no name, outracing the stormwind;
We leap to the infinite dark like the sparks from the anvil.
Thou leadest, O God! All's well with Thy troopers that follow.

Tryste Noel

The Ox he openeth wide the doore,
    And from the Snowe he calls her inne,
And he hath seen her smile therefore,
    Our Ladye without Sinne.
        Now soone from Sleep
        A Starre shall leap,
And soone arrive both King and Hinde:
            Amen, Amen:
But O the place co'd I but finde!

95

The Ox hath hushed his voyce and bent
　Trewe eyes of Pitty ore the Mow,
And on his lovelie Neck, forspent,
　The Blessed layes her Browe.
　　Around her Feet,
　　Full warme and sweete,
His bowerie Breath doth meeklie dwell:
　　　Amen, Amen:
But sore am I with Vaine Travel!

The Ox is Host in Judah stall
　And Host of more than onlie one,
For close she gathereth withal
　Our Lorde her littel Sonne.
　　Glad Hinde and King
　　Their Gyfte may bring,
But wo'd tonight my Teares were there,
　　　Amen, Amen:
Between her Bosom and His Hayre!

Ode for a Master Mariner Ashore

There in his room, whene'er the moon looks in,
And silvers now a shell, and now a fin,
And o'er his chart glides like an argosy,
Quiet and old sits he.
Danger! he hath grown homesick for thy smile.
Where hidest thou the while, heart's boast,
Strange face of beauty sought and lost,
Star-face that lured him out from boyhood's isle?

Blown clear from dull indoors, his dreams behold
Night-water smoke and sparkle as of old,
The taffrail lurch, the sheets triumphant toss
Their phosphor-flowers across.
Towards ocean's either rim the long-exiled
Wears on, till stunted cedars throw
A lace-like shadow over snow,
Or tropic fountains wash their agates wild.

Awhile, play up and down the briny spar
Odors of Surinam and Zanzibar,
Till blithely thence he ploughs, in visions new,
The Labradorian blue;
All homeless hurricanes about him break;
The purples of spent day he sees

From Samos to the Hebrides,
And drowned men dancing darkly in his wake.

Where the small deadly foam-caps, well descried,
Top, tier on tier, the hundred-mountainèd tide,
Away, and far away, his pride is borne,
Riding the noisy morn,
Plunges, and preens her wings, and laughs to know
The helm and tightening halyards still
Follow the urging of his will,
And scoff at sullen earth a league below.

Mischance hath barred him from his heirdom high,
And shackled him with many an inland tie,
And of his only wisdom made a jibe
Amid an alien tribe:
No wave abroad but moans his fallen state,
The trade-wind ranges now, the trade-wind roars!
Why is it on a yellowing page he pores?
Ah, why this hawser fast to a garden gate?

Thou friend so long withdrawn, so deaf, so dim,
Familiar Danger, O forget not him!
Repeat of thine evangel yet the whole
Unto his subject soul,
Who suffers no such palsy of her drouth,
Nor hath so tamely worn her chain,
But she may know that voice again,
And shake the reefs with answer of her mouth.

O give him back, before his passion fail,
The singing cordage and the hollow sail,
And level with those agèd eyes let be
The bright unsteady sea;
And move like any film from off his brain
The pasture wall, the boughs that run
Their evening arches to the sun,
The hamlet spire across the sown champaign;

And on the shut space and the trivial hour,
Turn the great floods! and to thy spousal bower,
With rapt arrest and solemn loitering,
Him whom thou lovedst bring:
That he, thy faithful one, with praising lip,
Not having, at the last, less grace
Of thee than had his roving race,
Sum up his strength to perish with a ship.

97

In Leinster

I try to knead and spin, but my life is low the while.
Oh, I long to be alone, and walk abroad a mile;
Yet if I walk alone, and think of naught at all,
Why from me that's young should the wild tears fall?

The shower-stricken earth, the earth-colored streams,
They breathe on me awake, and moan to me in dreams;
And yonder ivy fondling the broke castle-wall,
It pulls upon my heart till the wild tears fall.

The cabin-door looks down, a furze-lighted hill,
And far as Leighlin Cross the fields are green and still;
But once I hear the blackbird in Leighlin hedges call,
The foolishness is on me, and the wild tears fall!

ROBERT STEPHEN HAWKER

Aunt Mary: A Christmas Chant

Now, of all the trees by the king's highway,
        Which do you love the best?
O! the one that is green upon Christmas Day,
        The bush with the bleeding breast.
Now the holly with her drops of blood for me:
For that is our dear Aunt Mary's tree.

Its leaves are sweet with our Saviour's Name,
        'Tis a plant that loves the poor:
Summer and winter it shines the same
        Beside the cottage door.
O! the holly with her drops of blood for me:
For that is our kind Aunt Mary's tree.

'Tis a bush that the birds will never leave:
        They sing in it all day long;
But sweetest of all upon Christmas Eve
        Is to hear the robin's song.
'Tis the merriest sound upon earth or sea:
For it comes from our own Aunt Mary's tree.

So, of all that grows by the king's highway,
        I love that tree the best;
'Tis a bower for the birds upon Christmas Day,
        The bush of the bleeding breast.

98

O! the holly with her drops of blood for me:
For that is our sweet Aunt Mary's tree.

King Arthur's Waes-hael

Waes-hael for knight and dame;
   O merry be their dole;
Drink-hael! In Jesu's name
   We fill the tawny bowl;
But cover down the curving crest,
Mould of the Orient Lady's breast.

Waes-hael! yet lift no lid:
   Drain ye the reeds for wine.
Drink-hael! the milk was hid
   That soothed that Babe divine;
Hush'd, as this hollow channel flows,
He drew the balsam from the rose.

Waes-hael! thus glowed the breast
   Where a God yearned to cling;
Drink-hael! so Jesu pressed
   Life from its mystic spring;
Then hush and bend in reverend sign
And breathe the thrilling reeds for wine.

Waes-hael! in shadowy scene
   Lo! Christmas children we:
Drink-hael! behold we lean
   At a far Mother's knee;
To dream that thus her bosom smiled,
And learn the lip of Bethlehem's Child.

JAMES M. HAYES

Old Nuns

Our Lady smiles on youthful nuns,
   She loves them well.
Our Lady's smile like sunshine floods
   Each convent cell,
But fondest falls Our Lady's smile
   Where old nuns dwell;

Old nuns whose hearts are young with love
   For Mary's Son,

Old nuns whose prayers for faltering souls
    Have victory won,
Old nuns whose lives are beautiful
    With service done.

Their love a loveless world has saved
    From God's dread rod,
The paths where Sorrow walks with Sin
    Their feet have trod,
Their knees have worn the flags that pave
    The house of God.

Our Lady smiles on youthful nuns,
    She loves them well;
Our Lady's smile like sunshine floods
    Each convent cell;
But fondest falls Our Lady's smile
    Where old nuns dwell.

The Mother of the Rose

I kneel on Holy Thursday with the faithful worshipping
Where Christ is throned in splendor as the sacramental King.

I ever will remember it, that wondrous full-blown rose
Among the burning tapers on the altar of repose.

O blessed among roses all, to bloom in beauty there,
To give your heart unto your God and in His glory share.

In quiet fields beyond the town, near where the river flows
There is a humble garden where a gentle rose-tree grows.

To-night our Lord remembers on the altar of repose
This rose-tree in the fields afar, the mother of the rose.

The Transfiguration

He seeks the mountains where the olives grow,
    The Lord of Glory, veiled in humble guise;
His soul is shadowed with a coming woe,
    The grief of all the world is in His eyes:
His spirit struggles in the dark caress
Of anguish, pain and utter loneliness.

He always loved the mountain tops, for there
    Away from earth, He treads the mystic ways,

100

And sees the vision of the Fairest Fair,
    As Heaven dawns upon His raptured gaze;
The loneliness, the pain, the grief depart;
Surpassing gladness fills His Sacred Heart.

That day He stood upon the olive hill,
    And Peter, James and John in wonder saw
The burning glories of the God-head fill
    His soul with grandeur, and in holy awe
They fell upon the ground and cried for grace,
Lest they should die beholding God's own Face.

As minor chords that sob from strings of gold
    The Master speaks in accents sweet and sad:
The vision past, the chosen three behold
    No one but Jesus and their souls are glad.
The awe, the splendor and the glory gone,
How sweet the face of Christ to look upon!

EMILY H. HICKEY

Beloved, It Is Morn

Beloved, it is morn!
    A redder berry on the thorn,
    A deeper yellow on the corn,
For this good day new-born.
        Pray, Sweet, for me
        That I may be
        Faithful to God and thee.

Beloved, it is day!
    And lovers work, as children play,
    With heart and brain untired alway:
Dear love, look up and pray.
        Pray, Sweet, for me
        That I may be
        Faithful to God and thee.

Beloved, it is night!
    Thy heart and mine are full of light,
    Thy spirit shineth clear and white,
God keep thee in His sight!
        Pray, Sweet, for me
        That I may be
        Faithful to God and thee.

101

A Sea Story

Silence. A while ago
 Shrieks went up piercingly;
But now is the ship gone down;
 Good ship, well manned, was she.
There's a raft that's a chance of life for one,
 This day upon the sea.

A chance for one of two;
 Young, strong, are he and he,
Just in the manhood prime,
 The comelier, verily,
For the wrestle with wind and weather and wave,
 In the life upon the sea.

One of them has a wife
 And little children three;
Two that can toddle and lisp,
 And a suckling on the knee:
Naked they'll go, and hunger sore,
 If he be lost at sea.

One has a dream of home,
 A dream that well may be:
He never has breathed it yet;
 She never has known it, she.
But some one will be sick at heart
 If he be lost at sea.

"Wife and kids at home!—
 Wife, kids, nor home has he!—
Give us a chance, Bill!" Then,
 "All right, Jem!" Quietly
A man gives up his life for a man,
 This day upon the sea.

GERARD MANLEY HOPKINS, S.J.

Spring

Nothing is so beautiful as spring—
When weeds, in wheels, shoot long and lovely and lush;
Thrush's eggs look little low heavens, and thrush
Through the echoing timber does so rinse and wring
The ear, it strikes like lightnings to hear him sing;

102

The glassy peartree leaves and blooms, they brush
The descending blue; that blue is all in a rush
With richness; the racing lambs too have fair their fling.

What is all this juice and all this joy?
A strain of the earth's sweet being in the beginning
In Eden garden.—Have, get, before it cloy,
Before it cloud, Christ, lord, and sour with sinning,
Innocent mind and Mayday in girl and boy,
Most, O maid's child, thy choice and worthy the winning.

The Habit of Perfection

Elected Silence, sing to me
And beat upon my whorlèd ear,
Pipe me to pastures still and be
The music that I care to hear.

Shape nothing, lips; be lovely-dumb:
It is the shut, the curfew sent
From there where all surrenders come
Which only make you eloquent.

Be shellèd, eyes, with double dark
And find the uncreated light:
This ruck and reel which you remark
Coils, keeps, and teases simple sight.

Palate, the hutch of tasty lust,
Desire not to be rinsed with wine:
The can must be so sweet, the crust
So fresh that come in fasts divine!

Nostrils, your careless breath that spend
Upon the stir and keep of pride,
What relish shall the censers send
Along the sanctuary side!

O feel-of-primrose hands, O feet
That want the yield of plushy sward,
But you shall walk the golden street,
And you unhouse and house the Lord.

And, Poverty, be thou the bride
And now the marriage feast begun,
And lily-coloured clothes provide
Your spouse not laboured-at, nor spun.

103

The Starlight Night

Look at the stars! look, look up at the skies!
O look at all the fire-folk sitting in the air!
The bright boroughs, the circle-citadels there!
Down in dim woods the diamond delves! The elves'-eyes!
The grey lawns cold where gold, where quickgold lies!
Wind-beat whitebeam; airy abeles all on a flare!
Flake-doves sent floating out at a farmyard scare!—
Ah well! it is all a purchase, all is a prize.

Buy then! Bid then!—What?—Prayer, patience, alms, vows.
Look, look: a May-mess, like on orchard boughs!
Look! March-bloom, like on mealed-with-yellow sallows!
These are indeed the barn: withindoors house
The shocks. This piece-bright paling hides the spouse
Christ home, and the mother of Christ and all His hallows.

SCHARMEL IRIS

The Friar of Genoa

In Genoa a friar walked;
Of every sacred tale he talked;
Alone he dwelt, in prayer he knelt;
    "Ave Maria, Ave Maria!"
From dawn till dusk he sang.

His bruised and blistered feet were bare;
His head burned in the sunlight's glare.
On stones he slept, and worked and wept,
    "Ave Maria, Ave Maria!"
In every blow or pang.

Out of his dole he clothed the poor,
And every hardship did endure;
He blessed the meek and nursed the weak
    "Ave Maria, Ave Maria!"
With each succeeding day.

And begged for alms for those in need,
A kind word spoke with every deed,
With sinners dined and led the blind—
    "Ave Maria, Ave Maria!"
Until he passed away.

104

And is his work done? Ah, surprise!
Out of the tomb where low he lies
A perfume blows, as of a rose:
            "Ave Maria, Ave Maria!"
It sings in shade or sun.

And he who breathes it, him it feeds,
And stirs his heart to noble deeds;
And one has said, "He is not dead—
            Ave Maria, Ave Maria!
His life has just begun!"

LIONEL JOHNSON

The Dark Angel

Dark Angel, with thine aching lust
To rid the world of penitence:
Malicious Angel, who still dost
My soul such subtle violence!

Because of thee, no thought, no thing,
Abides for me undesecrate:
Dark Angel, ever on the wing,
Who never reachest me too late!

When music sounds, then changest thou
Its silvery to a sultry fire:
Nor will thine envious heart allow
Delight untortured by desire.

Through thee, the gracious Muses turn
To Furies, O mine Enemy!
And all the things of beauty burn
With flames of evil ecstasy.

Because of thee, the land of dreams
Becomes a gathering place of fears:
Until tormented slumber seems
One vehemence of useless tears.

When sunlight glows upon the flowers,
Or ripples down the dancing sea:
Thou, with thy troop of passionate powers,
Beleaguerest, bewilderest, me.

105

Within the breath of autumn woods,
Within the winter silences:
Thy venomous spirit stirs and broods,
O Master of impieties!

The ardour of red flame is thine,
And thine the steely soul of ice:
Thou poisonest the fair design
Of nature, with unfair device.

Apples of ashes, golden bright;
Waters of bitterness, how sweet!
O banquet of a foul delight,
Prepared by thee, dark Paraclete!

Thou art the whisper in the gloom,
The hinting tone, the haunting laugh:
Thou art the adorner of my tomb,
The minstrel of mine epitaph.

I fight thee, in the Holy Name!
Yet, what thou dost is what God saith:
Tempter! should I escape thy flame,
Thou wilt have helped my soul from Death:

The second Death, that never dies,
That cannot die, when time is dead:
Live Death, wherein the lost soul cries,
Eternally uncomforted.

Dark Angel, with thine aching lust!
Of two defeats, of two despairs:
Less dread, a change to drifting dust,
Than thine eternity of cares.

Do what thou wilt, thou shalt not so,
Dark Angel! triumph over me:
Lonely, unto the Lone I go;
Divine, to the Divinity.

Te Martyrum Candidatus

Ah, see the fair chivalry come, the companions of Christ!
White Horsemen, who ride on white horses, the Knights of
    God!
They, for their Lord and their Lover who sacrificed
All, save the sweetness of treading, where He first trod!

106

These through the darkness of death, the dominion of night,
Swept, and they woke in white places at morning tide:
They saw with their eyes, and sang for joy of the sight,
They saw with their eyes the eyes of the Crucified.

Now, whithersoever He goeth, with Him they go:
White Horsemen, who ride on white horses, oh fair to see!
They ride, where the rivers of Paradise flash and flow,
White Horsemen, with Christ their Captain: forever He!

Christmas and Ireland

The golden stars give warmthless fire,
   As weary Mary goes through night:
Her feet are torn by stone and briar;
   She hath no rest, no strength, no light:
O Mary, weary in the snow,
     Remember Ireland's woe!

O Joseph, sad for Mary's sake!
   Look on our earthly Mother, too:
Let not the heart of Ireland break
   With agony the ages through:
For Mary's love, love also thou
     Ireland, and save her now!

Harsh were the folk, and bitter stern,
   At Bethlehem, that night of nights.
For you no cheering hearth shall burn:
   We have no room here, you no rights.
O Mary and Joseph; hath not she,
     Ireland, been even as ye?

The ancient David's royal house
   Was thine, Saint Joseph! wherefore she,
Mary, thine ever-virgin Spouse,
   To thine own city went with thee.
Behold! thy citizens disown
     The heir of David's throne!

Nay, more! The very King of Kings
   Was with you, coming to His own:
They thrust Him forth to lowliest things;
   The poor, meek beasts of toil alone
Stood by, when came to piteous birth
     The God of all the earth.

And she, our Mother Ireland, knows
    Insult, and infamies of wrong:
Her innocent children clad with woes,
    Her weakness trampled by the strong:
And still upon her Holy Land
    Her pitiless foemen stand.

From Manger unto Cross and Crown
    Went Christ: and Mother Mary passed
Through Seven Sorrows, and sat down
    Upon the Angel Throne at last.
Thence, Mary! to thine own Child pray,
    For Ireland's hope this day!

She wanders amid winter still,
    The dew of tears is on her face:
Her wounded heart takes yet its fill
    Of desolation and disgrace.
God still is God! And through God she
    Foreknows her joy to be.

The snows shall perish at the spring,
    The flowers pour fragrance round her feet:
Ah, Jesus! Mary! Joseph! bring
    This mercy from the Mercy Seat!
Send it, sweet King of Glory, born
    Humbly on Christmas Morn!

To My Patrons

Thy spear rent Christ, when dead for me He lay:
    My sin rends Christ, though never one save He
Perfectly loves me, comforts me. Then pray,
    Longinus Saint! the Crucified, for me.

Hard is the holy war, and hard the way:
    At rest with ancient victors would I be.
O faith's first glory from our England! pray,
    St. Alban! to the Lord of Hosts, for me.

Fain would I watch with thee, till morning gray,
    Beneath the stars austere: so might I see
Sunrise, and light, and joy, at last. Then pray,
    John Baptist Saint! unto the Christ, for me.

Remembering God's coronation day;
    Thorns for His crown; His throne, a Cross: to thee

Heaven's kingdom dearer was than earth's. Then pray
   Saint Louis! to the King of kings, for me.

Thy love loved all things: thy love knew no stay,
   But drew the very wild beasts round thy knee.
O lover of the least and lowest! pray,
   Saint Francis! to the Son of Man, for me.

Bishop of souls in servitude astray,
   Who didst for holy service set them free:
Use still thy discipline of love, and pray,
   Saint Charles! unto the world's High Priest, for me.

Our Lady of the Snows

Far from the world, far from delight,
Distinguishing not day from night;
Vowed to one sacrifice of all
The happy things, that men befall;
Pleading one sacrifice, before
Whom sun and sea and wind adore;
Far from earth's comfort, far away,
We cry to God, we cry and pray
For men, who have the common day.
Dance, merry world! and sing: but we,
Hearing, remember Calvary:
Get gold, and thrive you! but the sun
Once paled; and the centurion
Said: *This dead man was God's own Son.*
Think you, we shrink from common toil,
Works of the mart, works of the soil;
That, prisoners of strong despair,
We breathe this melancholy air;
Forgetting the dear calls of race,
And bonds of house, and ties of place;
That, cowards, from the field we turn,
And heavenward, in our weakness, yearn?
Unjust! unjust! while you despise
Our lonely years, our mournful cries:
You are the happier for our prayer;
The guerdon of our souls, you share.
Not in such feebleness of heart,
We play our solitary part;
Not fugitives of battle, we
Hide from the world, and let things be:
But rather, looking over earth,
Between the bounds of death and birth;

109

And sad at heart, for sorrow and sin,
We wondered, where might help begin.
And on our wonder came God's choice,
A sudden light, a clarion voice,
Clearing the dark, and sounding clear:
And we obeyed: behold us, here!
In prison bound, but with your chains:
Sufferers, but of alien pains.
Merry the world, and thrives apace,
Each in his customary place:
Sailors upon the carrying sea,
Shepherds upon the pasture lea,
And merchants of the town; and they,
Who march to death, the fighting way;
And there are lovers in the spring,
With those, who dance, and those, who sing:
The commonwealth of every day,
Eastward and westward, far away,
Once the sun paled; once cried aloud
The Roman, from beneath the cloud:
This day the Son of God is dead!
Yet heed men, what the Roman said?
They heed not: we then heed for them,
The mindless of Jerusalem;
Careless, they live and die: but we
Care, in their stead, for Calvary.
O joyous men and women! strong,
To urge the wheel of life along,
With strenuous arm, and cheerful strain,
And wisdom of labourous brain:
We give our life, our heart, our breath,
That you may live to conquer death;
That, past your tomb, with souls in health,
Joy may be yours, and blessed wealth;
Through vigils of the painful night,
Our spirits with your tempters fight:
For you, for you, we live alone,
Where no joy comes, where cold winds moan:
Nor friends have we, nor have we foes;
Our Queen is of the lonely Snows.
Ah! and sometimes, our prayers between,
Come sudden thoughts of what hath been:
Dreams! And from dreams, once more we fall
To prayer: *God save, Christ keep, them all.*
And thou, who knowest not these things,
Hearken, what news our message brings!
Our toils, thy joy of life forgot:
Our lives of prayer forget thee not.

Cadgwith

My windows open to the autumn night,
In vain I watched for sleep to visit me:
How should sleep dull mine ears, and dim my sight,
Who saw the stars, and listened to the sea?

Ah, how the City of our God is fair!
If, without sea and starless though it be,
For joy of the majestic beauty there,
Men shall not miss the stars, nor mourn the sea.

A Friend

All, that he came to give,
He gave, and went again:
I have seen one man live,
I have seen one man reign,
With all the graces in his train.

As one of us, he wrought
Things of the common hour:
Whence was the charmed soul brought,
That gave each act such power;
The natural beauty of a flower?

Magnificence and grace,
Excellent courtesy:
A brightness on the face,
Airs of high memory:
Whence came all these, to such as he?

Like young Shakespearian kings,
He won the adoring throng:
And, as Apollo sings,
He triumphed with a song:
Triumphed, and sang, and passed along.

With a light word he took
The hearts of men in thrall:
And, with a golden look,
Welcomed them, at his call
Giving their love, their strength, their all.

No man less proud than he,
Nor cared for homage less;
Only, he could not be

Far off from happiness:
Nature was bound to his success.

Weary, the cares, the jars
The lets, of every day:
But the heavens filled with stars,
Chanced he upon the way:
And where he stayed, all joy would stay.

Now, when sad night draws down,
When the austere stars burn:
Roaming the vast stars burn:
My thoughts and memories yearn
Toward him, who never will return.

Yet I have seen him live,
And owned my friend, a king:
All, that he came to give,
He gave, and I, who sing
His praise, bring all I have to bring.

By the Statue of King Charles at Charing Cross

Sombre and rich, the skies;
    Great glooms and starry plains.
Gently the night wind sighs;
    Else a vast silence reigns.

The splendid silence clings
    Around me: and around
The saddest of all kings
    Crowned, and again discrowned.

Comely and calm, he rides
    Hard by his own Whitehall:
Only the night wind glides:
    No crowds, nor rebels, brawl.

Gone, too, his court: and yet,
    The stars his courtiers are;
Stars in their stations set;
    And every wandering star.

Alone he rides, alone,
    The fair and fatal king:
Dark night is all his own,
    That strange and solemn thing.

Which are more full of fate:
    The stars; or those sad eyes?
Which are more still and great:
    Those brows; or the dark skies?

Although his whole heart yearn
    In passionate tragedy:
Never was face so stern
    With sweet austerity.

Vanquished in life, his death
    By beauty made amends:
The passing of his breath
    Won his defeated ends.

Brief life, and hapless? Nay:
    Through death, life grew sublime.
Speak after sentence? Yea:
    And to the end of time.

Armoured he rides, his head
    Bare to the stars of doom:
He triumphs now, the dead,
    Beholding London's gloom.

Our wearier spirit faints,
    Vexed in the world's employ:
His soul was of the saints;
    And art to him was joy.

King, tried in fires of woe!
    Men hunger for thy grace:
And through the night I go,
    Loving thy mournful face.

Yet, when the city sleeps;
    When all the cries are still:
The stars and heavenly deeps
    Work out a perfect will.

The Throne of the King

The sun was setting, and its golden glow
Deepened the shadows on the village street,
And reverent touched the beauty of the head
Of Him who sat, in thought, beside the well
Of Nazareth. Two women came to fill
Their earthen jars; and sent their burdens down
To where the water lay; then drew them up.
But still the Boy, unmoved, gazed steadily
Upon the distant hills, that girded round
Jerusalem, the City of the Soul.

His eyes were deep as some unfathomed sea,
That tosses wreckage on its billowed crest;
But hides its treasures ever in the caves,
That men shall never touch, or touching die.
"How strange the Boy," one woman softly said
As back they went, their burdens on their heads.
"Yet he is Joseph's Son," the other spoke,
"And Joseph is my neighbor, a just man;
But not more lettered than the other men,
Your own and mine. He is not priest nor scribe
That he could teach such wisdom to his Son.
And it doth sometimes seem the Boy is wise
Beyond His years, with knowledge overmuch."
"His mother, whom I know," her friend replied,
"As Mary, sweeps the shavings from the floor,
Cooks the poor fare for Joseph and her Son,
Cares for the water, and her jar brings here
As we do every day, who know not much
Beyond the things we hear from holy men.
Yet strange is Mary too; I know not where
To match the peace that's on her tranquil brow;
Though, through it all, I've seen the Shadow there
The dread of days to come, though all resigned.
So like His mother is this only Son
In beauty, in the peace that's on His face;
But sometimes, deeper still, the Shadow falls
Across His features. Look! behold it now.
For it doth speak the dread of awful things,
More awful than the ruin of a world!"

A-down the street there rang a clatter loud
Of horses dashing in a maddened run,

And sounds of wheels swift rolling on the pave.
The women shrank affrighted to the wall,
And cowered there in trembling, mortal fear.
In view the charging horses passed along
Straight to the well, no driver grasped the reins,
For he had fallen to the stony street.
Yet never moved the Boy, nor turned His eyes
From off the hills that held them so intent.
But from a doorway rushed a stranger lad
Who grasped the bit of one, and held him fast.
The others, panting, stopped so near the Boy
That, on His face He must have felt the heat
Which steaming rose from their perspiring flanks,
As now they stood, foam-flecked and trembling by.
The driver came and meekly murmured thanks,
Before he led his charges back again
To where his master waited for the steeds.
"He gave me naught but words, and I did save
The steeds. The chariot, too, would have been dashed
All broken on the stones, had I not come."
The lad was angered, but the Boy moved not,
Though from the distant hills His gaze was drawn.
"Dost thou not know," the lad said, wonderingly,
"How near was Death to thee a moment since?"

The Boy, now fully aroused, smiled at the lad
All kindly, as a loving father smiles
Upon his child that waked him unaware,
Whose sleep nor storm nor clatter could affect,
Yet at the touch of little baby hands
Opens wide his eyes, that twinkle joyfully.
"No nearer to grim Death," the Boy replied,
"Was I than thou, my friend, art near it now.
Thou seekest Joseph and hast wandered far
From distant Jaffa, where thy father died.
Thou'rt Fidus named. From Joseph thou wouldst learn
The craftsman's art, and how to handle tools
To work with wood, that thou thyself may'st be
Like him, a craftsman skilled in his own trade."
"A prophet Thou!" the lad in wonder cried.
"Come with me," made He answer. "I am known
As Joseph's Son; so I will speak for thee."

As evening fell on Nazareth's burning street
Each day these two would wander out alone;
And by the well, or in a quiet glade
Seated, would hold their talk, with none to hear.

115

Yet converse scarce it was; with ears intent,
Fidus did always listen, while the Boy
Poured out a tale of Kings and Prophets old;
Of marvels that they worked to testify
Unto a King whom yet the earth would see,
A King of all Judea and the world;
Whose glory, mounting even to the stars
Would dim with rich effulgence, their great light.
The Sun of Justice He, the Moon of night
That had for ages settled o'er the earth.
He told of wonders that the King would do
Before He mounted to His mighty throne.
He told of love surpassing every love
That earth had seen, and of His Kingdom wide;
Till all on fire Fidus hung'red to see
The King Himself, and worship at His throne.
"A Roman though I am," he oft would cry,
"Thy King I'd welcome and for Him I'd serve."
"Yet thou art craftsman and no soldier thou."
"A craftsman too can serve his loyal due."
"How wouldst thou serve?" the Boy inquiring spoke.
"When Joseph bids me go, that I can learn no more,
This I can do—to build for Him His throne."

The Shadow swept across the boyish face—
The Shadow Fidus once had seen before;
And he was silent, for in awe he stood
When that mysterious shade shut off the light
That shone out from the radiant brow.
The Shadow was not fear, nor dread of death;
But dread of something worse than death could bring.
It was as if a lily, broken, bent,
But yet unsullied, now was stained with filth
By impious hand; more cruel far than death
The marring of the whiteness death had spared:
Or like a stream, that through its mountain bed
Had raced unfettered, toward the amber sea,
And o'er the rapids and the pebbles dashed
Clear, cold and placid when the mouth is reached;
Then, death unfeared before it, ready now
To give back to the ocean all it gave,
Into its pureness poured a stream so dark
That tainted all its life, when life was lost.

'Twas thus the Shadow seemed; but soon it passed,
And smiling boyhood turned a happy face
The while he said: "So thou wouldst build His throne?
But dost thou know the form that throne will take?"

116

" 'T will be a throne," Fidus replied, "so high
That all may see Him, while from it He reigns,
And know that He has come unto His own."
"Aye," quick the Boy made answer, "it shall be
Uplifted high that every man may see;
Not Jews alone but even ye of Rome;
And men from Britain too, on farthest shore
Of Rome's great Empire: they shall see and know
The King who reigns upon that living throne;
And in the islands of unchartered seas
The King shall lifted be, that all may know;
And worlds still undiscovered shall bow down
To do Him homage, yet shall hate His name.
For homage goes with hate, and hate will be
The measure of the homage that shall swell
In paeans great around the royal throne."

Fidus looked wond'ring at the Boy who spoke,
As if the right to build the throne were His
And He could give it to the friend who asked
This only boon, as pledge of love untold.
"And I would build it strong so it could go
O'er sea and land, and last for aye and aye."
"So thou wouldst build the throne?" again the Boy
Half musing spoke. Across His face once more
The Shadow fell; and, as he stood, His hands
He lifted up and out, as if in prayer.
Another Shadow fell upon the ground,
The arms and body strangely like a Cross.
Fidus was silent till the prayer was done.
The sun now set, and all the shadows passed.
They, arm in arm, ran fast to Joseph's house.
But, at the door they paused and, said the Boy:
"Thou must remember ever this thy day
When I the promise gave that I can keep,
For thou shalt build His throne!"

The years passed on,
And Fidus to the Roman hosts returned
Where, welcomed as a soldier's clever son,
He wrought in wood for all the legions there
In Jaffa, where his father had been killed.
For eighteen years he stayed beside the sea
And, working at the trade that Joseph taught,
He never once forgot the precious pledge
The Boy had made. But never saw nor heard
Aught of his friend. Then he was sent away
By Pilate's call, unto Jerusalem.

117

The evening of the day when he arrived
Great turmoil swept along the Jaffa road,
And near the Gate of Gardens, where the hill
Called Calvary lifted up its rocky head.
He heard the crowds discuss a Wonder-Man
The priests had taken, and was on His way
To judgment. "Out on such a King," cried one,
"Himself He can not save from shameful death.
Tomorrow's sun will see Him lifted up
Above the hill, and throw the Shadow of
A Cross upon you fools who thought Him King."
And on the faces dark of all around,
Fidus saw Hate he could not understand.
Then up a vision rose of Nazareth
When evening fell; a Boy of beauty rare,
With a strange Shadow on His lovely face,
Standing with arms outstretched in prayer,
The glory of the setting sun upon His head.
But long and grim the shadow of a Cross
Before Him as He stood. Then to his mind
Came swift the stories of the mighty King,
And then the promise: "Thou shalt build His throne."

Alas! the long and wav'ring years had swept
The dreams of youth away; but still remained
The love, that hungered now to feel the hand
Within his own of Mary's Son. The day
Rose brightly in the East. At Pilate's door
He met by chance a captain he had known
In Jaffa, who bade him attentive wait
Within the hall, amongst the soldiers there.
But soon a tumult rose without the doors;
The Wonder-Man was coming to be judged.
Then, as the cries increased, his friend came in.
"Make thou a Cross," he said, "We have but two
And, if I judge aright, three shall be sent
Beyond the wall this day to Calvary."
No more of shouting Fidus heard, for he
Alone made ready a great Cross of wood;
And, that his craftsman skill should be confessed,
He made it well, both strong and workmanlike.
" 'Tis fit," he said, "to serve a King," and smiled
At his grim jest; then went he on his way.

Out in the streets the crowd was surging on
Along the way that leads to Calvary's hill.
And o'er it Fidus saw his Cross; and then,
Sometimes, a thorn-crowned head with waving hair

118

Blood-clotted now, and stained a deeper hue;
And Hate seemed in the air vibrating round.
When sudden, like a bell that sweetly rings
Above a storm, and seems a messenger
Of Peace and Love, there woke upon his soul
From out the sleeping past, some prophet words:
"For homage goes with hate, and hate shall be
The measure of the homage that shall swell
In paeans great around the royal throne."

The surging crowd hid from his eyes the things
He did not care to see, but faint he heard
The hammer strokes, that seemed to drive the nails
Deep in his heart. Then turned he to a man
Who silent stood beside him, and he said:
"A stranger I, from Jaffa, yesternight
I came. This man? What evil hath He done?"
"I know not any wrong that He hath done,"
Came answer fast. "I only know the good
That He had wrought. Behold my eyes that see!
Once they were dark. He passed me by one day
And loud I cried: 'O Son of David, mercy show
That I may see.' He touched me and I saw."
Another silent man near Fidus stood,
To him he spoke, "And friend, what knowest thou?"
"I know that now I live though I was dead;
For I had gone into the ending tomb
All spiced for rest and bound with linen bands;
And He did come, and He did call me forth.
I heard His voice that sounded far away,
As if I stood within a valley deep,
And some one, from the mountain crest,
Kept calling me. Then clearer was the Voice;
As if on wings, I soared aloft to Him,
Who had the Power to bid me come or stay.
Again my heart did beat and vital blood
Surged through my wid'ning veins. I lived again."
Then Fidus quick recalled a wondrous thing:
He saw the Boy in Joseph's little shop,
A sick lamb refuged in His tender arms.
He gently stroked the lamb and then the pain
Was gone from out its piteous pleading eyes.
And, lo, the man felt hot tears on his cheeks.

The Cross was raised, and faint the outline stood
'Twixt Fidus and the lurid, murky sky
That threatened from afar a terror dark.
Then swift it came, for all of darkness dread

119

That air could hold, fell down upon the earth.
The stumbling crowd in panic slunk away;
But Fidus groped through darkness to the Cross.
He heard a moan of sorrow. Well he knew
The voice of Mary, she of Joseph's house.
His heart stood still; the Vision came again:
That evening fair—the Boy—the distant hills—
The Shadow of the Cross upon the earth
As He stood silent all absorbed in prayer—
The promise that himself should build a throne.
"Aye," so the Boy had said, "for it shall be
Raised up on high that every man may see,
Not Jews alone, but even ye of Rome;
And men from Britain too, on farthest shore
Of Rome's great Empire: they shall see and know
The King who reigns upon that living throne;
And, in the islands of uncharted seas
The King shall lifted be that all may know;
And worlds still undiscovered shall bow down
To do Him homage, yet shall hate His name.
For homage goes with hate, and hate will be
The measure of the homage that shall swell
In paeans great around His royal throne."

A lightning flash! The rocks asunder rent,
The tombs burst open and the dead arose.
One moment Fidus saw the Crucified
Ere darkness fell again around the Cross.
But in that moment a new vision rose;
He saw the hill rise high, and higher still,
Till over all the mountains of the world
It towering stood; and nations, worshipping
Gazed on a mighty throne that bore a King!
Blood red the jewels in His crown of thorns,
With ermined pain that wrapped Him all about,
Deep in His hands the orb and sceptre nails,
Quite gone the Shadow of the primal sin
And, on His brow, fulfilled the ancient pledge
Of Earth's Redemption.

The Housewife's Prayer

Lady, who with tender word
Didst keep the house of Christ the Lord,
Who didst set forth the bread and wine
Before the Living Wheat and Vine,
Reverently didst make the bed
Whereon was laid the holy head
That such a cruel pillow prest
For our behoof, on Calvary's crest;
Be beside me while I go
About my labors to and fro.
Speed the wheel and speed the loom,
Guide the needle and the broom,
Make my bread rise sweet and light,
Make my cheese come foamy white,
Yellow may my butter be
As cowslips blowing on the lea.
Homely though my tasks and small,
Be beside me at them all.
Then when I shall stand to face
Jesu in the judgment place,
To me thy gracious help afford,
Who art the Handmaid of the Lord.

Brother Juniper

As unto Francis Poverty,
So Folly was a bride to thee.
Not the jade that fashions quips
For the smiles of mocking lips,
And in the face of stony Death
Capers till she's out of breath,
But the maid that moves and sings
About divinely foolish things,
She that gives her substance all
For love, and laughs to find it small,
She that drew God's Son to be
A butt, a jest on Calvary,
And 'neath the leper's guise doth know
The King in his incognito.

The world is grown too wise, and we
Go our sad ways sensibly.
O, would that our lean souls might win
Some grace of thine, God's harlequin,

121

Whose days were lavished like fool's gold
Upon His pleasures manifold.
"Would God," cried Francis, on his knees,
"I had a forest of such trees!"

GEORGE PARSONS LATHROP

The Child's Wish Granted

Do you remember, my sweet, absent son,
How in the soft June days forever done
You loved the heavens so warm and clear and high;
And, when I lifted you, soft came your cry—
"Put me 'way up—'way up in the blue sky"?

I laughed and said I could not—set you down,
Your gray eyes wonder-filled beneath that crown
Of bright hair gladdening me as you raced by,
Another Father now, more strong than I,
Has borne you voiceless to your dear blue sky.

Charity

Unarmed she goeth, yet her hands
Strike deeper awe than steel-caparisoned bands,
No fatal hurt of foe she fears—
Veiled, as with mail, in mist of gentle tears.

'Gainst her thou canst not bar the door;
Like air she enters; where none dared before.
Even to the rich she can forgive
Their regal selfishness—and let them live!

ROSE HAWTHORNE LATHROP

A Song before Grief

Sorrow, my friend,
When shall you come again?
The wind is slow, and the bent willows send
Their silvery motions wearily down the plain.

The bird is dead
That sang this morning through the summer rain!

Sorrow, my friend,
I owe my soul to you.
And if my life with any glory end
Of tenderness for others, and the words are true,
Said, honoring, when I'm dead—
Sorrow, to you, the mellow praise, the funeral wreath, are due.

And yet, my friend,
When love and joy are strong,
Your terrible visage from my sight I rend
With glances to blue heaven. Hovering along,
By mine your shadow led,
"Away!" I shriek, "nor dare to work my new-sprung mercies
    wrong!"

Still, you are near:
Who can your care withstand?
When deep eternity shall look most clear,
Sending bright waves to kiss the trembling land,
My joy shall disappear—
A flaming torch thrown to the golden sea by your pale hand.

The Clock's Song

Eileen of four,
Eileen of smiles;
Eileen of five,
Eileen of tears;
Eileen of ten, of fifteen years,
Eileen of youth
And woman's wiles;
Eileen of twenty,
In love's land,
Eileen all tender
In her bliss,
Untouched by sorrow's treacherous kiss,
And the sly weapons in life's hand—
Eileen aroused to share all fate,
Eileen a wife,
Pale, beautiful,
Eileen most grave and dutiful,
Mourning her dreams in queenly state.
Eileen! Eileen! . . .

123

EDMUND LEAMY, Sr.

Ireland

I loved a love—a royal love—
    In the golden long ago;
And she was fair as fair could be.
The foam upon the broken sea,
The sheen of sun, or moon, or star,
The sparkle from the diamond spar,
Not half so rare and radiant are
    As my own love—my royal love—
      In the golden long ago.

And she had stately palace halls—
    In the golden long ago;
And warriors, men of stainless swords,
Were seated at her festive boards,
Fierce champions of her lightest words,
While hymned the bard the chieftain's praise,
And sang their deed of battle days,
    To cheer my love, my royal love,
      In the golden long ago.

She wore a stately diadem—
    In the golden long ago;
Wrought by a cunning craftsman's hand,
And fashioned from a battle brand,
Full fit for the queen of a soldier land;
Her sceptre was a sabre keen,
Her robe a robe of radiant green,
    My queenly love, my royal love,
      In the golden long ago.

Alas for my love, my royal love,
    Of the golden long ago!
For gone are all her warrior bands,
And rusted are her battle brands,
And broken her sabre bright and keen,
And torn her robe of radiant green,
A slave where she was a stainless queen,
    My own love, my royal love,
      Of the golden long ago.

But there is hope for my royal love
    Of the golden long ago;
Beyond the broad and shining sea
Gathers a stubborn chivalry,

124

That yet will come to make her free,
And hedge her round with gleaming spears,
And crown her queen of all the years,
  My own love, my royal love,
    Of the golden long ago.

EDMUND LEAMY

Music Magic

Perhaps there is no magic in this dull old world of ours;
Perhaps there are no fairy tales to gladden heart-break hours;
Perhaps there is no beauty, and perhaps all things are wrong;
But still there is the wonder of a little, old-time song!

A squeaking and battered old organ, rattling a moss-covered
    tune,
Stood in the street of the city, there, in the heat of the noon;
Banging of roses and sunshine, thrilling of lands far away,
Whispering songs of my childhood—sorrowful, simple and
    gay;
I was a child for a moment, filled with a child's petty fears,
Dreaming, and dreaming, and dreaming, never a thought of
    the tears.
Then as the music softened, singing of love and of life,
Brought it back thought of the old days, far from the toil and
    the strife,
Glimmer of gold in the star-light, shimmer of silk by the sea;
Words that were whispered, half-spoken, dreams that were
    never to be.
Sweet intermingled with sadness, what is as dear as the past?
Is there a day in the future that is as fair as the last?
Music, oh, music the master, there in the heat of the noon,
A squeaking and battered old organ, rattling a moss-covered
    tune,
Carried me back in my dreaming, far, to the long, long ago;
Feeling, 'way down in my heart-chords, hope I thought never
    could glow;
Brought to me, who was a failure, beaten and crossed in the
    fight,
Help in the hour of the darkness—pointed the way to the
    light.

Perhaps there is no magic in this dull, old world of ours;
Perhaps there are no fairy tales to gladden heart-break hours;

Perhaps there is no beauty and perhaps all things are wrong;
But still there is the wonder of a little, old-time song!

My Ship

My ship is an old ship and her sails are grey and torn,
And in the dim and misty night she seems a thing forlorn;
Her battered sides are beetle black, her decks are scarred and
    old,
And heavy rise the musty scents from out her crumbling hold.

The young ships in the tide-way with a sneering smile sail by,
And fair they flash their white sails against a sun-drenched
    sky,
And fleet they run before the clouds that usher in a blow,
But could a storm coerce my ship whene'er she wished to go!

My ship is an old ship and her sails are torn and grey,
And she's not white and beautiful, nor fragile such as they,
But she has sailed o'er every sea to every land a-gleam,
And on her decks make merry now the wraiths of youthful
    dream!

Gethsemane

Breathes there a man who claimeth not
One lonely spot,
His own Gethsemane,
Whither with his inmost pain
He fain
Would weary plod,
Find the surcease that is known
In wind a-moan
And sobbing sea,
Cry his sorrow hid of men,
And then—
Touch hands with God.

Visions

I never watch the sun set a-down the Western skies
But that within its wonderness I see my mother's eyes;
I never hear the West wind sob softly in the trees
But that there comes her broken call far o'er the distant seas;
And never shine the dim stars but that my heart would go
Away and back to olden lands and dreams of long ago.

126

A rover of the wide world, when yet my heart was young
The sea came whispering to me in well-beloved tongue,
And oh! the promises she held of golden lands a-gleam
That clung about my boy-heart and filled mine eyes with
      dream,
And Wanderlust came luring me till 'neath the stars I swore
That I would be a wanderer for ever, ever more.

A rover of the wide world, I've seen the Northern lights
A-flashing countless colours in the knife-cold wintry nights;
I've watched the Southern Cross ablaze o'er smiling, sunny
      lands,
And seen the lazy sea caress palm-sheltered, silvery sands;
Still wild unrest is scouring me, the Wanderlust of yore,
And I must be a wanderer for ever, ever more.

And yet, I see the sun set a-down the Western skies
And glimpse within the wonderness my mother's pleading
      eyes;
And yet I hear the West wind sob softly in the trees,
That vainly cloaks her broken call far o'er the distant seas;
And still when shine the dim stars my wander heart would go
Away and back to her side, and dreams of long ago.

My Lips Would Sing

My lips would sing a song for you, a soulful little song for
      you,
  A plaintive little song for you, upon a summer's day;
But for the very life of me, the merry, merry life of me,
  The laughter-loving life of me, I cannot but be gay.

For oh, the sun is shining, Dear, and who could be repining,
      Dear,
  And who would be unhappy, Dear, when all the world is
      young?
So I will hum a melody, a mirthful little melody,
  A joyous little melody that never yet was sung.

And you shall hear of Fairyland, of Kings and Queens of
      Fairyland,
  Of men and maids of Fairyland, and Love shall be the
      theme,
And straight before your brimming eyes, a golden glint of
      Paradise
  Shall steal, my Dear, to still your sighs, and give you back
      your dream.

And you will taste of happiness, a tiny bit of happiness,
  A wistful bit of happiness, upon a summer's day;
And just a little smile from you, a sunny little smile from you,
  A trembly little smile from you shall be a poet's pay!

SHANE LESLIE

Ireland, Mother of Priests

The fishwife sits by the side
Of her childing bed,
Her fire is deserted and sad,
Her beads are long said;
Her tears ebb and flow with the sea,
Her grief on the years,
But little she looks to the tide,
And little she hears:
For children in springtime play round
Her sorrowing heart,
To win them their feeding she loves
To hunger apart;
Her children in summer she counts
Awhile for her own;
But winter is ever the same,
The loved ones are flown.
Far over the sea they are gone,
Far out of her ken
They travel the farthest of seas
As fishers of men.
Yet never a word to her sons
To keep them at home,
And never a motherly cry
Goes over the foam;
She sits with her head in her hands,
Her eyes on the flame,
And thinks of the others that played,
Yet left her the same,
With vesture she wove on the loom
Four-coloured to be,
And lanterns she trimmed with her hair
To light them to sea.
Oh, far have the living ones gone,
And further the dead,
For spirits come never to watch
The fisherwife's bed;

And sonless she sits at the hearth,
And peers in the flame,
She knows that their fishing must come
As ever it came—
A fishing that never set home,
But seaways it led,
For God who has taken her sons
Has buried her dead.

RUTH TEMPLE LINDSAY

The Hunters

The Lion, he prowleth far and near,
   Nor swerves for pain or rue;
He heedeth nought of sloth nor fear,
   He prowleth—prowleth through
The silent glade and the weary street,
   In the empty dark and the full noon heat;
And a little Lamb with aching feet—
   He prowleth too.

The Lion croucheth alert, apart—
   With patience doth he woo;
He waiteth long by this shuttered heart,
   And the Lamb—He waiteth too.
Up the lurid passes of dreams that kill,
   Through the twisting maze of the great Untrue,
The Lion followeth the fainting will—
   And the Lamb—He followeth too.

From the tickets dim of the hidden way
   Where the debts of Hell accrue,
The Lion leapeth upon his prey:
   But the Lamb—He leapeth too.
Ah! loose the leash of the sins that damn,
   Mark Devil and God as goals,
In the panting love of a famished Lamb,
   Gone mad with the need of souls.

The Lion, he strayeth near and far;
   What heights hath he left untrod?
He crawleth nigh to the purest star,
   On the trail of the saints of God.
And throughout the darkness of things unclean,
   In the depths where the sin-ghouls brood,

There prowleth ever with yearning mien—
    A lamb as white as Blood!

WILLIAM LIVINGSTON

In Cherry Lane

In Cherry Lane the blossoms blow
    In wreaths of white around the trees,
And spread their petals wide, as though
    They longed for nectar-seeking bees.

O'erhead, the arching boughs that spring
    From pillar trunks look down and smile
On lowly currant shrubs that cling
    Around their feet along the aisle.

In Cherry Lane the sunbeams steal
    Through many a leaf and branch above,
And tender shoots come forth to feel
    The touches of a wondrous love.

And life grows warmer with the hours,
    Unmoved, unchilled by human pang,
Till from the stems now robed in flowers
    The great red drops in clusters hang.

Ah, Mother mine! white blossoms came
    And filled my soul with thoughts of thee,
Who art to those that love thy name
    What honeyed buds are to the bee.

Thou art the floweret white and fair,
    A virgin from thy stainless birth,
The fruitful stem designed to bear
    A Saviour to our sinful earth.

And when the cherries, ripe and red,
    Come forth upon the breast of June,
They'll tell me of a heart that bled,
    By men forgotten all too soon.

Ah, precious drops! through future days
    Preserve my soul from spot or stain,
With tender thoughts of love and praise
    That once were mine in Cherry Lane.

S. M. M.

Surrender

If thou art merely conscious clay—ah, well,
Tire not such stuff with futile, tread-mill climb
Which lifts to leave thee level with the slime;
Nor think that death can break thy earth-born spell;
Clay hath no heel Achillean, vulnerable.
Be animate till some deliberate time
Shall choke and crunch thee to potential grime,
For thou art fit for neither heaven nor hell.

But He who made thee cousin to the clod
First plunged thee in the Spirit which is He,
Whence thou hast risen, divinely armed and shod
To scale the ramparts of eternity.
Already stricken with the shafts of God,
Thou fallest prisoner to the Deity.

DENIS A. McCARTHY

Saint Brigid

Brigid, the daughter of Duffy, she wasn't like other young
      things,
Dreaming of lads for her lovers, and twirling her bracelets and
      rings;
Combing and coiling and curling her hair that was black as
      the sloes,
Painting her lips and her cheeks that were ruddy and fresh as
      the rose.
Ah, 'twasn't Brigid would waste all her days in such follies as
      these—
Christ was the Lover she worshipped for hour after hour on
      her knees;
Christ and His Church and His poor—and 'twas many a mile
      that she trod
Serving the loathsomest lepers that ever were stricken by God.

Brigid, the daughter of Duffy, she sold all her jewels and
      gems,
Sold all her finely-spun robes that were braided with gold to
      the hems;
Kept to her back but one garment, one dress that was faded
      and old,

131

Gave all her goods to the poor who were famished with hunger and cold.
Ah, 'twasn't Brigid would fling at the poor the hard word like a stone—
Christ the Redeemer she saw in each wretch that was ragged and lone;
Every wandering beggar who asked for a bite or a bed
Knocked at her heart like the Man who had nowhere to shelter His head.

Brigid, the daughter of Duffy, she angered her father at last.
"Where are your dresses, my daughter? Crom Cruach! You wear them out fast!
Where are the chains that I bought you all wrought in red gold from the mine?
Where the bright brooches of silver that once on your bosom would shine?"
Ah, but 'twas he was the man that was proud of his name and his race,
Proud of their prowess in battle and proud of their deeds in the chase!
Knew not the Christ, the pale God whom the priests from afar had brought in,
Held to the old Gaelic gods that were known to Cuchullin and Finn.

Brigid, the daughter of Duffy, made answer, "O father," said she,
"What is the richest of raiment, and what are bright jewels to me?"
Lepers of Christ must I care for, the hungry of Christ must I feed;
How can I walk in rich robes when His people and mine are in need?"
Ah, but 'twas she didn't fear for herself when he blustered and swore,
Meekly she bowed when he ordered his chariot brought to the door;
Meekly obeyed when he bade her get in at the point of his sword,
Knowing whatever her fate she'd be safe with her Lover and Lord.

Brigid, the daughter of Duffy, was brought to the court of the King,
(Monarch of Leinster, MacEnda, whose praises the poets would sing).
"Hither, O monarch," said Duffy, "I've come with a maiden to sell;

132

Buy her and bind her to bondage—she's needing such discipline well!"
Ah, but 'twas wise was the King. From the maid to the chieftain he turned;
Mildness he saw in her face, in the other 'twas anger that burned;
"This is no bondmaid, I'll swear it, O chief, but a girl of your own.
Why sells the father the flesh of his flesh and the bone of his bone?"

Brigid, the daughter of Duffy, was mute while her father replied—
"Monarch, this maid has no place as the child of a chieftain of pride.
Beggars and wretches whose wounds would the soul of a soldier affright,
Sure, 'tis on these she is wasting my substance from morning till night!"
Ah, but 'twas bitter was Duffy; he spoke like a man that was vext.
Musing, the monarch was silent; he pondered the question perplexed.
"Maiden," said he, "if 'tis true, as I've just from your father heard tell,
Might it not be, as my bondmaid, you'd waste all my substance as well?"

Brigid, the daughter of Duffy, made answer. "O monarch," she said,
"Had I the wealth from your coffers, and had I the crown from your head—
Yea, if the plentiful yield of the broad breasts of Erin were mine,
All would I give to the people of Christ who in poverty pine."
Ah, but 'twas then that the King felt the heart in his bosom upleap,
"I am not worthy," he cried, "such a maiden in bondage to keep!
Here's a king's sword for her ransom, and here's a king's word to decree
Never to other than Christ and His poor let her servitude be!"

The Poor Man's Daily Bread

Not only there where jewelled vestments blaze,
    And princely prelates bow before Thy shrine,
Where myriads line the swept and garnished ways

Through which is borne Thy majesty divine—
O Jesus of the ever-loving heart,
    Not only there Thou art!

But where the lowliest church its cross uplifts
    Above the city's sordidness and sin;
Where all unheeded human wreckage drifts
    And drowns amid the foulness and the din—
There, too, anear the very gates of hell,
    O Saviour, dost Thou dwell!

Oh, meet it is that round Thy altar thrones,
    Thy highest priests should ministering throng
With silken robe, with gold and precious stones,
    With solemn chant and loud triumphant song:
What beauty that the world could give would be
    Too beautiful for Thee?

And yet to those that work with grimy hands
    And sweaty brows in ditches and in drains,
Thou comest with a love that understands
    Their labor ill-requited, and their pains.
Who knows so well as Thou what they endure,
    O Father of the poor?

And so, deep-hid in many a city street,
    Or far where lonely workers break the soil,
Are shrines where Thou, the Merciful, dost meet,
    In love's embrace, the weary ones that toil.
For them Thy hospitable board is spread,
    With Thee, Thy very Self, their daily Bread!

Rosa Mystica

O Mystic Rose, in God's fair garden growing,
O Mystic Rose, in Heaven's high courtyard blowing—
Make sweet, make sweet the pathway I am going,
        O Mystic Rose!
The darkling, deathward way that I am going,
        O Mystic Rose!

O Rose, more white than snow-wreath in December!
O Rose, more red than sunset's dying ember,
My sins forget, my penitence remember,
        O Mystic Rose!
Though all should fail, I pray that thou remember,
        O Mystic Rose!

134

O Mystic Rose, the moments fly with fleetness;
To judgment I, with all my incompleteness—
But thou, make intercession by thy sweetness,
    O Mystic Rose!
Be near to soothe and save me by the sweetness,
    O Mystic Rose!

THOMAS MacDONAGH

What Is White?

What is white?
    The soul of the sage, faith-lit,
The trust of Age,
    The infant's untaught wit.
What more white?
    The face of Truth made known,
The voice of Youth
    Singing before her throne.

Wishes for My Son

Now, my son, is life for you—
And I wish you joy of it—
Joy of power in all you do,
Deeper passion, better wit
Than I had who had enough,
Quicker life and length thereof,
More of every gift but love.

Love I have beyond all men,
Love that now you share with me—
What have I to wish you then
But that you be good and free,
And that God to you may give
Grace in stronger days to live?

For I wish you more than I
Ever knew of glorious deed,
Though no rapture passed me by
That an eager heart could heed,
Though I followed heights and sought
Things the sequel never brought.

135

Wild and perilous holy things
Flaming with a martyr's blood,
And the joy that laughs and sings
Where a foe must be withstood,
Joy of headlong happy chance
Leading on the battle dance.

But I found no enemy,
No man in a world of wrong,
That Christ's word of Charity
Did not render clean and strong—
Who was I to judge my kind,
Blindest groper of the blind?

God to you may give the sight
And the clear undoubting strength
Wars to knit for single right,
Freedom's war to knit at length,
And to win, through wrath and strife,
To the sequel of my life.

But for you, so small and young,
Born on Saint Cecilia's Day,
I in more harmonious song
Now for nearer joys should pray—
Simple joys: the natural growth
Of your childhood and your youth,
Courage, innocence and truth:

These for you, so small and young,
In your hand and heart and tongue.

THOMAS D'ARCY McGEE

To Ask Our Lady's Patronage for a Book on Columbus

Star of the Sea, to whom, age after age,
    The maiden kneels whose lover sails the sea;
Star, that the drowning death-pang can assuage,
    And shape the soul's course to eternity;
Mother of God, to Egypt's realm exiled,
    Mother of God, in Bethlehem's crib confined,
Thee do I ask to aid my anxious mind,
    And make this book find favour with thy Child.

136

Of one who lived and laboured in thy ray,
   I would rehearse the striving and success;
Through the dense past I ne'er shall find my way,
   Unless thou helpest, holy Comfortress;
A world of doubt and darkness to evade;
   An ocean all unknown to Christian kind;
Another world by nature's self arrayed,
   O'er the wide waste of waves, I seek to find.

SEUMAS MacMANUS

Resignation

Be still, sad soul, be still,
Bend you to Heaven's high will.
When the toilsome race is run,
And the summit strove for won—
When secrets are unsealed,
All hidden things revealed,
All mysteries made known,
The good we doubted shown,
Vexed questionings at rest,
I'll say, "Well, God knew best."
Me thought you went full soon,
In the rapture of the noon,
In the glory of the sun,
Your noble work begun—
In your grasp the magic wand
That would raise a stricken land—
A while you fain would stay;
But the call brooked no delay:
You sighed, and bowed your head,
And they put you with the dead.
Our God is kind, and He
Will blunt the shaft to me;
Will stay the dripping woe
Ere the chalice overflow;
May let me end the race
With the high sun on my face,
And the hot blood bounding free,
Through the beating veins of me.
At most but some sad hours
And He'll call me when night lowers.
Oh, at the trysting gate,
With radiant face you'll wait!
With arms in love outspread

137

To take a weary head,
And clasp it to your breast
Where always it found rest.
You'll speak no word for joy,
But, crooning o'er your boy,
Draw him into the light,
Where nevermore comes night.

In Dark Hour

I turn my steps where the Lonely Road
   Winds far as the eye can see,
And I bend my back for the burden sore
   That God has reached down to me.

I have said farewell to the sun-kissed plains,
   To joy I gave good-bye;
Now the bleak wide wastes of the world are mine,
   And the winds that wail in the sky.

No bright flower blooms, no sweet bird calls,
   Nor hermit ever abode,
Not a green thing lifts one lowly leaf,
   O God, on the Lonely Road!

The thick dank mists come stealing down,
   And press me on every side.
With never a voice to cheer me on,
   And never a hand to guide.

I shall cry in my need for a Voice and Hand,
   And the solace of love-wet eyes—
And an icy clutch will close on my heart,
   When Echo, the mocker, replies.

I know my good soul will fail me not,
   When Forms from the Dark round me creep,
And whisper 'twere sweet to journey no more,
   But lay down the burden and sleep.

(*Look onward and up, O Heart of my Heart,*
   Where the road strikes the skies afar!
To cheer you, and guide, thro' your darkest hour,
   Behold yon beckoning Star!)

I set my face to the grey wild wastes,
   I bend my back to the load—
Dear God be kind with the heart-sick child
   Who steps on the Lonely Road.

Hymn for Pentecost

Pure Spirit of the always-faithful God,
Kindler of Heaven's true light within the soul!
From the lorn land our sainted fathers trod,
Ascends to Thee our cry of hope and dole.
Thee, Thee we praise;
To Thee we raise
Our choral hymn in these awakening days:
O send us down anew that fire
Which of old lived in David's and Isaiah's lyre.

Centuries had rolled, and earth lay tombed in sleep,
The nightmare-sleep of nations beneath kings;
And far abroad o'er liberty's great deep
Death's angel waved his black and stilling wings.
Then struck Thine hour!
Thou, in Thy power,
But breathedst, and the free stood up, a tower;
And tyranny's thrones and strongholds fell,
And men made jubilee for an abolished hell.

And she, our mother-home, the famed, the fair,
The golden house of light and intellect,
Must she still groan in her intense despair?
Shall she lie prone while Europe stands erect?
Forfend this, Thou
To whom we vow
Souls even our giant wrongs shall never bow:
Thou wilt not leave our green flag furled,
Nor bear that we abide the byword of the world.

Like the last lamp that burned in Tullia's tomb
Through ages, vainly, with unwaning ray;
Our star of hope lights but a path of gloom
Whose false track leads us round and round alway.
But Thou canst open
A gate from hope
To victory! Thou canst nerve our arms to cope
With looming storm and danger still,
And lend a thunder-voice to the land's lightning will.

Descend, then, Spirit of the Eternal King!
To Thee, to Him, to His avenging Son,
The Triune of God, in boundless trust we cling;
His help once ours, our nationhood is won.
We watch the time

139

Till that sublime
Event shall thrill the free of every clime.
Speed, mighty Spirit! speed its march,
And thus complete for earth mankind's triumphal arch.

Dark Rosaleen

O my dark Rosaleen,
   Do not sigh, do not weep!
The priests are on the ocean green,
   They march along the deep.
There's wine from the royal Pope
   Upon the ocean green,
And Spanish ale shall give you hope,
   My dark Rosaleen!
   My own Rosaleen!
Shall glad your heart, shall give you hope,
Shall give you health, and help, and hope,
   My dark Rosaleen!

Over hills and through dales
   Have I roamed for your sake;
All yesterday I sailed the sails
   On river and on lake.
The Erne, at its highest flood,
   I dashed across unseen,
For there was lightning in my blood,
   My dark Rosaleen!
   My own Rosaleen!
Oh! there was lightning in my blood,
Red lightning through my blood,
   My dark Rosaleen!

All day long, in unrest,
   To and fro do I move,
The very soul within my breast
   Is wasted for you, love!
The heart in my bosom faints
   To think of you, my Queen,
My life of life, my saint of saints,
   My dark Rosaleen!
   My own Rosaleen!
To hear your sweet and sad complaints,
My life, my love, my saint of saints,
   My dark Rosaleen!

Woe and pain, pain and woe,
   Are my lot, night and noon,

To see your bright face clouded so,
    Like to the mournful moon.
But yet will I rear your throne
    Again in golden sheen;
'Tis you shall reign, shall reign alone,
    My dark Rosaleen!
    My own Rosaleen!
'Tis you shall have the golden throne,
'Tis you shall reign, and reign alone,
    My dark Rosaleen!

Over dews, over sands,
    Will I fly for your weal:
Your holy, delicate white hands
    Shall girdle me with steel.
At home in your emerald bowers,
    From morning's dawn till e'en,
You'll pray for me, my flower of flowers,
    My dark Rosaleen!
    My own Rosaleen!
You'll think of me through daylight's hours,
My virgin flower, my flower of flowers,
    My dark Rosaleen!

I could scale the blue air,
    I could plough the high hills,
Oh, I could kneel all night in prayer,
    To heal your many ills!
And one beamy smile from you
    Would float like light between
My toils and me, my own, my true,
    My dark Rosaleen!
    My own Rosaleen!
Would give me life and soul anew,
A second life, a soul anew,
    My dark Rosaleen!

Oh! the Erne shall run red
    With redundance of blood,
The earth shall rock beneath our tread,
    And flames wrap hill and wood,
And gun-peal and slogan-cry
    Wake many a glen serene,
Ere you shall fade, ere you shall die,
    My dark Rosaleen!
    My own Rosaleen!
The Judgment Hour must first be nigh,
Ere you shall fade, ere you can die,
    My dark Rosaleen!

THEODORE MAYNARD

A Song of Colours

Gold for the crown of Mary,
   Blue for the sea and sky,
Green for the woods and the meadows
   Where small white daisies lie,
And red for the colour of Christ's blood
   When He came to the cross to die.

These things the high God gave us
   And left in the world He made—
Gold for the hilt's enrichment,
   And blue for the sword's good blade,
And red for the roses a youth may set
   On the white brows of a maid.

Green for the cool, sweet gardens
   Which stretch about the house,
And the delicate new frondage
   The winds of spring arouse,
And red for the wine which a man may drink
   With his fellows in carouse.

Blue and green for the comfort
   Of tired hearts and eyes,
And red for that sudden hour which comes
   With danger and great surprise,
And white for the honour of God's throne
   When the dead shall all arise.

Gold for the cope and chalice,
   For kingly pomp and pride,
And red for the feathers men wear in their caps
   When they win a war or a bride,
And red for the robe which they dressed God in
   On the bitter day He died.

The World's Miser

A miser with an eager face
Sees that each roseleaf is in place.

He keeps beneath strong bolts and bars
The piercing beauty of the stars.

The colours of the dying day
He hoards as treasure—well He may!—

And saves with care (lest they be lost)
The dainty diagrams of frost.

He counts the hairs of every head,
And grieves to see a sparrow dead.

Among the yellow primroses
He holds His Summer palaces,

And sets the grass about them all
To guard them as His spearmen small.

He fixes on each wayside stone
A mark to show it as His own,

And knows when raindrops fall through air
Whether each single one be there,

That gathered into ponds and brooks.
They may become His picture books,

To show in every spot and place
The living glory of His face.

Cecidit, Cecidit Babylon Magna!

The aimless business of your feet,
    Your swinging wheels and piston rods,
The smoke of every sullen street
    Have passed away with all your gods.

For in a meadow far from these
    A hodman treads across the loam,
Bearing his solid sanctities
    To that strange altar called his home.

I watch the tall, sagacious trees
    Turn as the monks do, every one;
The saplings, ardent novices,
    Turning with them towards the sun,

That Monstrance held in God's strong hands,
    Burnished in amber and in red;
God, His own Priest, in blessing stands;
    The earth, adoring, bows her head.

143

The idols of your market place,
　　Your high debates, where are they now?
Your lawyers' clamour fades apace—
　　A bird is singing on the bough!

Three fragile, sacramental things
　　Endure, though all your pomps shall pass—
A butterfly's immortal wings,
　　A daisy, and a blade of grass.

A Song of Laughter

The stars with their laughter are shaken;
　　The long waves laugh at sea;
And the little Imp of Laughter
　　Laughs in the soul of me.

I know the guffaw of a tempest,
　　The mirth of a blossom and bud—
But I laugh when I think of how Cuchulain laughed
　　At the crows with their bills in his blood.

The mother laughs low at her baby,
　　The bridegroom with joy in his bride—
And I think that Christ laughed when they took Him with
　　　staves
　　On the night before He died.

Apocalypse

Shall summer wood where we have laughed our fill;
　　Shall all your grass so good to walk upon;
Each field that we have loved, each little hill,
　　Be burnt like paper—as hath said Saint John?

Then not alone they die! For God hath told
　　How all His plains of mingled fire and glass,
His walls of hyacinth, His streets of gold,
　　His aureoles of jewelled light shall pass,

That He may make us nobler things that these,
　　And in her royal robes of blazing red
Adorn His bride. Yea, with what mysteries
　　And might and mirth shall she be diamonded.

144

And what new secrets shall our God disclose;
　　Or set what suns of burnished brass to flare;
Or what empurpled bloom to oust the rose;
　　Or what strange grass to glow like angels' hair!

What pinnacles of silvery tracery,
　　What dizzy, rampired towers shall God devise
Of topaz, beryl and chalcedony
　　To make Heaven pleasant to His children's eyes!

And in what cataclysms of flame and foam
　　Shall the first Heaven sink—as red as sin—
When God hath cast aside His ancient home
　　As far too mean to house His children in.

ALICE MEYNELL

A General Communion

I saw the throng, so deeply separate,
　　Fed at one only board—
The devout people, moved, intent, elate,
　　And the devoted Lord.

Oh struck apart! not side from human side,
　　But soul from human soul,
As each asunder absorbed the multiplied,
　　The ever unparted whole.

I saw this people as a field of flowers,
　　Each grown at such a price
The sum of unimaginable powers
　　Did no more than suffice.

A thousand single central daisies they,
　　A thousand of the one;
For each the entire monopoly of day;
　　For each, the whole of the devoted sun.

The Shepherdess

She walks—the lady of my delight—
　　A shepherdess of sheep.
Her flocks are thoughts. She keeps them white;
　　She guards them from the steep;

145

She feeds them on the fragrant height,
   And folds them in for sleep.

She roams maternal hills and bright,
   Dark valleys safe and deep.
Into that tender breast at night
   The chastest stars may peep.
She walks—the lady of my delight—
   A shepherdess of sheep.

She holds her little thoughts in sight,
   Though gay they run and leap.
She is so circumspect and right;
   She has her soul to keep.
She walks—the lady of my delight—
   A shepherdess of sheep.

Christis in the Universe

With this ambiguous earth
His dealings have been told us. These abide:
The signal to a maid, the human birth,
The lesson, and the young Man crucified.

But not a star of all
The innumerable host of stars has heard
How He administered this terrestrial ball.
Our race have kept their Lord's entrusted Word.

Of His earth-visiting feet
None knows the secret, cherished, perilous,
The terrible, shamefast, frightened, whispered, sweet,
Heart-shattering secret of His way with us.

No planet knows that this
Our wayside planet, carrying land and wave,
Love and life multiplied, and pain and bliss,
Bears, as chief treasure, one forsaken grave,

Nor, in our little day,
May his devices with the heavens be guessed,
His pilgrimage to tread the Milky Way
Or His bestowals there be manifest.

But in the eternities,
Doubtless we shall compare together, hear
A million alien Gospels, in what guise
He trod the Pleiades, the Lyre, the Bear.

146

O, be prepared, my soul!
To read the inconceivable, to scan
The million forms of God those stars enroll
When, in our turn, we show to them a Man.

"I Am the Way"

Thou art the Way.
Hadst Thou been nothing but the goal,
I cannot say
If Thou hadst ever met my soul.

I cannot see—
I, child of process—if there lies
An end for me,
Full of repose, full of replies.

I'll not reproach
The road that winds, my feet that err.
Access, approach
Art Thou, Time, Way, and Wayfarer.

Unto Us a Son Is Given

Given, not lent,
And not withdrawn—once sent,
This Infant of mankind, this One,
Is still the little welcome Son.

New every year,
New born and newly dear,
He comes with tidings and a song,
The ages long, the ages long;

Even as the cold
Keen winter grows not old,
As childhood is so fresh, foreseen,
And spring in the familiar green.

Sudden as sweet
Come the expected feet.
All joy is young, and new all art,
And He, too, whom we have by heart.

147

To a Daisy

Slight as thou art, thou art enough to hide
Like all created things, secrets from me,
And stand a barrier to eternity.
And I, how can I praise thee well and wide
From where I dwell—upon the hither side?
Thou little veil for so great mystery,
When shall I penetrate all things and thee,
And then look back? For this I must abide.
Till thou shalt grow and fold and be unfurled
Literally between me and the world.
Then I shall drink from in beneath a spring.
And from a poet's side shall read his book.
O daisy mine, what will it be to look
From God's side even of such a simple thing?

The Newer Vainglory

Two men went up to pray; and one gave thanks,
      Not with himself—aloud,
With proclamation, calling on the ranks
      Of an attentive crowd.

"Thank God, I clap not my own humble breast,
      But other ruffians' backs,
Imputing crime—such is my tolerant haste—
      To any man that lacks.

"For I am tolerant, generous, keep no rules,
      And the age honors me.
Thank God, I am not as these rigid fools,
      Even as this Pharisee."

Via, et Veritas, et Vita

"You never attained to Him." "If to attain
Be to abide, then that may be."
"Endless the way, followed with how much pain!"
"The way was He."

WILFRID MEYNELL

The Folded Flock

I saw the shepherd fold the sheep,
With all the little lambs that leap.

O Shepherd Lord, so I would be
Folded with all my family.

Or go they early, come they late,
Their mother and I must count them eight.

And how, for us, were any heaven
If we, sore-stricken, saw but seven?

Kind Shepherd, as of old Thou'lt run
And fold at need a straggling one.

HELEN LOUISE MORIARTY

Convent Echoes

Clear on the air, their pulsing cadence pealing,
    I hear a sweet refrain,
While o'er my thoughts a gentle mist is stealing,
    And mem'ries come again,

Of quiet halls where dusk is slow descending,
    Where peace has spread her wings.
Soft music in the distance only lending
    More charms where twilight clings.

Anon appear the black-robed nuns, their faces
    Serene in sweet repose;
Across their brows the world has left no traces
    Of earthly dreams or woes.

Now loud on air the organ music swelling,
    They reach the chapel door—
The sweet faint incense stealing upward, telling
    'Tis Benediction's hour.

Now low-bowed heads, and hearts to Him ascending
    On incense laden air.

149

Ah surely Heaven must smile with ear attending
    The nun's low whispered prayer.

Fond memory lingers on those dim old hallways—
    Lingers and drops a tear,
And kind affection drapes the picture always
    Through each succeeding year.

JOHN HENRY CARDINAL NEWMAN

England

Tyre of the West, and glorying in the name
    More than in Faith's pure fame!
O trust not crafty fort nor rock renown'd
    Earn'd upon hostile ground;
Wielding Trade's master-keys, at thy proud will
To lock or loose its waters, England! trust not still.

Dread thine own power! Since haughty Babel's prime,
    High towers have been man's crime.
Since her hoar age, when the huge moat lay bare,
    Strongholds have been man's snare.
Thy nest is in the crags; ah, refuge frail!
Mad counsels in its hour, or traitors, will prevail.

He who scann'd Sodom for His righteous men
    Still spares thee for thy ten;
But, should vain tongues the Bride of Heaven defy,
    He will not pass thee by;
For, as earth's kings welcome their spotless guests,
So gives He them by turn, to suffer or be blest.

The Pillar of the Cloud

Lead, kindly Light, amid the encircling gloom,
    Lead Thou me on!
The night is dark, and I am far from home—
    Lead Thou me on!
Keep Thou my feet; I do not ask to see
The distant scene—one step enough for me.

I was not ever thus, nor pray'd that Thou
    Shouldst lead me on.

150

I lov'd to choose and see my path; but now
　　　Lead Thou me on!
I lov'd the garish day, and, spite of fears,
Pride rul'd my will; remember not past years.

So long Thy power hath bless'd me, sure it still
　　　Will lead me on,
O'er moor and fen, o'er crag and torrent, till
　　　The night is gone;
And with the morn those angel faces smile
Which I have lov'd long since, and lost awhile.

The Greek Fathers

Let heathen sing thy heathen praise,
Fall'n Greece! the thought of holier days
　　　In my sad heart abides;
For sons of thine in Truth's first hour
Were tongues and weapons of His power,
Born of the Spirit's fiery shower,
　　　Our fathers and our guides.

All thine is Clement's varied page;
And Dionysius, ruler sage,
　　　In days of doubt and pain;
And Origen with eagle eye;
And saintly Basil's purpose high
To smite imperial heresy,
　　　And cleanse the Altar's stain.

From thee the glorious preacher came,
With soul of zeal and lips of flame,
　　　A court's stern martyr-guest;
And thine, O inexhaustive race!
Was Nazianzen's heaven-taught grace;
And royal-hearted Athanase,
　　　With Paul's own mantle blessed.

Relics of Saints

"The Fathers are in dust, yet live to God":
　　So says the Truth; as if the motionless clay
Still held the seeds of life beneath the sod,
　　Smouldering and straggling till the judgment day.

151

And hence we learn with reverence to esteem
　　Of these frail houses, though the grave confines;
Sophist may urge his cunning tests, and deem
　　That they are earth;—but they are heavenly shrines.

The Sign of the Cross

Whene'er across this sinful flesh of mine
　　I draw the Holy Sign,
All good thoughts stir within me, and renew
　　Their slumbering strength divine;
Till there springs up a courage high and true
　　To suffer and to do.

And who shall say, but hateful spirits around,
　　For their brief hour unbound,
Shudder to see, and wail their overthrow?
　　While on far heathen ground
Some lonely saint hails the fresh odour, though
　　Its source he cannot know?

CHARLES L. O'DONNELL, C.S.C.

To St. Joseph

St. Joseph, when the day was done
　　And all your work put by,
You saw the stars come one by one
　　Out in the violet sky.

You did not know the stars by name,
　　But there sat at your knee
One who had made the light and flame
　　And all things bright that be.

You heard with Him birds in the tree
　　Twitter "Good-night" o'erhead—
The Maker of the world must see
　　His little ones to bed.

Then when the darkness settled round,
　　To Him your prayers were said;
No wonder that your sleep was ground
　　The angels loved to tread.

The Dead Musician

[In memory of Brother Basil, organist for half a century at
the University of Notre Dame]

He was the player and the played upon,
He was the actor and the acted on,
Artist, and yet himself a substance wrought;
God played on him as he upon the keys,
Moving his soul to mightiest melodies
Of lowly serving, hid austerities,
And holy thought that our high dream out-tops—
He was an organ where God kept the stops.
      Naught, naught
Of all he gave us came so wondrous clear
As that he sounded to the Master's ear.

Wedded he was to the immortal Three,
Poverty, Obedience and Chastity,
And in a fourth he found them all expressed,
For him all gathered were in Music's breast,
     And in God's house
  He took her for his spouse—
High union that the world's eye never scans
     Nor world's way knows.
Not any penny of applauding hands
He caught, nor would have caught,
    Not any thought
    Save to obey
  Obedience that bade him play,
    And for his bride
  To have none else beside,
That both might keep unflecked their virgin snows.

Yet by our God's great law
Such marriage issue saw,
As they who cast away may keep,
     Who sow not reap.
    In Chastity entombed
    His manhood bloomed,
    And children not of earth
    Had spotless birth.
With might unmortal was he strong
    That he begot
    Of what was not,
Within the barren womb of silence, song.
    Yea, many sons he had
  To make his sole heart glad—
Romping the boundless meadows of the air,

153

Skipping the cloudy hills, and climbing bold
The heavens' nightly stairs of starry gold.
      Nay, winning heaven's door
        To mingle evermore
With deathless troops of angel harmony.
      He filled the house of God
      With servants at his nod,
A music-host of moving pageantry.
Lo, this priest, and that an acolyte:
      Ah, such we name aright
        Creative art,
To body forth love slumbering at the heart. . . .
      Fools, they who pity him,
        Imagine dim
Days that the world's glare brightens not.
        Until the seraphim
    Shake from their flashing hair
    Lightnings, and weave serpents there,
        His days we reckon fair. . . .

        Yet more he had than this;
        Lord of the liberative kiss,
        To own and yet refrain,
        To hold his hand in reign.
High continence of his high power,
That turns from virtue's very flower,
      In loss of that elected pain
        A greater prize to gain.
As one who long had put wine by
      Would now himself deny
      Water, and thirsting die.
So, sometimes he was idle at the keys,
Pale fingers on the aged ivories;
        Then, like a prisoned bird,
        Music was seen, not heard,
Then were his quivering hands most strong
With blood of the repressèd song,—
    A fruitful barrenness. Oh, where
        Out of angelic air,
    This side the heavens' spheres
    Such sight to start and hinder tears.
Who knows, perhaps while silence throbbed
He heard the *De Profundis* sobbed
    By his own organ at his bier today—
    It is the saints' anticipative way,
    He knew both hand and ear were clay.
        That was one thought
        Never is music wrought,
For silence only could that truth convey.

154

Widowed of him, his organ now is still,
His music-children fled, their echoing feet yet fill
The blue, far reaches of the vaulted nave,
The heart that sired them, pulseless in the grave.
Only the song he made is hushed, his soul,
Responsive to God's touch, in His control
Elsewhere shall tune the termless ecstasy
    Of one who all his life kept here
        An alien ear,
Homesick for harpings of eternity.

The Son of God

The fount of Mary's joy
    Revealed now lies,
For, lo, has not the Boy
    His Father's eyes?

THOMAS O'HAGAN

Giotto's Campanile

O pulsing heart with voice attuned
    To all the soul builds high,
Framing in notes of love divine
    A drama of the sky,
Across the Arno's flowing tide
    The notes chime on the air,
Deep as the mysteries of God
    And tender as a prayer.

Here, where the Poet of Sorrows dwelt,
    Whose altar Love had built,
And framed his morn in dreams so pure
    That knew not stain nor guilt:
O *Vita Nuova!* Earthly Love
    Then changed to love Divine;
Transfigured at the wedding-feast,
    Earth's grapes are heavenly wine.

Where cowled monk with soul of fire
    Struck vice athwart the face,
With God's anointed sword of truth
    That flashed with beams of grace.
O bitter days of war and strife!

155

Heaven's ardor was too great;
    The Empire of the earth held sway
        And sealed with saddest fate.

Methinks I hear from thy strong lips,
    O century-dowered bell!
The story of the Whites and Blacks,
    As banners rose or fell;
Methinks I hear an epic voice,
    Full of God's love and power,
With accent of an Exile sad
    Speaking from out thy tower!

JOHN BOYLE O'REILLY

Name of Mary

Dear, honored name, beloved for human ties,
    But loved and honored first that One was given
In living proof, to erring mortal eyes,
    That our poor flesh is near akin to heaven.

Sweet word of dual meaning: one of grace,
    And born of our kind Advocate above;
And one, by mercy linked to that dear face
    That blessed my childhood with its mother-love,

And taught me first the simple prayer: "To thee,
    Poor banished sons of Eve, we send our cries."
Through mist of years, those words recall to me
    A childish face upturned to loving eyes.

And yet, to some the name of Mary bears
    No special meaning and no gracious power;
In that dear word they seek for hidden snares,
    As wasps find poison in the sweetest flower.

But faithful hearts can see, o'er doubts and fears,
    The Virgin-link that binds the Lord to earth;
Which, to the upturned trusting face, appears
    Greater than angel, though of human birth.

The sweet-faced moon reflects, on cheerless night,
    The rays of hidden sun that rise to-morrow;
So, unseen God still lets his promised light,
    Through holy Mary, shine upon our sorrow.

MARY A. O'REILLY

A Christmas Carol

Night in the far Judean land,
    The pregnant air is still,
The sky one blue unclouded band,
    Seems drooping o'er each hill.
The hills then toward each other bend,
Some mighty secret to portend.
    Gloria in excelsis Deo.

The sheep in near-by pastures browse,
    Some bleat as if in pain;
The youthful shepherds watch and drowse,
    Then drowse and watch again;
When lo! a light from Heaven appears
Which makes them huddle in their fears.
    Gloria in excelsis Deo.

God's glory shone around them there,
    And then an angel cried—
"Fear not, for I good tidings bear
    To you, and all beside.
For unto you is born this day
A Savior, Christ the Lord." We pray—
    Gloria in excelsis Deo.

Then swinging from the skies there came
    Groups of the heavenly host,
Praising the Lord in sweet acclaim—
    The burden of their toast—
"Glory to God on High," again—
His "Peace on earth, good will to men."
    Gloria in excelsis Deo.

Within a stable sweet with hay,
    And warm with breath of kine,
The Baby and His Mother lay,
    O, mystery divine!
The bed of straw a cloud appears,
We hear the music of the spheres.
    Gloria in excelsis Deo.

Dear maiden mother, let us now,
    While to your breast He clings,
In humble adoration bow
    With shepherds and with kings,

157

And at His feet our off'ring be
Praise, love, faith, hope and charity.
Gloria in excelsis Deo.

SHAEMAS O'SHEEL

Roma Mater Sempaeterna

The blue skies bend and are about her furled,
A maiden mantle; and with lilies bright
The sun daywhiles doth crown her, and at night
With stars her garment's border is empearled.
Not a king's favorite, perfumed and curled,
Is half so fair; no queen of martial might
So potent as the Mother of the Light,
The Mary of the Cities of the World!
Eternal Mother, at whose breasts of white
The infant Church was suckled and made strong
With the sweet milk of heavenly Truth and Love,
O thou that art all nations set above,
Strengthen us still because the way is long,
Mary of Cities, Mother of the Light!

Mary's Baby

Joseph, mild and noble, bent above the straw:
A pale girl, a frail girl, marvelling he saw;
"O my love, my Mary, my bride, I pity thee!"
"Nay, dear," said Mary, "all is well with me!"
  "Baby, my Baby, O my Babe," she sang.
  Suddenly the golden night all with music rang.

Angels leading shepherds, shepherds leading sheep:
The silence of worship broke the mother's sleep.
All the meek and lowly of the world were there;
Smiling she showed them that her Child was fair.
  "Baby, my Baby," kissing Him she said.
  Suddenly a flaming star through the heavens sped.

Three old men and weary knelt them side by side,
The world's wealth forswearing, majesty and pride;
Worldly might and wisdom before the Babe bent low:
Weeping, maid Mary said "I love Him so!"
  "Baby, my Baby," and the Baby slept.
  Suddenly on Calvary all the olives wept.

They Went Forth to Battle

They went forth to battle, but they always fell;
Their eyes were fixed above the sullen shields;
Nobly they fought and bravely, but not well,
And sank heart-wounded by a subtle spell.
They knew not fear that to the foeman yields,
They were not weak, as one who vainly wields
A futile weapon, yet the sad scrolls tell
How on the hard-fought field they always fell.

It was a secret music that they heard,
A sad sweet plea for pity and for peace;
And that which pierced the heart was but a word,
Though the white breast was red-lipped where the sword
Pressed a fierce cruel kiss, to put surcease
On its hot thirst, but drank a hot increase.
Ah, then by some strange troubling doubt were stirred,
And died for hearing what no foeman heard.

They went forth to battle but they always fell;
Their might was not the might of lifted spears;
Over the battle-clamor came a spell
Of troubling music, and they fought not well.
Their wreaths are willows and their tribute, tears;
Their names are old sad stories in men's ears;
Yet they will scatter the red hordes of Hell
Who went to battle forth and always fell.

He Whom a Dream Hath Possessed

He whom a dream hath possessed knoweth no more of
        doubting,
    For mist and the blowing of winds and the mouthing of
        words he scorns;
Not the sinuous speech of schools he hears, but a knightly
        shouting,
    And never comes darkness down, yet he greeteth a million
        morns.

He whom a dream hath possessed knoweth no more of
        roaming;
    All roads and the flowing of waves and the speediest flight
        he knows,
But wherever his feet are set, his soul is forever homing,
    And going he comes, and coming he heareth a call and goes.

159

He whom a dream hath possessed knoweth no more of sorrow,
  At death and the dropping of leaves and the fading of suns
      he smiles,
For a dream remembers no past and scorns the desire of a
      morrow,
  And a dream in a sea of doom sets surely the ultimate isles.

He whom a dream hath possessed treads the impalpable
      marches,
  From the dust of the day's long road he leaps to a laughing
      star,
And the ruin of worlds that fall he views from eternal arches,
  And rides God's battle-field in a flashing and golden car.

CONDÉ BENOIST PALLEN

Maria Immaculata

How may I sing, unworthy I,
Our Lady's glorious sanctity?
She whose celestial shoon
Rest on the hornèd moon
In Heaven's highest galaxy;
She whom the poet sang of old
In that rare vision told
In soft Tuscan speech of gold,
The spotless spouse and mother-maid
The goodliest sapphire in Heaven's floor inlaid,
Around whom wheels the circling flame
Of the rapt seraph breathing Mary's name,
While choir to choir replies
In growing harmonies
Through all the glowing spheres of Paradise,
Till universal Heaven's glad estate
Rings jubilation to their queen immaculate.

Ah me! Unworthy I to sing
The stainless mother of my King,
My King and Lord,
The Incarnate Word,
Heaven itself comprest
Within her virgin breast!
How may my faltering rhyme
Sing of Eternity in time,
Omnipotence in human frailty exprest,
Our earthly garden fragrant with celestial thyme.
What Muse, though great Urania guide her flight,

160

May dare the sacrosanct and awful height
Of that mysterious sublime
Within the secret counsels of the Infinite!
Omniscence there supreme and sole
Clasps the beginning and the whole
Of Love beyond created sight,
Uncreate and quintessential light!
Before the splendor of that ray
Cherub and seraph fall away
Dazzled and broken by excess
Of everpowering blessedness,
Yet panting for the fulness of the bliss
That breathes consuming fire from Love's unkenned abyss.
Not through that fiery sphere my way,
But here where shines the veilèd day,
The flames of mystery insteeped
In this our mortal clay;
For in her maiden breast asleep
Lies all the Love of Heaven's deep,
The holy circle of her zone
Incarnate Love's terrestrial throne.

The great archangel veils his face
Before her: "Hail, full of grace!"
And Heaven is clasped of earth;
While all the wheeling spheres with all their choirs
Around her wheel seraphic fires.
Eden rises to its second birth;
Again the prime estate
Of man is renovate,
And all the elder worth renewed in her immaculate;
Virgin and spouse of Him
Who breathes the virtue of the Seraphim,
Virgin and mother of the Eternal Son,
Daughter, Virgin, Spouse in one!
The spotless mate of spotless Dove,
The one great miracle of God's love,
From all eternity the chosen bride,
Save only her none, none
Exempt from sin's dominion;
Save only her of Adam's race
Or heavenly line, none full of grace;
On her alone, on her alone
The torrent of His love poured down
The deep abundance of its flood
Into the pure channels of her maidenhood,
The fleckless mirror of her grace
Reflecting all the beauty of His face.

She looks with human eyes
Into the eyes of Paradise;
Upon her virgin breast the Babe divine
Gazes again into her eyne;
O vanity of words to tell
The wonder of that spell,
The ravishment of bliss
Upwelling from the deep abyss
Of Love incarnate gazing in the eyes
Of his terrestrial paradise!
See Heaven within her arms,
Gathered against all harms,
Innocence by innocence addrest,
Virgin love by virgin love carest,
The sinless mother and the sinless Son
For Heaven and earth to gaze upon!
Her living image on her knee,
O the depths of her maternity!
Her God, her Infant at her breast,
O Love beyond all utterance exprest,
The Eternal Word in virgin flesh made manifest!

Ye sons of Adam rejoice
With exultant voice!
Shake off your chains! Arise!
The ancient dragon has no power
O'er Jesse's virgin flower,
And stricken 'neath a maiden's sandal lies.
Nor may his venomed breath so much
As her garment's outer margin touch;
And sin's torrential flood,
That whelmed all Adam's flesh and blood,
Its loathsome stream turns back
Before her footsteps' radiant track.

Rejoice, children of men!
Behold again
Your flesh rejuvenate
In her immaculate!
Rejoice with exceeding joy,
For in her free from sin's alloy
Your renovated race
In plenitude of grace
Dare look again unshamed upon its Maker's Face!
Chosen to bear the Eternal Word,
In her your more than dignity restored;
In her the more than golden worth
Of Eden's prime when Heaven was linked with earth;

162

Unstained by Adam's guilty forfeiture,
In her your long corrupted flesh made pure;
For of her, flesh of flesh and bone of bone,
Eternal Love builds up His stainless throne!

Rejoice and be glad this day!
In jubilation lay
Your tribute at her feet,
Spotless and most meet,
The mystic rose of Jesse's root,
To bear the heavenly fruit;
Wisdom's seat and Heaven's gate,
Our surest advocate,
Mother of God immaculate!
Be glad, O Adam's clay,
Be glad this happy day.
And with accordant voice acclaim
Our spotless Lady's stainless fame;
Be ye exceeding glad and sing
The mother of our King.
And though unworthy be my strain,
She is too tender not to deign
To lend a gracious ear
To this her children's humble prayer:
Mother of Mercy, hear!
Mother whose face is likest His,
Who our Redeemer is,
Grant us one day to share
Thy happiness in gazing on His face,
Who found thee without spot and full of grace!

The Raising of the Flag

Lift up the banner of our love
To the kiss of the winds above,
The banner of the world's fair hope,
Set with stars from the azure cope,
When liberty was young,
And yet unsung
Clarioned her voice among
The trodden peoples, and stirred
The pulses with her word,
Till the swift flood red
From the quick heart sped,
Flushing valor's cheek with flame
At sounding of her august sacred name!

Lift up the banner of the stars,
The standard of the double bars,
Red with the holy tide
Of heroes' blood, who died
At the feet of liberty,
Shouting her battle-cry
Triumphantly
As they fell like sickled corn
In that first resplendent morn
Of freedom, glad to die
In the dawn of her clear eye!

Lift up the flag of starry blue
Caught from the crystal hue
Of central heaven's glowing dome,
Where the great winds largely roam
In unrestrainèd liberty;
Caught from the cerulean sea
Of midmost ocean tossing free,
Flecked with the racing foam
Of rushing waters, as they leap
Unbridled from the laughing deep
In the gulfs of liberty!

Lift up the banner red
With the blood of heroes shed
In victory!
Lift up the banner blue
As heaven, and as true
In constancy!
Lift up the banner white
As sea foam in the light
Of liberty;
The banner of the triple hue,
The banner of the red and white and blue,
Bright ensign of the free!

Lift up the banner of the days to come,
When cease the trumpet and the rolling drum;
When peace in the nest of love
Unfolds the wings of the dove,
Brooding o'er the days to-be,
Peace born of freedom's might,
Peace sprung from the power of right,
The peace of liberty!

Lift up the flag of high surprise
To greet the gladdened eyes

Of peoples far and near,
The glorious harbinger
Of earth's wide liberties,
Streaming pure and clear
In freedom's lofty atmosphere!

Lift up our hearts to Him who made to shine
In Heaven's arch the glorious sign
Of mercy's heavenly birth
To all the peoples of the earth,
The pledge of peace divine!
And let our glorious banner, too,
The banner of the rainbow's hue,
In heaven's wide expanse unfurled,
Be for a promise to the world
Of peace to all mankind;
Banner of peace and light,
Banner of red and blue and white,
Red as the crimson blood
Of Christ's wide brotherhood,
Blue with the unchanging hope
Of heaven's steadfast sun,
White as the radiant sun
The whole earth shining on!

The Babe of Bethlehem

O cruel manger, how bleak, how bleak!
    For the limbs of the Babe, my God;
Soft little limbs on the cold, cold straw;
    Weep, O eyes, for thy God!

Bitter ye winds in the frosty night
    Upon the Babe, my God,
Piercing the torn and broken thatch;
    Lament, O heart, for thy God!

Bare is the floor, how bare, how bare
    For the Babe's sweet mother, my God;
Only a stable for mother and Babe;
    How cruel thy world, my God!

Cast out, cast out, by his brother men
    Unknown the Babe, my God;
The ox and the ass alone are there;
    Soften, O heart, for thy God!

Dear little arms and sweet little hands,
    That stretch for thy mother, my God;
Soft baby eyes to the mother's eyes;
    Melt, O heart, for thy God!

Waxen touches on mother's heart,
    Fingers of the Babe, my God;
Dear baby lips to her virgin breast,
    The virgin mother of God.

The shepherds have come from the hills to adore
    The Babe in the manger, my God;
Mary and Joseph welcome them there;
    Worship, O soul, thy God!

But I alone may not come near
    The Babe in the manger, my God;
Weep for thy sins, O heart, and plead
    With Mary the mother of God.

May I not come, oh, just to the door,
    To see the Babe, my God;
There will I stop and kneel and adore,
    And weep for my sins, O God!

But Mary smiles, and rising up,
    In her arms the Babe, my God,
She comes to the door and bends her down,
    With the Babe in her arms, my God!

Her sinless arms in my sinful arms
    Place the Babe, my God;
"He has come to take thy sins away";
    Break, O heart, for thy God!

COVENTRY PATMORE

The Toys

My little son, who look'd from thoughtful eyes
And mov'd and spoke in quiet grown-up wise,
Having my law the seventh time disobey'd,
I struck him, and dismiss'd
With hard words and unkiss'd,
His Mother, who was patient, being dead.
Then fearing lest his grief should hinder sleep
I visited his bed,
But found him slumbering deep,
With darken'd eyelids, and their lashes yet
From his late sobbing wet.
And I, with moan,
Kissing away his tears, left others of my own;
For, on a table drawn beside his head,
He had put, within his reach,
A box of counters and a red-vein'd stone,
A piece of glass abraded by the beach,
And six or seven shells,
A bottle with bluebells
And two French copper coins, ranged there with careful art,
To comfort his sad heart.
So when that night I pray'd
To God, I wept, and said:
Ah, when at last we lie with trancèd breath,
Not vexing Thee in death,
And Thou rememberest of what toys
We made our joys,
How weakly understood
Thy great commanded good,
Then, fatherly not less
Than I whom Thou hast moulded from the clay,
Thou'lt leave Thy wrath, and say,
"I will be sorry for their childishness."

"If I Were Dead"

"If I were dead, you'd some time say, poor Child!"
The dear lips quiver'd as they spake,
And the tears break
From eyes, which, not to grieve me, brightly smiled.
Poor Child, poor Child!
I seem to hear your laugh, your talk, your song.
It is not true that Love will do no wrong.

Poor Child!
And did you think, when you so cried and smiled,
How I, in lonely nights, should lie awake,
And of those words your full avengers make?
Poor Child, poor Child!
And now, unless it be
That sweet amends thrice told are come to thee,
O God, have Thou *no* mercy upon me!
Poor Child!

Departure

It was not like your great and gracious ways!
Do you, that have nought other to lament,
Never, my Love, repent
Of how, that July afternoon,
You went,
With sudden, unintelligible phrase,
And frightened eye,
Upon your journey of so many days
Without a single kiss, or a good-bye?
I knew, indeed, that you were parting soon;
And so we sate, within the low sun's rays,
You whispering to me, for your voice was weak,
Your harrowing praise.
Well, it was well
To hear you such things speak,
And I could tell
What made your eyes a growing gloom of love,
As a warm South-wind sombres a March grove.
And it was like your great and gracious ways
To turn your talk on daily things, my Dear,
Lifting the luminous, pathetic lash
To let the laughter flash,
Whilst I drew near,
Because you spoke so low that I could scarcely hear.
But all at once to leave me at the last,
More at the wonder than the loss aghast,
With huddled, unintelligible phrase,
And frighten'd eye,
And go your journey of all days
With not one kiss, or a good-bye,
And the only loveless look the look with which you passed;
'Twas all unlike your great and gracious ways.

Regina Coeli

Say, did his sisters wonder what could Joseph see
In a mild, silent little Maid like thee?
And was it awful, in that narrow house,
With God for Babe and Spouse?
Nay, like thy simple, female sort, each one
Apt to find Him in Husband and in Son,
Nothing to thee came strange in this.
Thy wonder was but wondrous bliss:
Wondrous, for, though
True Virgin lives not but does know,
(Howbeit none ever yet confess'd,)
That God lies really in her breast,
Of thine He made His special nest!
And so
All mothers worship little feet,
And kiss the very ground they've trod;
But, ah, thy little Baby sweet,
Who was indeed thy God!

PADRAIC PEARSE

Ideal

[Translated by Thomas MacDonagh]

Naked I saw thee,
  O beauty of beauty!
And I blinded my eyes
  For fear I should flinch.

I heard thy music,
  O sweetness of sweetness!
And I shut my ears
  For fear I should fail.

I kissed thy lips,
  O sweetness of sweetness!
And I hardened my heart
  For fear of my ruin.

I blinded my eyes,
  And my ears I shut,

169

I hardened my heart
  And my love I quenched.

I turned my back
  On the dream I had shaped,
And to this road before me
  My face I turned.

I set my face
  To the road here before me,
To the work that I see,
  To the death that I shall meet.

CHARLES PHILLIPS

Music

There is a hunger in my heart tonight,
  A longing in my soul, to hear
The voice of heaven o'er the noise of earth
  That doth assail mine ear.

For we are exiled children of the skies,
  Lone and lost wanderers from home. . . .
The stars come out like lamps in windows lit
  Far, far from where we roam;

Like candles lit to show the long late way,
  Dear kindly beacons sure and bright;
But O, the heavy journeying, and O
  The silence of the night!—

The dark and vasty silences that lie
  Between the going and the goal!
Will not God reach a friendly hand to lift
  And land my weary soul?

Will not God speak a friendly word to me
  Above the tumult and the din
Of earthly things—one little word to hush
  The voice of care and sin? . . .

He speaks! He answers my poor faltering prayer!
  He opens heaven's lattice wide;
He bids me bathe my brow in heavenly airs
  Like to a flowing tide!

He calls; He gives unto my famished soul,
    Unto my eager heart, its meed:
He breathes upon me with the breath of song,
    And O, my soul is freed,

And I am lifted up and up, and held
    A little while—a child, to see
The beauties of my Father's house, which shall
    No more be shut from me!

JOSEPH MARY PLUNKETT

I See His Blood upon the Rose

I see His blood upon the rose
    And in the stars the glory of His eyes,
His body gleams amid eternal snows,
    His tears fall from the skies.

I see His face in every flower;
    The thunder and the singing of the birds
Are but His voice—and carven by His power
    Rocks are His written words.

All pathways by His feet are worn,
    His strong heart stirs the ever-beating sea,
His crown of thorns is twined with every thorn,
    His cross is every tree.

The Stars Sang in God's Garden

The stars sang in God's garden;
The stars are the birds of God;
The night-time is God's harvest,
Its fruits are the words of God.

God ploughed His fields at morning,
God sowed His seed at noon,
God reaped and gathered in His corn
With the rising of the moon.

The sun rose up at midnight,
The sun rose red as blood,
It showed the Reaper, the dead Christ,
Upon His cross of wood.

171

For many live that one may die,
And one must die that many live—
The stars are silent in the sky
Lest my poor songs be fugitive.

MAY PROBYN

"Is It Nothing to You?"

We were playing on the green together,
    My sweetheart and I—
Oh, so heedless in the gay June weather,
    When the word went forth that we must die.
Oh, so merrily the balls of amber
    And of ivory tossed we to the sky,
While the word went forth in the King's chamber,
    That we both must die.

Oh, so idly, straying through the pleasaunce,
    Plucked we here and there
Fruit and bud, while in the royal presence
    The King's son was casting from his hair
Glory of the wreathen gold that crowned it,
    And, ungirding all his garment fair,
Flinging by the jewelled clasp that bound it,
    With his feet made bare,

Down the myrtled stairway of the palace,
    Ashes on his head,
Came he, through the rose and citron alleys,
    In the rough sark of sackcloth habited,
And in a hempen halter—oh! we jested,
    Lightly, and we laughed as he was led
To the torture, while the bloom we breasted
    Where the grapes grew red.

Oh, so sweet the birds, when he was dying,
    Piped to her and me—
Is no room this glad June day for sighing—
    He is dead, and she and I go free!
When the sun shall set on all our pleasure
    We will mourn him—What, so you decree
We are heartless?—Nay, but in what measure
    Do you more than we?

The Bees of Myddleton Manor (17th Century)

Buzzing, buzzing, buzzing, my golden-belted bees:
My little son was seven years old—the mint-flower touched
    his knees;
    Yellow were his curly locks;
    Yellow were his stocking-clocks;
His plaything of a sword had a diamond in its hilt;
    Where the garden beds lay sunny,
    And the bees were making honey,
"For God and the king—to arms! to arms!" the day long
    would he lilt.
Smock'd in lace and flowered brocade, my pretty son of seven
Wept sore because the kitten died, and left the charge uneven.
    "I head one battalion, mother—
    Kitty," sobbed he, "led the other!
    And when we reach'd the bee-hive bench
    We used to halt and storm the trench:
    If we could plant our standard here,
    With all the bees a-buzzing near,
    And fly the colors safe from sting,
    The town was taken for the king!"
Flirting flitting over the thyme, by bees with yellow band—
My little son of seven came close, and clipp'd me by the hand;
    A wreath of mourning cloth was wound
    His small left arm and sword-hilt round,
And on the thatch of every hive a whisp of black was bound.
"Sweet mother, we must tell the bees, or they will swarm
    away:
Ye little bees!" he called, "draw nigh, and hark to what I say,
And make us golden honey still for our white wheaten bread,
    Though never more
    We rush on war
    With Kitty at our head:
        Who'll give the toast
        When swords are cross'd,
    Now Kitty lieth dead?"
Buzzing, buzzing, buzzing, my bees of yellow girth:
My son of seven changed his mood, and clasp'd me in his
    mirth.
"Sweet mother, when I grow a man and fall on battlefield,"
He cried, and down in the daisied grass upon one knee he
    kneel'd,
"I charge thee, come and tell the bees how I for the king lie
    dead;
And thou shalt never lack fine honey for thy wheaten bread!"

Flitting, flitting, flitting, my busy bees, alas!
No footsteps of my soldier son came clinking through the
    grass.
    Thrice he kiss'd me for farewell;
    And far on the stone his shadow fell;
He buckled spurs and sword-belt on, as the sun began to
    stoop,
Set foot in stirrup, and sprang to horse, and rode to join his
    troop.
    To the west he rode, where the winds were at play,
    And Monmouth's army mustering lay;
    Where Bridgewater flew her banner high,
    And gave up her keys, when the Duke came by;
    And the maids of Taunton paid him court
    With colors their own white hands had wrought;
    And red as a field, where blood doth run,
    Sedgemoor blazed in the setting sun.

Broider'd sash and clasp of gold, my soldier son, alas!
The mint was all in flower, and the clover in the grass:
        "With every bed
        In bloom," I said,
      "What further lack the bees,
        That they buzz so loud,
        Like a restless cloud,
      Among the orchard trees?"
No voice in the air, from Sedgemoor field,
Moan'd out how Grey and the horse had reel'd;
Met me no ghost, with haunting eyes,
That westward pointed 'mid its sighs,
And pull'd apart a bloody vest,
And show'd the sword-gash in his breast.

Empty hives, and flitting bees, and sunny morning hours;
I snipp'd the blossom'd lavender, and the pinks, and the
    gillyflowers;
    No petal trembled in my hold—
    I saw not the dead stretched stark and cold
    On the trampled turf at the shepherd's door,
    In the cloak and the doublet Monmouth wore,
    With Monmouth's scarf and headgear on,
    And the eyes, not clos'd, of my soldier son;
I knew not how, ere the cocks did crow, the fight was fought
    in the dark,
With naught for guide but the enemy's guns, when the flint
    flash'd out a spark,
Till, routed at first sound of fire, the cavalry broke and fled,
And the hoofs struck dumb, where they spurned the slain,
    and the meadow stream ran red;

I saw not the handful of horsemen spur through the dusk, and
     out of sight,
My soldier son at the Duke's left hand, and Grey that rode
     on his right.

Buzzing, buzzing, buzzing, my honey-making bees,
They left the musk, and the marigolds and the scented faint
     sweet peas;
They gather'd in a darkening cloud, and sway'd, and rose to
     fly;
A blackness on the summer blue, they swept across the sky.
Gaunt and ghastly with gaping wounds—(my soldier son,
     alas!)
Footsore and faint, the messenger came halting through the
     grass.
The wind went by and shook the leaves—the mint-stalk shed
     its flower—
And I miss'd the murmuring round the hives, and my boding
     heart beat slower.
     His soul we cheer'd with meat and wine;
     With woman's craft and balsam fine
     We bathed his hurts, and bound them soft,
     While west the wind played through the croft,
     And the low sun dyed the pinks blood red,
     And, straying near the mint-flower shed,
     A wild bee wantoned o'er the bed.

He told how my son, at the shepherd's door, kept watch in
     Monmouth's clothes,
While Monmouth donned the shepherd's frock, in hope to
     cheat his foes.
     A couple of troopers spied him stand,
     And bade him yield to the king's command:
     "Surrender, thou rebel as good as dead,
     A price is set on thy traitor head!"
     My soldier son, with secret smile,
     Held both at bay for a little while,
     Dealt them such death blow as he fell,
     Neither was left the tale to tell;
     With dying eyes that asked no grace,
     They stared on him for a minute's space,
     And felt that it was not Monmouth's face.
Crimsoned through was Monmouth's cloak, when the soldier
     dropped at their side—
"Those knaves will carry no word," he said, and he smiled
     in his pain, and died.
"Two days," told the messenger, "did we lie
     Hid in the fields of peas and rye,
     Hid in the ditch of brake and sedge,

175

With the enemy's scouts down every hedge,
Till Grey was seized, and Monmouth seized, that under the
    fern did crouch,
Starved and haggard, and all unshaved, with a few raw peas in
    his pouch."

No music soundeth in my ears, but a passing bell that tolls
For gallant lords with head on block—sweet Heaven receive
    their souls!
  And a mound, unnamed, in Sedgemoor grass,
  That laps my soldier son, alas!
    The bloom is shed—
    The bees are fled—
  Middleton luck it's done and dead.

ADELAIDE ANNE PROCTER

A Legend

The Monk was preaching: strong his earnest word,
  From the abundance of his heart he spoke,
And the flame spread—in every soul that heard
  Sorrow and love and good resolve awoke:—
The poor lay Brother, ignorant and old,
  Thanked God that he had heard such words of gold.

"Still let the glory, Lord, be thine alone"—
  So prayed the Monk, his heart absorbed in praise:
"Thine be the glory: if my hands have sown
  The harvest ripened in Thy mercy's rays,
It was Thy blessing, Lord, that made my word
  Bring light and love to every soul that heard.

"O Lord, I thank Thee that my feeble strength
  Has been so blest; that sinful hearts and cold
Were melted at my pleading,—knew at length
  How sweet Thy service and how safe Thy fold:
While souls that loved Thee saw before them rise
  Still holier heights of loving sacrifice."

So prayed the Monk: when suddenly he heard
  An Angel speaking thus: "Know, O my son,
The words had all been vain, but hearts were stirred,
  And saints were edified, and sinners won,
By his, the poor lay Brother's humble aid
  Who sat upon the pulpit stair and prayed."

176

The Sacred Heart

What wouldst thou have, O soul,
   Thou weary soul?
Lo! I have sought for rest
On the Earth's heaving breast,
   From pole to pole.
Sleep—I have been with her,
   But she gave dreams;
Death—nay, the rest he gives
   Rest only seems.
Fair nature knows it not—
   The grass is growing;
The blue air knows it not—
   The winds are blowing:
Not in the changing sky,
   The stormy sea,
Yet somewhere in God's wide world
   Rest there must be.
Within thy Saviour's Heart
   Place all thy care,
And learn, O weary soul,
   Thy Rest is there.

What wouldst thou, trembling soul?
   Strength for the strife,—
Strength for this fiery war
   That we call Life.
Fears gather thickly round;
   Shadowy foes,
Like unto armed men,
   Around me close.
What am I, frail and poor,
   When griefs arise?
No help from the weak earth,
   Or the cold skies.
Lo! I can find no guards,
   No weapons borrow;
Shrinking, alone I stand,
   With mighty sorrow.
Courage, thou trembling soul,
   Grief thou must bear,
Yet thou canst find a strength
   Will match despair;
Within thy Saviour's Heart—
   Seek for it there.

What wouldst thou have, sad soul,
  Oppressed with grief?—
Comfort: I seek in vain,
  Nor find relief.
Nature, all pitiless,
  Smiles on my pain;
I ask my fellow men,
  They give disdain.
I asked the babbling streams,
  But they flowed on;
I asked the wise and good,
  But they gave none.
Though I have asked the stars,
  Coldly they shine.
They are too bright to know
  Grief such as mine.
I asked for comfort still,
  And I found tears,
And I have sought in vain
  Long, weary years.
Listen, thou mournful soul,
  Thy pain shall cease;
Deep in His sacred Heart
  Dwells joy and peace.

Yes, in that Heart divine
  The Angels bright
Find, through eternal years,
  Still new delight.
From thence his constancy
  The martyr drew,
And there the virgin band
  Their refuge knew.
There, racked by pain without,
  And dread within,
How many souls have found
  Heaven's bliss begin.
Then leave thy vain attempts
  To seek for peace;
The world can never give
  One soul release;
But in thy Saviour's Heart
  Securely dwell,
No pain can harm thee, hid
  In that sweet cell.
Then fly, O coward soul,
  Delay no more:
What words can speak the joy
  For thee in store?

What smiles of earth can tell
    Of peace like thine?
Silence and tears are best
    For things divine.

The Annunciation

How pure, and frail, and white,
    The snowdrops shine!
Gather a garland bright
    For Mary's shrine.

For, born of winter snows,
    These fragile flowers
Are gifts to our fair Queen
    From Spring's first hours.

For on this blessèd day
    She knelt at prayer;
When, lo! before her shone
    An Angel fair.

"Hail, Mary!" thus he cried,
    With reverent fear:
She, with sweet wondering eyes,
    Marvelled to hear.

Be still, ye clouds of Heaven!
    Be silent, Earth!
And hear an Angel tell
    Of Jesus' birth,

While she, whom Gabriel hails
    As full of grace,
Listens with humble faith
    In her sweet face.

Be still—Pride, War, and Pomp,
    Vain Hopes, vain Fears,
For now an Angel speaks,
    And Mary hears.

"Hail, Mary!" lo, it rings
    Through ages on;
"Hail Mary!" it shall sound,
    Till Time is done.

179

"Hail, Mary!" infant lips
  Lisp it to-day;
"Hail, Mary!" with faint smile
  The dying say.

"Hail, Mary!" many a heart
  Broken with grief,
In that angelic prayer
  Has found relief.

And many a half-lost soul,
  When turned at bay,
With those triumphant words
  Has won the day.

"Hail, Hary, Queen of Heaven!"
  Let us repeat,
And place our snowdrop wreath
  Here at her feet.

Our Daily Bread

Give us our daily Bread,
  O God, the bread of strength!
For we have learnt to know
  How weak we are at length.
As children we are weak,
  As children must be fed;—
Give us Thy Grace, O Lord,
  To be our daily Bread.

Give us our daily Bread:—
  The bitter bread of grief.
We sought earth's poisoned feasts
  For pleasure and relief;
We sought her deadly fruits,
  But now, O God, instead,
We ask thy healing grief
  To be our daily Bread.

Give us our daily Bread
  To cheer our fainting soul;
The feast of comfort, Lord,
  And peace, to make us whole:
For we are sick of tears,
  The useless tears we shed;—
Now give us comfort, Lord,
  To be our daily Bread.

Give us our daily Bread,
    The Bread of Angels, Lord,
For us, so many times,
    Broken, betrayed, adored:
His Body and His Blood;—
    The feast that Jesus spread:
Give Him—our life, our all—
    To be our daily Bread!

JAMES RYDER RANDALL

My Maryland

The despot's heel is on thy shore,
            Maryland!
His torch is at thy temple door,
            Maryland!
Avenge the patriotic gore
That flecked the streets of Baltimore,
And be the battle-queen of yore,
            Maryland, my Maryland!

Hark to an exiled son's appeal,
            Maryland!
My Mother State, to thee I kneel,
            Maryland!
For life and death, for woe and weal,
Thy peerless chivalry reveal,
And gird thy beauteous limbs with steel,
            Maryland, my Maryland!

Thou wilt not cower in the dust,
            Maryland!
Thy beaming sword shall never rust,
            Maryland!
Remember Carroll's sacred trust,
Remember Howard's warlike thrust,
And all thy slumberers with the just,
            Maryland, my Maryland!

Come! 'tis the red dawn of the day,
            Maryland!
Come with thy panoplied array,
            Maryland!
With Ringgold's spirit for the fray,
With Watson's blood at Monterey,

181

With fearless Lowe and dashing May,
      Maryland, my Maryland!

Dear Mother, burst the tyrant's chain,
      Maryland!
Virginia should not call in vain,
      Maryland!
She meets her sisters on the plain,—
"Sic semper!" 'tis the proud refrain
That baffles minions back amain,
      Maryland!
Arise in majesty again,
      Maryland, my Maryland!

Come! for thy shield is bright and strong,
      Maryland!
Come! for thy dalliance does thee wrong,
      Maryland!
Come to thine own heroic throng
Stalking with Liberty along,
And chant thy dauntless slogan-song,
      Maryland, my Maryland!

I see the blush upon thy cheek,
      Maryland!
For thou wast ever bravely meek,
      Maryland!
But lo! there surges forth a shriek,
From hill to hill, from creek to creek,
Potomac calls to Chesapeake,
      Maryland, my Maryland!

Thou wilt not yield the vandal toll,
      Maryland!
Thou wilt not crook to his control,
      Maryland!
Better the fire upon thee roll,
Better the shot, the blade, the bowl,
Than crucifixion of the soul,
      Maryland, my Maryland!

I hear the distant thunder hum,
      Maryland!
The Old Line's bugle, fife and drum,
      Maryland!
She is not dead, nor deaf, nor dumb;
Huzza! she spurns the Northern scum!
She breathes! She burns! She'll come! She'll come!
      Maryland, my Maryland!

Magdalen

The Hebrew girl, with flaming brow,
   The banner-blush of shame,
Sinks at the sinless Saviour's knees
   And dares to breathe His name.
From the full fountain of her eyes
   The lava-globes are roll'd—
They wash His feet; she spurns them off
   With her ringlet-scarf of gold.

The Meek One feels the eloquence
   Of agonizing prayer,
The burning tears, the suppliant face,
   The penitential hair;
And when, to crown her brimming woe,
   The ointment box is riven—
"Rise, daughter, rise! Much hast thou loved:
   Be all thy sins forgiven!"

Dear God! The prayer of good and pure,
   The canticles of light,
Enrobe Thy throne with gorgeous skies,
   As incense in Thy sight;
May the shivered vase of Magdalen
   Soothe many an outcast's smart,
Teaching what fragrant pleas may spring
   From out a *broken heart!*

Why the Robin's Breast Was Red

The Saviour, bowed beneath His cross, climbed up the dreary
   hill,
And from the agonizing wreath ran many a crimson rill;
The cruel Roman thrust Him on with unrelenting hand,
Till, staggering slowly 'mid the crowd, He fell upon the sand.

A little bird that warbled near, that memorable day,
Flitted around and strove to wrench one single thorn away;
The cruel spike impaled his breast—and thus 'tis sweetly said,
The robin has his silver vest incarnadined with red.

Ah, Jesu! Jesu! Son of man! my dolor and my sighs
Reveal the lesson taught by this winged Ishmael of the skies.
I, in the palace of delight or cavern of despair,
Have plucked no thorns from Thy dear brow, but planted
   thousands there!

183

AGNES REPPLIER

Le Repos en Egypte: The Sphinx

All day I watch the stretch of burning sand;
   All night I brood beneath the golden stars;
Amid the silence of a desolate land,
   No touch of bitterness my reverie mars.
Built by the proudest of a kingly line,
   Over my head the centuries fly fast;
The secrets of the mighty dead are mine;
   I hold the key of a forgotten past.

Yet, ever hushed into a rapturous dream,
   I see again that night. A halo mild
Shone from the liquid moon. Beneath her beam
   Traveled a tired young Mother and the Child.
Within mine arms she slumbered, and alone
   I watched the Infant. At my feet her guide
Lay stretched o'erwearied. On my breast of stone
   Rested the Crucified.

JAMES JEFFREY ROCHE

Nature the False Goddess

The vilest work of vilest man,
   The cup that drugs, the sword that slays,
The purchased kiss of courtesan,
   The lying tongue of blame or praise,

The cobra's fang, the tiger's tongue,
   The python's murderous embrace—
The wrath of any living thing
   A man may fear but gravely face.

But thou, cold Mother, knowest naught
   Of love, of hate, or joy, or woe;
Thy bounties come to man unsought,
   Thy curses fall on friend and foe.

Thou bearest balm upon thy breath,
   Or sowest poison in the air;
And if man reapeth life or death,
   Thou dost not know, thou dost not care.

184

Thou art God's instrument of fate,
    Obedient, mighty, soulless, blind,
No demon to propitiate,
    No deity in love enshrined.

Let him who turns from God away
    To Bel or Moloch bend the knee;
Defile his soul to wood or clay,
    Or thrill with voodoo's ecstasy.

Seek any fetish undivine,
    Be any superstition's thrall,
From Heaven or Hell will come a sign;
    But thou alone art deaf to all.

Andromeda

They chained her fair young body to the cold and cruel stone;
The beast begot of sea and slime had marked her for his own;
The callous world beheld the wrong, and left her there alone.
Base caitiffs who belied her, false kinsmen who denied her,
            Ye left her there alone!
My Beautiful, they left thee in thy peril and thy pain;
The night that hath no morrow was brooding on the main:
But, lo! a light is breaking of hope for thee again;
'Tis Perseus's sword a-flaming, thy dawn of day proclaiming
            Across the western main.
O Ireland! O my country! he comes to break thy chain!

Three Doves

Seaward, at morn, my doves flew free;
At eve they circled back to me.
The first was Faith; the second, Hope;
The third, the whitest, Charity.

Above the plunging surges play
Dream-like they hovered, day by day.
At last they turned, and bore to me
Green signs of peace thro' nightfall gray,

No shore forlorn, no loveliest land
Their gentle eye had left unscanned,
'Mid hues of twilight-heliotrope
Or daybreak fires by heaven-breath fanned.

185

Quick visions of celestial grace—
Hither they waft, from earth's broad space,
Kind thoughts for all humanity,
They shine with radiance from God's face.

Ah, since my heart they choose for home,
Why loose them,—forth again to roam?
Yet look; they rise with loftier scope
They wheel in flight toward Heaven's pure dome.

Fly, messengers that find no rest
Save in such toil as makes man blest!
Your home is God's immensity;
We hold you but at His behest.

The Way of the World

The hands of the King are soft and fair
   They never knew labor's strain
The hands of the Robber redly wear
   The bloody brand of Cain.
But the hands of the Man are hard and scarred
   With the scars of toil and pain.

The slaves of Pilate have washed his hands
   As white as a kings might be.
Barrabas with wrists unfettered stands
   For the world has made him free.
But Thy palms toil-worn by nails are torn,
   O Christ, on Calvary.

JOHN JEROME ROONEY

Ave Maria

Lady, thy soldier I would be,
   This day I choose thy shield,
And go, thrice-armored for the fight,
   Forth to the world's wide field.

There I shall meet the dark allies,
   The Flesh, the Fiend, the World.
And fiercely shall their darts of fire
   Upon my heart be hurled.

But I will raise my buckler strong
    Betwixt me and the foe,
And, with the spirit's flaming sword,
    Shall give them blow for blow.

Lady, thy sailor I would be,
    This day I sign my name
To sail the high seas of the earth
    For glory of thy fame.

The tempest may besiege my bark,
    The pirate lie in wait:
The perils of the monstrous deep
    May tempt o'erwhelming fate:

Yet, wheresoe'er my ship may steer
    Upon the waters wide,
Thy name shall be my compass sure,
    Thy star my midnight guide.

Thy poet, Lady, I would be
    To sing thy peerless praise;
Thy loyal bard, I'd bring to thee
    Heart-music from all lays.

Soft melody, outpoured in June
    By God's dear feathered throng,
Would mingle with the organ's roll
    To glorify my song;

And Dante's voice and Petrarch's strain
    And Milton's matchless line
Would lend to my poor minstrel note
    A harmony divine.

Lady, I choose to be thy son;
    For Mother thee I choose;
O, for thy sweet and holy Child,
    Do not my claim refuse!

Alone and motherless am I:
    Tho' strong, I long for rest—
The thunder of the world's applause
    Is not a mother's breast.

Ave Maria! Shield us all.
    Thy sons we choose to be.
Mother of grace, we raise our hearts,
    Our hearts, our love to thee!

187

Revelation

The Lord God said to His angel: "Let the old things pass
    away.
They have heaped the earth with slaughter, their sin obscures
    the day.
Roll up the night on a curtain: let the stars fade one by one:
Out of the face of the heavens my anger shall blot the sun.
For the man I made and breathed on, filled with my breath
    of breath,
Hath sown the seas with hatred, his skies are dark with death.
The babe is slain at the bosom, the babe who beholds my face;
A welter of woe he leaves it,—the dream of my love and
    grace.

"Love was the dower I gave him, love the light of his days,
Love the core of his being, love, and the upward gaze.
Hate is the meat he feeds on, hate is his daily bread:
His drink is the blood of his brother, whom Cain hath stricken
    dead.
I said to the man in the Garden: 'Where is thy brother, Cain?'
'Am I my brother's keeper?' now comes the answer again."
The Lord God said to His angel: "This Thing is accursed and
    a lie:
It hath sinned from the Law I gave it, and surely it shall die."

"The beasts of the field are patient, the birds rejoice in song—
But what is this Thing of blood-lust, and where does it belong?
Lo, I shall establish a judgment: Let the old things pass away:
They have heaped the fields with slaughter: their sin defiles
    the day.
They have laid on the weak sore burdens, on the just, their
    whips and ban:
For a handful of crimsoned silver they have kissed the Son
    of Man.
Roll back the scroll of the heavens; from out of the womb of
    birth
Come forth new heavens untainted; come forth, renewed, the
    Earth!"

Marquette on the Shores of the Mississippi

Here, in the midnight of the solemn wood,
He heard a roar as of a mighty wind,—
The onward rush of waters unconfined
Trampling in legions thro' the solitude.

Then lo! before him swept the conquering flood,
Free as the freedom of the truth-strong mind
Which hills of Doubt could neither hide nor bind,
Which, all in vain, the valley mounds withstood!

With glowing eye he saw the prancing tide
With yellow mane rush onward thro' the night
Into the vastness he had never trod:
Nor dreamt of conquest of that kingdom wide
As down the flood his spirit took its flight
Seeking the long-lost children of his God!

The Empire Builder

This is the song of the Empire Builder,
    Who out of the ends of the earth,
Thro' travail of war and of carnage
    Brings strange, new realms to birth.

This is the boast of the Empire Builder:
    Give heed to the deeds of his hands
And scorn thou not the glory he hath
    In his gold and his wasted lands.

He hath counted his neighbors' cattle
    With the cold, gray eye of greed:
He hath marked for his own the fields of wheat
    Where he never had sown the seed:

The vine-clad cot by the hillside,
    Where the farmer's children play,—
"This shall fit in my plan," he said;
    "What use for such as they?"

And so, in the dusk of evening,
    He brought his armèd men,
And where had shone the clustering grapes
    There stretched a waste again.

Homeless, the children wandered
    Thro' the fields their father won:
No more shall they feel his clasp and kiss—
    Aye, never beneath the sun.

Vex, vex not the Empire Builder,
    Nor babble of Mercy's shield;
Hath he not his vaster issue—
    The linking of field to field?

189

Hath he not noted the boundary
  That lies 'twixt "mine and thine"?
Hath he not said, " 'Twere better for thee
  If thine henceforth be mine"?

And so doth the Empire Builder,
  From out of the ends of the earth,
Thro' travail of war and of carnage
  Bring strange, new realms to birth—

Realms builded on broken hearthstones,
  The triumph of Rapine's hour—
That one may boast in the halls of Fame
  And sit in the seats of Power!

This is the song of the Empire Builder,
  Who built not of wasted lands,
But who builded a kingdom of golden deeds
  And of things not made by hands!

The fields of the spirit were his to roam,
  The paths where the love-flowers grew:
He felt the breath of the spirits' spring
  In every wind that blew:

It came not laden with dying groans
  And homeless orphans' cries:
It blew from the mountains of the Lord
  And the fields of Paradise.

This is the boast of the Empire Builder
  Who built not of mouldering clay:
That the kingdom He built, not made by hands,
  Shall never pass away!

The mind cannot measure its boundaries,
  All Space is its outer gate:
It is broader than ever a man conceived
  And more durable than Fate.

This is the Empire our brother built,
  In His little hour of Earth,
Thro' the spirit's travail of righteous deeds
  And the spirit's glad rebirth.

He had silenced the boast of the Empire Builder,
  With his gold and wasted lands,
By his deathless kingdom of golden deeds
  And of things not made by hands.

This is the kingdom our brother built:
  It is good: it hath sufficed;—
For who can measure the glory he keeps
  With our Elder Brother, Christ?

The Men behind the Guns

A cheer and salute for the Admiral, and here's to the Captain
    bold,
And never forget the Commodore's debt when the deeds of
    might are told!
They stand to the deck through the battle's wreck when the
    great shells roar and screech—
And never they fear when the foe is near to practice what
    they preach:
But off with your hat and three times three for Columbia's
    true-blue sons,
The men below who batter the foe—the men behind the guns!

Oh, light and merry of heart are they when they swing into
    port once more,
When, with more than enough of the "green-backed stuff,"
    they start for their leave-o'-shore;
And you'd think, perhaps, that the blue-bloused chaps who
    loll along the street
Are a tender bit, with salt on it, for some fierce "mustache"
    to eat—
Some warrior bold, with straps of gold, who dazzles and fairly
    stuns
The modest worth of the sailor boys—the lads who serve the
    guns.

But say not a word till the shot is heard that tells the fight is
    on,
Till the long, deep roar grows more and more from the ships
    of "Yank" and "Don,"
Till over the deep the tempests sweep of fire and bursting
    shell,
And the very air is a mad Despair in the throes of a living
    hell;
Then down, deep down, in the mighty ship, unseen by the
    midday suns,
You'll find the chaps who are giving the raps—the men be-
    hind the guns!

Oh, well they know the cyclones blow that they loose from
    their cloud of death,

191

And they know is heard the thunder-word their fierce ten-
    incher saith!
The steel decks rock with the lightning shock, and shake with
    the great recoil,
And the sea grows red with the blood of the dead and reaches
    for his spoil—
But not till the foe has gone below or turns his prow and runs
Shall the voice of peace bring sweet release to the men behind
    the guns!

MATTHEW RUSSELL, S.J.

A Thought from Cardinal Newman

The world shines bright for inexperienced eyes,
And death seems distant to the gay and strong,
And in the youthful heart proud fancies throng,
And only present good can nature prize.
How then shall youth o'er these low vapours rise,
And climb the upward path so steep and long?
And how, amid earth's sights and sounds of wrong,
Walk with pure heart and face raised to the skies?

By gazing on the infinitely Good,
Whose love must quell, or hallow every other—
By living in the shadow of the Rood,
For He that hangs there is our Elder Brother,
Who dying gave to us Himself as food,
And His own Mother as our nursing Mother.

ABRAM J. RYAN

The Conquered Banner

Furl that Banner, for 'tis weary;
Round its staff 'tis drooping dreary:
    Furl it, fold it—it is best;
For there's not a man to wave it,
And there's not a sword to save it,
And there's not one left to lave it
In the blood which heroes gave it,
And its foes now scorn and brave it:
    Furl it, hide it—let it rest!

192

Take that Banner down! 'tis tattered;
Broken is its staff and shattered;
And the valiant hosts are scattered,
    Over whom it floated high.
Oh, 'tis hard for us to fold it,
Hard to think there's none to hold it,
    Now must furl it with a sigh!

Furl that Banner!—furl it sadly!
Once ten thousands hailed it gladly,
And ten thousands wildly, madly,
    Swore it should forever wave;
Swore that foeman's sword should never
Hearts like theirs entwined dissever
Till that flag should float forever
    O'er their freedom or their grave!

Furl it! for the hands that grasped it,
And the hearts that fondly clasped it,
    Cold and dead are lying low;
And that Banner—it is trailing
While around it sounds the wailing
    Of its people in their woe.

For, though conquered, they adore it—
Love the cold, dead hands that bore it,
Weep for those who fell before it,
Pardon those who trailed and tore it;
And oh, wildly they deplore it.
    Now to furl and fold it so!

Furl that Banner! True, 'tis gory,
Yet 'tis wreathed around with glory,
And 'twill live in song and story
    Though its folds are in the dust!
For its fame on brightest pages,
Penned by poets and by sages,
Shall go sounding down the ages—
    Furl its folds though now we must.

Furl that Banner, softly, slowly!
Treat it gently—it is holy,
    For it droops above the dead.
Touch it not—unfold it never;
Let it droop there, furled forever—
    For its people's hopes are fled!

A Child's Wish

I wish I were the little key
    That locks Love's Captive in,
And lets Him out to go and free
    A sinful heart from sin.

I wish I were the little bell
    That tinkles for the Host,
When God comes down each day to dwell
    With hearts He loves the most.

I wish I were the chalice fair,
    That holds the Blood of Love,
When every gleam lights holy prayer
    Upon its way above.

I wish I were the little flower
    So near the Host's sweet face,
Or like the light that half an hour
    Burns on the shrine of grace.

I wish I were the altar where,
    As on His mother's breast,
Christ nestles, like a child, fore'er
    In Eucharistic rest.

But, oh, my God, I wish the most
    That my poor heart may be
A home all holy for each Host
    That comes in love to me.

The Sword of Robert Lee

Forth from its scabbard, pure and bright
    Flashed the sword of Lee!
Far in the front of the deadly fight,
High o'er the brave in the cause of Right,
Its stainless sheen, like a beacon bright,
    Led us to Victory.

Out of its scabbard, where, full long,
    It slumbered peacefully,
Roused from its rest by the battle's song,
Shielding the feeble, smiting the strong,
Guarding the right, avenging the wrong,
    Gleamed the sword of Lee.

194

Forth from its scabbard, high in air
  Beneath Virginia's sky—
And they who saw it gleaming there,
And knew who bore it, knelt to swear
That where that sword led they would dare
  To follow—and to die.

Out of its scabbard! Never hand
  Waved sword from stain as free,
Nor purer sword led braver band,
Nor braver bled for a brighter land,
Nor brighter land had a cause so grand,
  Nor cause a chief like Lee!

Forth from its scabbard! How we prayed
  That sword might victor be;
And when our triumph was delayed,
And many a heart grew sore afraid,
We still hoped on while gleamed the blade
  Of noble Robert Lee.

Forth from its scabbard all in vain
  Bright flashed the sword of Lee;
'Tis shrouded now in its sheath again,
It sleeps the sleep of our noble slain,
Defeated, yet without a stain,
  Proudly and peacefully.

Song of the Mystic

I walk down the Valley of Silence—
  Down the dim voiceless Valley—alone!
And I hear not the fall of a footstep
  Around me, save God's and my own;
And the hush of my heart is as holy
  As hovers where angels have flown!

Long ago was I weary of voices
  Whose magic my heart could not win;
Long ago was I weary of noises
  That fretted my soul with their din;
Long ago was I weary of places
  Where I met but the human—and sin.

I walked through the world with the worldly;
  I craved what the world never gave;

195

And I said: "In the world, each Ideal
    That shines like a star on life's wave,
Is wrecked on the shores of the Real,
    And sleeps like a dream in a grave."

And still did I pine for the Perfect,
    And still found the false with the true;
I sought 'mid the human for heaven,
    And caught a mere glimpse of its blue;
And I wept when the clouds of the mortal
    Veiled even that glimpse from my view.

And I toiled on, heart-tired of the Human;
    And I moaned 'mid the mazes of men;
Till I knelt, long ago, at an altar
    And heard a voice call me. Since then
I walk down the Valley of Silence
    That lies far beyond human ken.

Do you ask what I found in the Valley?
    'Tis my trysting-place with the Divine;
And I fell at the feet of the Holy,
    And above me a voice said: "Be mine!"
And there rose from the depths of my spirit
    An echo—"My heart shall be thine."

Do you ask how I live in the Valley?
    I weep—and I dream—and I pray.
But my tears are as sweet as the dewdrops
    That fall on the roses in May;
And my prayers, like a perfume from censers,
    Ascendeth to God, night and day.

In the hush of the Valley of Silence,
    I dream all the songs that I sing;
And the music floats down the dim Valley,
    Till each finds a word for a wing,
That to men, like the Dove of the Deluge,
    A message of Peace they may bring.

But far on the deep there are billows
    That never shall break on the beach;
And I have heard songs in the Silence
    That never shall float into speech;
And I have had dreams in the Valley
    Too lofty for language to reach.

196

And I have seen Thoughts in the Valley—
　Ah, me! how my spirit was stirred!
And they wear holy veils on their faces,
　Their footsteps can scarcely be heard;
They pass through the Valley, like virgins
　Too pure for the touch of a word!

Do you ask me the place of the Valley,
　Ye hearts that are harrowed by Care?
It lieth afar, between mountains,
　And God and His angels are there;
And one is the dark mount of Sorrow,
　And one the bright mountain of Prayer.

ELIZABETH SETON

Mary, Virgin and Mother

Oh, Virgin Joy of all the world art thou,
In whose white, fragrant steps the countless throng
On souls elect doth follow God with song:
Creation's Queen, whose bright and holy brow
The multitude of saints, like stars, endow
With changeful splendors, flashing far and strong:
The Maid unshadow'd by the primal wrong:
God's Lily, chosen in His shrine to bow.

All these thy glories are, and still a grace
More high, more dread, and yet more sweet and fair,
Doth bind thy royal brows, O Mary blest.
God called thee Mother; yea, His sacred face
The tender likeness of thine own doth wear.
And thou art ours—we trust Him for the rest.

DORA SIGERSON

The Wind on the Hills

Go not to the hills of Erin
　When the night winds are about;
Put up your bar and shutter,
　And so keep the danger out.

197

For the good-folk whirl within it,
  And they pull by the hand,
And they push you by the shoulder,
  Till you move to their command.

And lo! you have forgotten
  What you have known of tears,
And you will not remember
  That the world goes full of years;

A year there is a lifetime,
  And a second but a day;
And an older world will greet you
  Each morn you come away.

Your wife grows old with weeping,
  And your children one by one
Grow grey with nights of watching,
  Before your dance is done.

And it will chance some morning
  You will come home no more;
Your wife sees but a withered leaf
  In the wind about the door.

And your children will inherit
  The unrest of the wind;
They shall seek some face elusive,
  And some land they never find.

When the wind is loud, they sighing
  Go with hearts unsatisfied,
For some joy beyond remembrance,
  For some memory denied.

And all your children's children,
  They cannot sleep or rest,
When the wind is out in Erin
  And the sun is in the West.

JOHN LANCASTER SPALDING

Believe and Take Heart

What can console for a dead world?
We tread on dust which once was life;
To nothingness all things are hurled:
What meaning in a hopeless strife?
        Time's awful storm
        Breaks but the form.

Whatever comes, whatever goes,
Still throbs the heart whereby we live;
The primal joys still lighten woes,
And time which steals doth also give.
        Fear not, be brave:
        God can thee save.

The essential truth of life remains,
Its goodness and its beauty too,
Pure love's unutterable gains,
And hope which thrills us through and through:
        God has not fled,
        Souls are not dead.

Not in most ancient Palestine,
Nor in the lightsome air of Greece,
Were human struggles more divine,
More blessed with guerdon of increase:
        Take thou thy stand
        In the workers' band.

Hast then no faith? Thine is the fault:—
What prophets, heroes, sages, saints,
Have loved, on thee still makes assault,
Thee with immortal things acquaints.
        On life then seize:
        Doubt is disease.

199

CHARLES WARREN STODDARD

The Bells of San Gabriel

[The Mission of San Gabriel the Archangel, near Los Angeles, founded in 1771, was, for a time, the most flourishing mission in California]

Thine was the corn and the wine,
　The blood of the grape that nourished;
The blossom and fruit of the vine
　That was heralded far away.
　When the wine and fig-tree flourished,
The promise of peace and of glad increase
　Forever and ever and aye.
What then wert thou, and what art now?
　Answer me, O, I pray!

　　　　And every note of every bell
　　　　Sang Gabriel! rang Gabriel!
　　　In the tower that is left the tale to tell
　　　　Of Gabriel, the Archangel.

Oil of the olive was thine;
　Flood of the wine-press flowing,
Blood of the Christ was the wine—
　Blood of the Lamb that was slain.
Thy gifts were fat of the kine
　Forever coming and going
Far over the hills, the thousand hills—
　Their lowing a soft refrain.
What then wert thou, and what are now?
　Answer me once again!

　　　　And every note of every bell
　　　　Sang Gabriel! rang Gabriel!
　　　In the tower that is left the tale to tell
　　　　Of Gabriel, the Archangel.

Seed of the corn was thine—
　Body of Him thus broken
And mingled with blood of the vine—
　The bread and the wine of life.
Out of the good sunshine.
　They were given to thee as a token—
The body of Him, and the blood of Him,
　When the gifts of God were rife.
What then wert thou, and what art now?
　After the weary strife?

200

And every note of every bell
  Sang Gabriel! rang Gabriel!
In the tower that is left the tale to tell
  Of Gabriel, the Archangel.

Where are they now, O bells?
  Where are the fruits of the Mission?
Garnered, where no one dwells,
  Shepherd and flock are fled.
O'er the Lord's vineyard swells
  The tide that with fell perdition
Sounded their doom and fashioned their tomb
  And buried them with the dead.
What then wert thou, and what art now?
  The answer is still unsaid.

    And every note of every bell
      Sang Gabriel! rang Gabriel!
    In the tower that is left the tale to tell
      Of Gabriel, the Archangel.

Where are they now, O tower!
  The locusts and wild honey?
Where is the sacred dower
  That the bride of Christ was given?
Gone to the wielders of power,
  The misers and minters of money;
Gone for the greed that is their creed—
  And these in the land have thriven.
What then wert thou, and what art now,
  And wherefore hast thou striven?

    And every note of every bell
      Sang Gabriel! rang Gabriel!
    In the tower that is left the tale to tell
      Of Gabriel, the Archangel.

Stigmata

In the wrath of the lips that assail us,
  In the scorn of the lips that are dumb,
The symbols of sorrow avail us,
  The joy of the people is come.
They parted Thy garments for barter,
  They follow Thy steps with complaint;
Let them know that the pyre of the martyr
  But purges the blood of the saint!

201

They have crucified Thee for a token,
    For a token Thy flesh crucified
Shall bleed in a heart that is broken
    For love of the wound in Thy side;
In pity for palms that were pleading,
    For feet that were grievously used,
There is blood on the brow that is bleeding
    And torn, as Thy brow that was bruised!

By Thee have we life, breath, and being;
    Thou hast knowledge of us and our kind;
Thou hast pleasure of eyes that are seeing,
    And sorrow of eyes that are blind;
By the seal of the mystery shown us—
    The wound that with Thy wounds accord—
O Lord, have mercy upon us!
    Have mercy upon us, O Lord!

Ave Maria Bells

At dawn, the joyful choir of bells,
    In consecrated citadels,
Flings on the sweet and drowsy air
A brief, melodious call to prayer;
    For Mary, Virgin meek and lowly,
    Conceived of the Spirit Holy,
As the Lord's angel did declare.

At noon, above the fretful street,
    Our souls are lifted to repeat
The prayer, with low and wistful voice:
"According to thy word and choice,
    Though sorrowful and heavy laden,
    So be it done to thy Handmaiden";
Then all the sacred bells rejoice.

At eve with roses in the west,
    The daylight's withering bequest,
Ring, prayerful bells, while blossom bright
The stars, the lilies of the night:
    Of all the songs the years have sung us,
    "The Word made Flesh had dwelt among us,"
Is still our ever-new delight.

SPEER STRAHAN, C.S.C.

The Poor

The poor I saw at the cloister gate
  Mutely beg with their patient eyes
An alms, for the love of Him who sate
  And supped with the poor in human guise.

And there were monks saw the nails' deep scars
  In the shrunken hands that reached for bread,
Who heard a Voice from beyond the stars
  In the broken thanks of them they fed.

I, too, at the gates of God each day
  Seek for an alms of strength and grace,
Beggar am I that wait and pray
  To feast my soul on His beauteous face.

The Promised Country

Fair must that promised country be
Whose streams rise from eternity
And One doth lead upon that way
Whose footfalls are the paths of day.

Nor lurking fear pursues them there,
As forward in the morning air
With Him the blessed ransomed go,
Their garments washen white as snow.

Alas! my days are very dim
That look up to the Seraphim.
Ah, Lord, some dawning may I be
One of that shining company!

Holy Communion

Disguised He stands without in the street;
Far come is He on heavy feet.
O heart of mine, open thy gate;
For darkness falls, and it is late!

Lord of the heaven's fairest height,
Homeless in the traveler's night,

Begging my hearth, my board, my cup,
That I, not He, may richly sup.

O soul of mine, the board begin,
And let this wondrous Beggar in!

CAROLINE D. SWAN

Stars of Cheer

The silent Christmas stars shine cool and clear
Above a world of mingled joy and woe;
On peaceful cottage homes, with thanks aglow
For royal bounty of the grape-crowned year;
And on red fields of blood, where many a tear
Is wiped away by Death, a gentle foe,
More merciful than they who bade it flow.
Shine, silver stars, rain down your blessed cheer!

Comfort the mourner with your Angel song!
The Christ-Child reigns. Behold His tiny hand
Upraised in benediction warm and sweet!
O'er every joy and every bitter wrong
The Babe of Bethlehem hath supreme command;
Come, worship, kings and peoples, at His feet!

JOHN BANNISTER TABB

Christ and the Pagan

I had no God but these,
The sacerdotal Trees,
And they uplifted me.
"I hung upon a tree."

The sun and moon I saw,
And reverential awe
Subdued me day and night.
"I am the perfect light."

Within a lifeless Stone—
All other Gods unknown—
I sought Divinity.
"The Corner-Stone am I."

204

For sacrificial feast
I slaughtered man and beast,
Red recompense to gain.
"So I, a Lamb, was slain.

"Yea; such My hungering Grace
That where ev'r My face
Is hidden, none may grope
Beyond eternal Hope."

Out of Bounds

A little Boy of heavenly birth,
   But far from home today,
Comes down to find His ball, the Earth,
   That Sin has cast away.
O comrades, let us one and all
Join in to get Him back His ball!

Father Damien

O God, the cleanest offering
Of tainted earth below,
Unblushing to Thy feet we bring—
"A leper white as snow!"

Recognition

When Christ went up to Calvary,
   His crown upon His head,
Each tree unto its fellow tree
   In awful silence said:
"Behold the Gardener is He
Of Eden and Gethsemane!"

"Is Thy Servant a Dog?"

So *must* he be, who in the crowded street,
Where shameless Sin and flaunting Pleasure meet,
Amid the noisome footprints finds the sweet
Faint vestige of Thy feet.

FRANCIS THOMPSON

Lilium Regis

O Lily of the King, low lies thy silver wing,
  And long has been the hour of thine unqueening;
And thy scent of Paradise on the night-wind spills its sighs,
  Nor any take the secrets of its meaning.
O Lily of the King, I speak a heavy thing,
  O patience, most sorrowful of daughters!
Lo, the hour is at hand for the troubling of the land,
  And red shall be the breaking of the waters.

Sit fast upon thy stalk, when the blast shall with thee talk,
  With the mercies of the King for thine awning,
And the just understand that thine hour is at hand,
  Thine hour at hand with power in the dawning.
When the nations lie in blood, and their kings a broken brood,
  Look up, O most sorrowful of daughters!
Lift up thy head and hark what sounds are in the dark,
  For His feet are coming to thee on the waters!

O Lily of the King, I shall not see, that sing,
  I shall not see the hour of thy queening!
But my Song shall see, and wake like a flower that dawn-winds
    shake,
  And sigh with joy the odours of its meaning.
O Lily of the King, remember then the thing
  That this dead mouth sang; and thy daughters,
As they dance before His way; sing there on the Day
  What I sang when night was on the waters!

To the English Martyrs

Rain, rain on Tyburn tree,
Red rain a-falling;
Dew, dew on Tyburn tree,
Red dew on Tyburn tree,
And the swart bird a-calling.
The shadow lies on England now
Of the deathly-fruited bough:
Cold and black with malison
Lies between the land and sun;
Putting out the sun, the bough
Shades England now!

The troubled heavens do wan with care,
And burthened with the earth's despair

Shiver a-cold; the starvèd heaven
Has want, with wanting man bereaven.
Blest fruit of the unblest bough,
Aid the land that smote you, now!
That feels the sentence and the curse
Ye died if so ye might reverse.
When God was stolen from out man's mouth,
Stolen was the bread; then hunger and drouth
Went to and fro; began the wail,
Struck root the poor-house and the jail.
Ere cut the dykes, let through that flood,
Ye writ the protest with your blood;
Against this night—wherein our breath
Withers, and the toiled heart perisheth—
Entered the *caveat* of your death.
Christ in the form of His true Bride,
Again hung pierced and crucified,
And groaned, "I thirst!" Not still ye stood—
Ye had your hearts, ye had your blood;
And pouring out the eager cup—
"The wine is weak, yet, Lord Christ, sup!"
Ah, blest! who bathed the parchèd Vine
With richer than His Cana-wine,
And heard, your most sharp supper past:
"Ye kept the best wine to the last!"

Ah, happy who
That sequestered secret knew,
How sweeter than bee-haunted dells,
The blosmy blood of martyrs smells!
Who did upon the scaffold's bed,
The ceremonial steel between you, wed
With God's grave proxy, high and reverend Death;
Or felt about your neck, sweetly,
(While the dull horde
Saw but the unrelenting cord)
The Bridegroom's arm, and that long kiss
That kissed away your breath, and claimed you His.
You did, with thrift of holy gain,
Unvenoming the sting of pain,
Hive its sharp heather-honey. Ye
Had sentience of the mystery
To make Abaddon's hookèd wings
Buoy you up to starry things;
Pain of heart, and pain of sense,
Pain the scourge, ye taught to cleanse;
Pain the loss became possessing;
Pain the curse was pain the blessing.

Chains, rack, hunger, solitude—these,
Which did your soul from earth release,
Left it free to rush upon
And merge in its compulsive Sun.
Desolated, bruised, forsaken,
Nothing taking, all things taken,
Lacerated and tormented,
The stifled soul, in naught contented,
On all hands straitened, cribbed, denied,
Can but fetch breath o' the Godward side.
Oh, to me, give but to me
That flower of felicity,
Which on your topmost spirit ware
The difficult and snowy air
Of high refusal! and the heat
Of central love which fed with sweet
And holy fire i' the frozen sod
Roots that ta'en hold on God.

Unwithering youth in you renewed
Those rosy waters of your blood—
The true *Fons Juventutis;* ye
Pass with conquest that Red Sea,
And stretch out your victorious hand
Over the Fair and Holy Land.
O, by the Church's pondering art
Late set and named upon the chart
Of her divine astronomy,
Through your influence from on high
Long ye shed unnoted! Bright
New cluster in our Northern night,
Cleanse from its pain and undelight
An impotent and tarnished hymn,
Whose marish exhalations dim
Splendours they would transfuse! And thou
Kindle the words which blot thee now,
Over whose sacred corse unhearsed
Europe veiled her face, and cursed
The regal mantle grained in gore
Of genius, freedom, faith, and More!

Ah, happy Fool of Christ, unawed
By familiar sanctities,
You served your Lord at holy ease!
Dear Jester in the Courts of God—
In whose spirit, enchanting yet,
Wisdom and love together met,

Laughed on each other for content!
That an inward merriment,
An inviolate soul of pleasure,
To your motions taught a measure
All your days; which tyrant king,
Nor bonds, nor any bitter thing,
Could embitter or perturb;
No daughter's tears, nor, more acerb,
A daughter's frail declension from
Thy serene example, come
Between thee and thy much content.
Nor could the last sharp argument
Turn thee from thy sweetest folly;
To the keen *accolade* and holy
Thou didst bend low a sprightly knee,
And jest Death out of gravity
As a too sad-visaged friend;
So, jocund, passing to the end
Of thy laughing martyrdom;
And now from travel art gone home
Where, since gain of thee was given,
Surely there is more mirth in heaven!

Thus, in Fisher and in thee,
Arose the purple dynasty,
The anointed Kings of Tyburn tree;
High in act and word each one:
He that spake—and to the sun
Pointed—"I shall shortly be
Above yon fellow." He too, he
No less high of speech and brave,
Whose word was: "Though I shall have
Sharp dinner, yet I trust in Christ
To have a most sweet supper." Priced
Much by men that utterance was
Of the doomed Leonidas—
Not more exalt than these, which note
Men who thought as Shakespeare wrote.

But more lofty eloquence
Than is writ by poet's pens
Lives in your great deaths: O these
Have more fire than poesies!
And more ardent than all ode,
The pomps and raptures of your blood!
By that blood ye hold in fee
This earth of England; Kings are ye:

And ye have armies—Want, and Cold,
And heavy Judgments manifold
Hung in the unhappy air, and Sins
That the sick gorge to heave begins,
Agonies and Martyrdoms,
Love, Hope, Desire, and all that comes
From the unwatered soul of man
Gaping on God. These are the van
Of conquest, these obey you; these,
And all the strengths of weaknesses,
That brazen walls disbed. Your hand,
Princes, put forth to the command,
And levy upon the guilty land
Your saving wars; on it go down,
Black beneath God's and heaven's frown;
Your prevalent approaches make
With unsustainable grace, and take
Captive the land that captived you;
To Christ enslave ye and subdue
Her so bragged freedom: for the crime
She wrought on you in antique time,
Parcel the land among you; reign,
Viceroys to your sweet Suzerain!
Till she shall know
This lesson in her overthrow:
Hardest servitude has he
That's jailed in arrogant liberty;
And freedom, spacious and unflawed,
Who is walled about with God.

The Hound of Heaven

I fled Him, down the nights and down the days;
   I fled Him, down the arches of the years;
I fled Him, down the labyrinthine ways
   Of my own mind; and in the midst of tears
I hid from Him, and under running laughter.
         Up vistaed hopes I sped;
         And shot, precipitated,
   Adown Titanic glooms of chasmèd fears,
From those strong Feet that followed, followed after.
        But with unhurrying chase,
        And unperturbèd pace,
    Deliberate speed, majestic instancy,
        They beat—and a Voice beat
        More instant than the Feet—
  "All things betray thee, who betrayest Me."

I pleaded, outlaw-wise,
By many a hearted casement, curtained red,
  Trellised with intertwining charities;
(For, though I knew His love who followèd,
    Yet was I sore adread
Lest, having Him, I must have naught beside).
But, if one little casement parted wide,
    The gust of His approach would clash it to:
    Fear wist not to evade, as Love wist to pursue.
Across the margent of the world I fled,
    And troubled the gold gateway of the stars,
    Smiting for shelter on their clangèd bars;
      Fretted to dulcet jars
And silvern chatter the pale ports o' the moon.
I said to Dawn, Be sudden; to Eve, Be soon;
    With thy young skiey blossoms heap me over
    From his tremendous Lover—
Float thy vague veil about me, lest He see!
    I tempted all His servitors, but to find
My own betrayal in their constancy,
In faith to Him their fickleness to me,
    Their traitorous trueness, and their loyal deceit.
To all swift things for swiftness did I sue;
    Clung to the whistling mane of every wind.
    But whether they swept, smoothly fleet,
The long savannahs of the blue;
    Or whether, Thunder-driven,
    They clanged his chariot 'thwart a heaven
Plashy with flying lightnings round the spurn o' their feet:—
    Fear wist not to evade as Love wist to pursue.
      Still with unhurrying chase,
      And unperturbèd pace,
    Deliberate speed, majestic instancy,
      Came on the following Feet,
      And a Voice above their beat—
    "Naught shelters thee, who wilt not shelter Me."

I sought no more that after which I strayed
      In face of man or maid;
But still within the little children's eyes
      Seems something, something that replies:
They at least are for me, surely for me!
I turned me to them very wistfully;
But just as their young eyes grew sudden fair
      With dawning answers there,
Their angel plucked them from me by the hair.
"Come then, ye other children, Nature's—share
With me" (said I) "your delicate fellowship;

Let me greet you lip to lip,
Let me twine with you caresses,
　　Wantoning
With our Lady-Mother's vagrant tresses,
　　Banqueting
With her in her wind-walled palace,
Underneath her azured dais,
Quaffing, as your taintless way is,
　　From a chalice
Lucent-weeping out of the dayspring."
　　　So it was done:
I in their delicate fellowship was one—
Drew the bolt of Nature's secrecies.
　　I knew all the swift importings
　　On the wilful face of skies;
　　I knew how the clouds arise
　　Spumèd of the wild sea-snortings;
　　　All that's born or dies
　　Rose and drooped with—made them shapers
Of mine own moods, or wailful or divine:
　　With them joyed and was bereaven.
　　I was heavy with the even,
　　When she lit her glimmering tapers
　　Round the day's dead sanctities.
　　I laughed in the morning's eyes.
I triumphed and I saddened with all weather,
　　　Heaven and I wept together,
And its sweet tears were salt with mortal mine;
Against the red throb of its sunset-heart
　　I laid my own to beat,
　　And share commingling heat;
But not by that, by that, was eased my human smart.
In vain my tears were wet on Heaven's grey cheek.
For ah! we know not what each other says,
　　These things and I; in sound *I* speak—
Their sound is but their stir, they speak by silences.
Nature, poor stepdame, cannot slake my drought;
　　Let her, if she would owe me,
Drop yon blue bosom-veil of sky, and show me
　　The breasts o' her tenderness:
Never did any milk of hers once bless
　　My thirsting mouth.
　　Nigh and nigh draws the chase,
　　With unperturbèd pace,
Deliberate speed, majestic instancy;
　　And past those noisèd fleet—
　　A Voice comes yet more fleet—
"Lo! naught contents thee who content'st not Me."

Naked I wait Thy love's uplifted stroke!
My harness piece by piece Thou hast hewn from me,
   And smitten me to my knee;
   I am defenceless utterly.
   I slept, methinks, and woke,
And, slowly gazing, find me stripped in sleep.
In the rash lustihead of my young powers,
      I shook the pillaring hours
And pulled my life upon me; grimed with smears,
I stand amid the dust o' the mounded years—
My mangled youth lies dead beneath the heap.
My days have crackled and gone up in smoke,
Have puffed and burst as sun-starts on a stream.
      Yea, faileth now even dream
The dreamer, and the lute the lutanist;
Even the linked fantasies, in whose blossomy twist
I swung the earth a trinket at my wrist,
Are yielding; cords of all too weak account
For earth with heavy griefs so overplussed.
         Ah! is Thy love indeed
A weed, albeit an amaranthine weed,
Suffering no flowers except its own to mount?
         Ah! must—
         Designer infinite!—
Ah! must Thou char the wood ere Thou canst limn with it?
My freshness spent its wavering shower i' the dust;
And now my heart is as a broken fount,
Wherein tear-drippings stagnate, spilt down ever
         From the dank thoughts that shiver
Upon the sighful branches of my mind.
         Such is; what is to be?
The pulp so bitter, how shall taste the rind?
I dimly guess what Time in mists confounds;
Yet ever and anon a trumpet sounds
From the hid battlements of Eternity;
Those shaken mists a space unsettle, then
Round the half-glimpsèd turrets slowly wash again
      But not ere him who summoneth
      I first have seen, enwound
With glooming robes purpureal, cypress-crowned;
His name I know, and what his trumpet saith.
Whether man's heart or life it be which yields
      Thee harvest, must Thy harvest fields
      Be dunged with rotten death?

         Now of that long pursuit
         Comes on at hand the bruit;
      That Voice is round me like a bursting sea:

"And is thy earth so marred,
Shattered in shard on shard?
Lo! all things fly thee, for thou fliest Me!
Strange, piteous, futile thing!
Wherefore should any set thee love apart?
Seeing none but I makes much of naught" (He said)
"And human love needs human meriting:
How hast thou merited—
Of all man's clotted clay the dingiest clot?
Alack, thou knowest not
How little worthy of any love thou art!
Whom wilt thou find to love ignoble thee
Save Me, save only Me?
All which I took from thee I did but take,
Not for thy harms,
But just that thou might'st seek it in My arms.
All which thy child's mistake
Fancies as lost, I have stored for thee at home:
Rise, clasp My hand, and come!"
Halts by me that footfall:
Is my gloom, after all,
Shade of His hand, outstretched caressingly?
"Ah, fondest, blindest, weakest,
I am He Whom thou seekest!
Thou dravest love from thee, who dravest Me."

The Dread of Height

["If ye were blind, ye should have no sin: but now ye say: We see:
    your sin remaineth."—John 9:41]

Not the Circean wine
Most perilous is for pain:
Grapes of the heaven's star-loaden vine,
Whereto the lofty-placed
Thoughts of fair souls attain,
Tempt with a more retributive delight,
And do disrelish all life's sober taste.
'Tis to have drunk too well
The drink that is divine,
Maketh the kind earth waste,
And breath intolerable.

Ah, me!
How shall my mouth content it with mortality?
Lo, secret music, sweetest music,

214

From distances of distance drifting its lone flight,
Down the arcane where Night would perish in night,
Like a god's loosened locks slips undulously:
Music that is to grievous of the height
For safe and low delight,
Too infinite
For bounded hearts which yet would girth the sea!
So let it be,
Though sweet be great, and though my heart be small:
So let it be,
O music, music, though you wake in me
No joy, no joy at all;
Although you only wake
Uttermost sadness, measure of delight,
Which else I could not credit to the height,
Did I not know,
That ill is statured to its opposite;
Did I not know,
And even of sadness so,
Of utter sadness, make
Of extreme sad a rod to mete
The incredible excess of unsensed sweet,
And mystic wall of strange felicity.
So let it be,
Though sweet be great, and though my heart be small,
And bitter meat
The food of gods for men to eat;
Yea, John ate daintier, and did tread
Less ways of heat,
Than whom to their wind-carpeted
High banquet-hall,
And golden love-feasts, the fair stars entreat.

But ah! withal,
Some hold, some stay,
O difficult Joy, I pray,
Some arms of thine,
Not only, only arms of mine!
Lest like a weary girl I fall
From clasping love so high,
And lacking thus thine arms, then may
Most hapless I
Turn utterly to love of basest rate;
For low they fall whose fall is from the sky.
Yea, who me shall secure
But I, of height grown desperate,
Surcease my wing, and my lost fate
Be dashed from pure

215

To broken writhings in the shameful slime:
Lower than man, for I dreamed higher,
Thrust down, by how much I aspire,
And damned with drink of immortality?
For such things be,
Yea, and the lowest reach of reeky Hell
Is but made possible
By foreta'en breath of Heaven's austerest clime.

These tidings from the vast to bring
Needeth not doctor nor divine,
Too well, too well
My flesh doth know the heart-perturbing thing;
That dread theology alone
Is mine,
Most native and my own;
And ever with victorious toil
When I have made
Of the deific peaks dim escalade,
My soul with anguish and recoil
Doth like a city in an earthquake rock,
As at my feet the abyss is cloven then,
With deeper menace than for other men,
Of my potential cousinship with mire;
That all my conquered skies do grow a hollow mock,
My fearful powers retire,
No longer strong,
Reversing the shook banners of their song.

Ah, for a heart less native to high Heaven,
A hooded eye, for jesses and restraint,
Or for a will accipitrine to pursue!—
The veil of tutelar flesh to simple livers given,
Or those brave-fledging fervours of the Saint,
Whose heavenly falcon-craft doth never taint,
Nor they in sickest time their ample virtue mew.

To My Godchild: Francis M. W. Meynell

This labouring, vast, Tellurian galleon,
Riding at anchor off the orient sun,
Had broken its cable, and stood out to space
Down some frore Arctic of the aerial ways:
And now, back warping from the inclement main,
Its vapourous shroudage drenched with icy rain,
It swung into its azure roads again;
When, floated on the prosperous sun-gale, you
Lit, a white halcyon auspice, 'mid our frozen crew.

216

To the Sun, stranger, surely you belong,
Giver of golden days and golden song;
Nor is it by an all-unhappy plan
You bear the name of me, his constant Magian.
Yet, ah! from any other that it came,
Lest fated to my fate you be, as to my name.
When at the first those tidings did they bring,
My heart turned troubled at the ominous thing:
Though well may such a title him endower,
For when a poet's prayer implores a poet's power.
The Assisian, who kept plighted faith to three,
To Song, to Sanctitude, and Poverty,
(In two alone of whom most singers prove
A fatal faithfulness of during love!);
He the sweet Sales, of whom we scarcely ken
How God he could love more, he so loved men;
The crown and crowned of Laura and Italy;
And Fletcher's fellow—from these, and not from me,
Take you your name, and take your legacy!

Or, if a right successive you declare
When worms, for ivies, intertwine my hair,
Take but this Poesy that now followeth
My clayey hest with sullen servile breath,
Made then your happy freedman by testating death.
My song I do but hold for you in trust,
I ask you but to blossom from my dust.
When you have compassed all weak I began,
Diviner poet, and ah! diviner man—
The man at feud with the perduring child
In you before Song's altar nobly reconciled—
From the wise heavens I half shall smile to see
How little a world, which owned you, needed me.
If, while you keep the vigils of the night,
For your wild tears make darkness all too bright,
Some lone orb through your lonely window peeps,
As it played lover over your sweet sleeps;
Think it a golden crevice in the sky,
Which I have pierced but to behold you by!

And when, immortal mortal, droops your head,
And you, the child of deathless song, are dead;
Then, as you search with unaccustomed glance
The ranks of Paradise for my countenance,
Turn not your tread along the Uranian sod
Among the bearded counsellors of God;
For, if in Eden as on earth are we,
I sure shall keep a younger company:

217

Pass where beneath their rangèd gonfalons
The starry cohorts shake their shielded suns,
The dreadful mass of their enridgèd spears:
Pass where majestical the eternal peers,
The stately choice of the great Saintdom, meet—
A silvern segregation, globed complete
In sandalled shadow of the Triune feet;
Pass by where wait, young poet-wayfarer,
Your cousined clusters, emulous to share
With you the roseal lightnings burning 'mid their hair;
Pass the crystalline sea, the Lampads seven:—
Look for me in the nurseries of Heaven.

KATHARINE TYNAN

Michael the Archangel

Not woman-faced and sweet, as look
The angels in the picture-book;
But terrible in majesty,
More than an army passing by.

His hair floats not upon the wind
Like theirs, but curled and closely twined:
Wrought with his aureole, so that none
Shall know the gold curls from the crown.

His wings he hath put away in steel,
He goes mail-clad from head to heel;
Never moon-silver hath outshone
His breastplate and his morion.

His brows are like a battlement,
Beautiful, brave and innocent;
His eyes with fires of battle burn—
On his strong mouth the smile is stern.

His horse, the horse of Heaven, goes forth,
Bearing him off to South and North,
Neighing far off, as one that sees
The battle over distances.

His fiery sword is never at rest,
His foot is in the stirrup prest;
Through all the world where wrong is done
Michael the Soldier rideth on.

Michael, Commander! Angels are
That sound the trumpet and that bear
The banners by the Throne, where is
The King one nameth on his knees.

Angels there are of peace and prayers,
And they that go with wayfarers,
And they that watch the house of birth,
And they that bring the dead from earth,

And mine own Angel. Yet I see,
Heading God's army gloriously,
Michael Archangel, like a sun,
Splendid beyond comparison!

Planting Bulbs

Setting my bulbs a-row
  In cold earth under the grasses,
Till the frost and the snow
  Are gone and the Winter passes—

Sudden a footfall light,
  Sudden a bird-call ringing;
And these in gold and in white
  Shall rise with a sound of winging.

Airy and delicate all,
  All go trooping and dancing
At Spring's call and footfall,
  Airily dancing, advancing.

In the dark of the year,
  Turning the earth so chilly,
I look to the day of cheer,
  Primrose and daffodilly.

Turning the sods and the clay
  I think on the poor sad people
Hiding their dead away
  In the churchyard, under the steeple.

All poor women and men,
   Broken-hearted and weeping,
Their dead they call on in vain,
   Quietly smiling and sleeping.

Friends, now listen and hear,
   Give over crying and grieving,
There shall come a day and a year
   When the dead shall be as the living.

There shall come a call, a footfall,
   And the golden trumpeters blowing
Shall stir the dead with their call,
   Bid them be rising and going.

Then in the daffodil weather
   Lover shall run to lover;
Friends all trooping together;
   Death and Winter be over.

Laying my bulbs in the dark,
   Visions have I of hereafter.
Lip to lip, breast to breast, hark!
   No more weeping, but laughter!

Sheep and Lambs

All in the April evening,
   April airs were abroad;
The sheep with their little lambs
   Passed me by on the road.

The sheep with their little lambs
   Passed me by on the road;
All in the April evening
   I thought on the Lamb of God.

The lambs were weary, and crying
   With a weak, human cry.
I thought on the Lamb of God
   Going meekly to die.

Up in the blue, blue mountains
   Dewy pastures are sweet;
Rest for the little bodies,
   Rest for the little feet.

But for the Lamb of God
  Up on a hilltop green
Only a cross of shame
  Two stark crosses between.

All in the April evening,
  April airs were abroad;
I saw the sheep with their lambs,
  And thought on the Lamb of God.

The Making of Birds

God made Him birds in a pleasant humour;
  Tired of planets and suns was He.
He said: "I will add a glory to summer,
  Gifts for my creatures banished from Me!"

He had a thought and it set Him smiling
  Of the shape of a bird and its glancing head,
Its dainty air and its grace beguiling:
  "I will make feathers," the Lord God said.

He made the robin; He made the swallow;
  His deft hands moulding the shape to His mood,
The thrush and the lark and the finch to follow,
  And laughed to see that His work was good.

He who has given men gift of laughter,
  Made in His image; He fashioned fit
The blink of the owl and the stork thereafter,
  The little wren and the long-tailed tit.

He spent in the making His wit and fancies;
  The wing-feathers He fashioned them strong;
Deft and dear as daisies and pansies,
  He crowned His work with the gift of song.

"Dearlings," He said, "make songs for my praises!"
  He tossed them loose to the sun and the wind,
Airily sweet as pansies and daisies;
  He taught them to build a nest to their mind.

The dear Lord God of His glories weary—
  Christ our Lord had the heart of a boy—
Made Him birds in a moment merry,
  Bade them soar and sing for His joy.

221

The Man of the House

Joseph, honoured from sea to sea,
This is your name that pleases me,
    "Man of the House."

I see you rise at the dawn and light
The fire and blow till the flame is bright.

I see you take the pitcher and carry
The deep well-water for Jesus and Mary.

You knead the corn for the bread so fine,
Gather them grapes from the hanging vine.

There are little feet that are soft and slow,
Follow you whithersoever you go.

There's a little face at your workshop door,
A little one sits down on your floor:

Holds His hands for the shavings curled,
The soft little hands that have made the world.

Mary calls you: the meal is ready:
You swing the Child to your shoulder steady.

I see your quiet smile as you sit
And watch the little Son thrive and eat.

The vine curls by the window space,
The wings of angels cover the face.

Up in the rafters, polished and olden,
There's a Dove that broods and his wings are golden.

You who kept Them through shine and storm,
A staff, a shelter kindly and warm,

Father of Jesus, husband of Mary,
Hold us your lilies for sanctuary!

Joseph, honoured from sea to sea,
Guard me mine and my own roof-tree,
    "Man of the House"!

THOMAS WALSH

Egidio of Coimbra (A.D. 1597)

The rumor came to Frei Egidio
In cloistered Santa Cruz, that out of Spain
King Philip's secret courier had fared
With orders under seal suspending all
The statutes of Coimbra that controlled
The contests for the professorial chairs,
And ordering the faculty to grant
Padre Francisco Suarez primacy
Among the masters theological.
And Frei Egidio, whose ancient name
Fonseca was relinquished when at court
It shone its brightest, who had ceaseless toiled
His score of years in cloister and in schools,
Unravelling knotty texts, disputing long
With monk and doctor of the Carmelites,
Dominicans and Trinitarians,
Consulting with the students, visiting,
Fawning and banqueting—himself and all
His faction in the University—
Now in the iron mandate from Madrid
Saw failure blight his hopes, and Santa Cruz
Eclipsed, through imposition unforeseen
Of Suarez de Toledo—only half
A monk!—a fledgling doctor in the Schools!—
And Frei Egidio unsleeping schemed
To check the rising of this Spanish star
Within Coimbra—and his henchmen went
Stealthy and sure to sow malignant seed
To choke the Hapsburg's new autocracy.

Stately was Frei Egidio, robust,
Swarthy and smooth his cheek; his raven locks
Piling about his tonsure in a crown.
Dark flashed his eye whene'er he rose to cast
His syllogistic spear across the lists,
Where many a mighty crest Minerva-crowned
Was forced to yield, or learnt the rapier thrust
Of his *distinguo* and *non-sequitur.*
Still more he shone when in procession moved
The doctors, masters, and licentiates,
With tufted caps, and rainbow gowns, and stoles,
And ring, and book across the steeps and squares,
While gallant youths pressed round on horse or foot

Holding his robe or stirrup through the town—
The *Catedratico da Vespera.*

But now this little shrivelled man sent out
From Salamanca—Philip's paragon!—
To rule Coimbra in theology!—
One of Loyola's strange and restless band
In the Collegio de Jesus—reproach
To every gorgeous doctor in the halls.
'Twas true he hid away within his house,
Came seldom to the festival or Acts,
Nor oft asserted his high presidence
O'er Frei Egidio—in craft or scorn,
It mattered not—for Frei Egidio
Would pluck him forth; no signet of the King
Could serve him here; the doctors of the Schools
Should learn how he, Fonseca, had been wronged.

With formal placards soon they smeared the walls
Of shrine and college, telling day and hour
And place, where Doutor Frei Egidio
Da Presentacao, of the Eremites
Of Sao Agostinho, titular
Da Vespera, would his conclusions hold
"De Voluntario et Involuntario"
Against all-comers, and imprimis there,
The Doutor Padre Suarez, titular
Da Prima of Coimbra, theologue
Of the *Collegia* and *Compania*
De Jesus. From near and far they came,
And took their stated rank, and filed
Into the Hall of Acts; the Chancellor
And Rector in their robes of silk, and fur,
And velvet, and great chains and seals of state;
The Bishop, and Inquisitor, and Dean,
And Chapter, in their purple; Canonists
In green; and Jurists in their scarlet gowns;
Frei Luiz of the Chair of Holy Writ,
In black and white of the Dominicans;
Frei Manoel of the Chair of Scotus, garbed
In white and brown of Carmel; titulars
In Peter Lombard and Durandus—sons
Of Bernard, Francis and Saint Benedict.

When each in order of his ancientry
Was seated in the tribune, and below
Ranged the licentiates, and bachelors,

And, out beyond, the thousand students—gay
In plumes and ruffs, or rags and disrepair—
There entered Bacharel Frei Constantino
Citing the *obligationes;* whereupon
Egidio began his argument
With exposition and arrangement clear,
And summary abrupt and crushing, as
His old experience in the courts had taught—
So free in tone and doctrine that the throng
Swayed on their benches, beating noisily
Great tomes together like the roll of drums.

Then silence for Suarez's *quodlibet;*
As half-reluctant, without emphasis,
His cold unwavering voice proposed the plan
Of his objection—when uproarious
Upon the instant, Frei Egidio
In tones of thunder shouted o'er the hall—
"Nego majorem!"—the scholastic world's
Unmitigated insult! How would he,
Spain's boasted theologian, reply
To Portugal's? The Jesuits around
Suarez's rostrum marvelled, whispered, turned,
And hid their faces, when they saw him bowed
Silent a moment, ere descending, calm,
He led them home across the jeering town.
Then the mad acclamations; bells of shrine
And monastery on the hills; the sweep
Of robes prelatical, the cavalcade
Of gorgeous nobles into Santa Cruz;
The blare of trumpets, and the lanterns strung
Yellow beneath the moon; the beggar throngs;
The maskers down the lanes; the nightingales
And river-songs of students wafted far
Across Mondego's Hills of Loneliness
And Meditation where Coimbra slept.

Thus triumphed Frei Egidio. But high
In the Collegio de Jesus the blow
Was red on every cheek; the Rector rose
In the community and said: "Padre
Francisco, not in fifty years have we
In our Coimbra known such sore defeat;
Tell me, I pray, had you no thought to save
Your honor and the honor of our schools—
You, boast of Rome and Salamanca's halls.—
You, to whom all the dialectic arts

Have been as play—could you not parry, feint,
Or bait Egidio until some chance
Or newer turn might save your argument?"
Suarez bowed and answered: "Better far
That we be humbled than a great man fall
To utter shame and ruin! Had I told
Egidio there that in denying thus
My proposition he was challenging
A solemn canon, word for word, prescribed
At Constance by the Universal Church—
Fetch me the Book of Councils—he was lost."

Scarce was the secret spoken, ere it stole
In rumor through the novice-court, and thence
Below to Santa Cruz—stole, like a cloud,
Black, ominous, across the starlit dome
Above the black *mosteiro,* where the moon
Revelled amid the sculptured lattices—
The marble ropes and palms memorial
Of old Da Gama and his caravels—
Upon the rose-paths and the trickling pools
Along the Cloister do Silencio.
There paced Fonseca, solitary guest
To catch the final crumbs, the laughter, far
Adown the stream, of lutes that mourned his feast,
When lo! a billet in his path!—*"Awake—"*
He read—*"at Constance 'twas decreed. Thy voice
Hath mocked the very words of Holy Church."*—
No more—yet in foreboding he made haste
To find his taper—fumbled through the stacks
In dust and chill—unclasped the folio
Liber Conciliorum—saw his doom—
Perchance the rack and secret prisons—writ
Upon the parchment!—Silence, mocking lutes!
Come, rain! come, whirlwind, blot the lanterns out:
Now knew he their insidious subterfuge—
The slippery Pharisees—to undermine
Coimbra's last bright paragon—they claimed
Another victim!— But his rage gave way
To grief; his scorn was all to blame; no scheme
Was theirs; Suarez spoke the Council's words
As duty bound him— With the break of day
Came self-renouncement to Egidio;
And in amaze to greet his ashen face
The sacristan laid out for him the alb
And chasuble of Requiem; resigned,
Like some bowed reed the storm has swept by night,

He took the chalice, veiled it 'gainst his breast,
And 'mid the first faint glimmer down the nave
Crept forth unto his mystic Calvary.

Coelo et in Terra

Earth is a jealous mother; from her breast
She will endure no separation long
From aught she bore;
So one by one
She claimeth evermore
The parent and the friend—
The loveliest and the best,
The meek, the faithful, and the strong—
Till, link by golden link undone,
The very tomb that seems
To youth the dismal gulf of all that's fair,
Becomes the chosen hearthstone of our dreams,
The wonder-house of all most rare,
Most deathless, and most dear;
Where the bereaved heart,
Life's exile held apart,
Would turn for love-warmth and abiding cheer,
Yea—earth can be so kind—
Then ye that rule the wind,
Are ye of less appeal?
Ye spirits of the stars
And regions where the suns
Themselves as atoms wheel
Beneath your thundering cars?
Cerulean ones!—
Or goddesses, or saints,
Or demiurge, or Trinities,
Wherewith heaven highest faints!
Are ye less kind than these
Dim vaults of clay,
Ye boasts and fathers of the ancient day?
Thou god Avernian, Dis!—behold
What timid form and old
Adown thy purple gulf descends
Unto the arch of Death—(Grim friend of friends!
Be thou placated!) 'Tis a mother, see,
Takes her first step—a child—into eternity!
Leave her not fearful there
Who was of love entire,
So gentle and so fair!—

227

Thy majesty and dread withhold
For the high head and bold,—
Imperial Death, mock not thyself with ire!
Nay—then it was not fear
That stayed her foot the while;
For now her lovely eyes,
Unclouded, brown,
Are lighted with their greeting smile—
The Hand awaited through the gloom
Is seen!—her whitened forehead lies
Upon the Shepherd's shoulder down—
Yea—her own Jesus comes—to lead
Unto the meadows where is Peace indeed!

A SUPPLEMENT TO
JOYCE KILMER'S
ANTHOLOGY OF
CATHOLIC POETS

Compiled by
JAMES EDWARD TOBIN

FOR

JEAN AND GENE

AND

SUSAN

MAURICE BARING

I Too Have Travelled

[To Hilaire Belloc, with a book of verses]

I too have travelled in the unknown land,
And anchored by the unfrequented shore;
I too have heard the Stygian waters roar,
And seen the foam of Lethe kiss the sand.

I too have trampled the enchanted grass,
And seen the phantom hunters gallop by,
And heard the faery bugle, and the sigh
Of banished gods that in the woodways pass.

And as a traveller brings his spoil to him
More richly graced in might and bravery,
So do I give to you these records dim

Of bright adventure in the fields forlorn;—
To you who heard the blast of Roland's horn,
And saw Iseult set sail for Brittany.

Vale

I am forever haunted by one dread,
That I may suddenly be swept away,
Nor have the leave to see you, and to say
Good-bye; then this is what I would have said:

I have loved summer and the longest day;
The leaves of June, the slumbrous film of heat,
The bees, the swallow, and the waving wheat,
The whistling of the mowers in the hay.

I have loved words which lift the soul with wings,
Words that are windows to eternal things.
I have loved souls that to themselves are true,

Who cannot stoop and know not how to fear,
Yet hold the talisman of pity's tear:
I have loved these because I have loved you.

231

ISABEL HARRISS BARR

Dialogue, without End

Question and answer—
Fire, without flame;
Answer and question,
Always the same.

Where, now, the guileless?
Whose is the blame?
Reply to the question
Always the same.

A paradox leans
On the arm of denial;
Truth is both victor
And victim of trial.

The question is born
Of a voice and a name;
The answer a circle—
Always the same.

The answer a circle
Of birth and of death,
Until man shakes off earth
And in heaven draws breath.

Morning Concert—Nantucket

Since neither Bach nor Paganini speak
The word I listen for—one, dutiful,
On guard, as if in fear that meaning break
Through counterpoint; the other, seeks to pull
Such heartstrings as I have, perhaps, too taut—
I close my ears. Now, inner tempests roar:
Waves, tossed and splintering midair, are caught
In sound. *Here, sunlight creeps across the floor;*
The glazed chintz hangings do not stir, each fold
Replete with scarlet flower, prim bird. The fall
Of tides that sweep away an outworn mould,
Unbridled, moves through this traditional
Décor . . . while beckoning, Ariel stands,
Poised on the threshold, beach plums in his hands.

232

ALFRED BARRETT, S.J.

Mint by Night

So quickly to have lost the summertime
Sends me home heartsick. Up the bank I climb
Trampling the hidden mint. I pause, and then
One breath of mint evokes all summer again.

You groping poets, blinded by too much
Of sea and sky, of taste and smell and touch,
Come out some night of tears and feel with me
How subtly mint assuages misery.

For mint by day is little more than grass
Tempting the casual cattle as they pass;
But mint by night is like the Holy Ghost,
Making its nearness known when needed most.

All redolent with promises of bright
Eternal summers to come is mint by night.
Come out and tramp with me some field untrod
When mint is like the very breath of God.

Summer must go and darkness come and death,
But night is heavy with God's very breath.
I will remember mint when frost comes on
And boughs are leafless and the last bird gone.

A Martyr's Mass

[Father Miguel Pro, S.J., executed at Mexico City, November 23,
     1927]

Kneeling he spoke the Names he loved the most
As the air was fanned by the whir of invisible wings;
He seemed like a priest about to breathe on the Host
     After the *Sanctus* rings.

"This is My Body," he said on his First-Mass-Day,
When the rose of priesthood slipped its snowy bud.
Lifting his chaliced heart now could he say
     At death, "This is My Blood."

233

Swift as an altar chime the rifles rang . . .
The stole of crimson flowing over his breast,
How bright it burned, and how his sealed lips sang
    The *Ite, missa est!*

ELIZABETH BELLOC

The Nightingale

In scented gardens of the south
By starlight did I hear thee sing.
A wild delight was in thy mouth.

It seemed a strange disproven thing
That they should tell of thy distress
Who said they heard thee sorrowing.

Thou hidden singer of the night,
From what deep wells of tenderness
Thy long-drawn note of love didst bring?

No salt was in that sacred spring
Of waters in the wilderness.

Thy song was of a sweet delight
Beyond the heart's imagining.

DANIEL BERRIGAN, S.J.

If Stones Can Dream

If stones can dream, after some hundred years
shouldering weight, making a wall inch onward
heaving it up a hill, braking its roll,
being only half above ground, taking the crack
of frost, the infernal sun, the insinuating sleepy moss;—
if stones can still aspire to stand up naked, a new creation
with horizon to see what they do, where the wall goes,
what shires, forests, it holds—
                              I suppose the dream
might rise, might arc, take color and stance of these

birches than fan out suddenly, bursting the wall
with powerful feet
                        so when we come on them, all that remains
of the neat arranged stones is a shambles. Lightning
    struck here,
is a first thought. But no: a lovely dream
shook from the mud the interminable years, and lives.

The Poet Prays Her

Mother, at that word your eloquent body spoke
I search another word vainly as Gabriel.
O witnessing your consent, he saw how love
planted an axis so deep in our human soil
that history, defeat, fear, aeons and nations
turned, would turn forever about your village room,
declaring like figures in time's rickety tower
this lightning strike, this only and central hour.

Whom the world could not contain is detained in you.
Since Love, in entering, so builds your hidden doorway,
consent again, receive me for child, I pray:
your nourishment, your silence, your face averted,
your hands serving excellent bread and meat; your heart
ages apart in its own country, its heaven descended
to four low walls and a dim evening fire.

HUGH FRANCIS BLUNT

Candlemas

They sold me candles by the pound,
And thought they only sold me wax;
They never guessed the things I found;
The values dealers cannot tax.

This candle for a Baby's eyes,
A pillared fire along the night,
A prophet of His paradise
To one redeemèd to the Light.

This candle for a bed of death,
For some old acolyte to hold,

Awaiting there with bated breath
For gates eternal to unfold.

Oh, many were the dreams I found
Among the boxes that I bought;
They sold me candles by the pound—
It was not wax, but stars, I got.

RAYMOND BOESCH, C. SS. R.

Life Is Leaving One Strange Port

Life is leaving one strange port,
Always for a stranger.
The sails elbowing past the clouds,
The anchor fished on deck like a captive crab,
The ship moulted from the land,
The perpetual voyage, the seamless seas.

Once the Gates of Hercules far aprow,
Two tiny men glaring over the straits,
Flushed in the violence of sunset.

Once an island close to the starboard,
Hump-backed, darkly malevolent,
With a blanched town
Caught in its fist, like a meatless bone.

These memories wanly flash
Leaving one strange port
Always for a stranger.

JOHN L. BONN, S.J.

Admonition

Nor ice nor fire shall harm you now.
   The snake shall guard his slender tooth;
The blast that cuts the horny bough
   Is temperate to youth

While through the branchings of the night
    Where the thorn withholds the fleet
Incontinently flame your white
    And unreprovèd feet.

But you shall beg for stone and steel,
    Sharp things that tore the world apart,
For even the thorn that pricked your heel
    To prick again your heart,
When death comes and you cannot weep,
    And beauty, and you cannot sigh;
No dream reproves the empty sleep
    Nor any tear, the eye.

Resurgence

Death again has swooped and flown
    And travelled trivially by.
A hawk is turned; a bird is blown
    Back to a big and vacant sky.

Dawn comes, noon follows, night returns.
    I hold the round and solid things
And wonder that the sleet still burns,
    The oil reeks, and the kettle sings.

Death came meaninglessly near
    And stopped, distracted from her chase.
I am a lost child waiting here.
    This is an unfamiliar place.

CHARLES A. BRADY

A Ballad of St. Thomas

[It was the great Chancellor's wont often to pray in jest: *Memento
    Mori*, a Latin pun which Colet found easy enough, but which,
    for a more degenerate age, may require some interpretation. It
    means both: Keep death in mind, and Remember More.]

Sir Thomas was a merry man, he laughed deep in his throat;
Erasmus was his parry man; King Harry roared till, "Marry,
        man,
You crack my sides, be wary, man," was all their jolly note.

237

His best jest was his first one, his last jest not his last one,
Both seared the beard of the ferry man, weird Charon in his
      boat.

Sir Thomas was a loyal one, he kept the King's great seal;
He was the loyal partisan; as far as toil of artisan
May cut the legal coil and moil he sheared for subject leal;
And all the while the hour-glass ran out for all his zeal.
And ever prayed this Tory: "Oh, Lord, *Memento Mori!*
At meal, at peal of mass-bell kneel, oh, gentles, seek your
      soul's high weal,
Oh, Lord, *Memento Mori!*"

Sir Thomas was a witty man, he pared Dom Luther's nails;
King Harry was a pretty man, but could not face this City
      man.
Oh, Lord, it is a pity, can a light wench tip the scales
Against the time their ditty ran so trippingly at Hales?
Memento Mori, Jesu Christ, his house of beasts, his vails,
His daughter Meg, good Mistress More, his beakers of brown
      ales,
But best of all remember, Christ, that joke he broke in gales.

St. Thomas was a saintly man, he came to headsman's block,
And still he quipped right quaintly then, and ever more, more
      faintly then
To Harry's ears came daintily then three crowings of the cock.
Memento Mori was his prayer from out the prisoner's dock.
Memento Mori gaily to the ticking of the clock,
Memento Mori as the axe was raised above the lips
That cracked the jest of times fourscore and never once did
      mock,
That never once did mock the Lord in times more than
      fourscore,
And for that More remembered God, his God remembered
      More.

KATHERINE BRÉGY

April Fools

O little frozen peach blossoms,
And shivering lilacs,
And magnolias bruised and multitudinous upon the ground—
Why did you not wait?
Why did you give the world so intemperate a trust?

238

For you clothed yourselves as brides
To meet your Bridegroom,
And went forth singing when the first trumpets began to
            sound:
Overnight the frost burnt you,
So quickly, quickly your loveliness turned brown with rust . . .

Will you remember, next year,
Foolish, credulous virgins?
Will you husband flower and fruit until the hour indubitably.
            strikes?
Will you sift false promise from true?
Will you be patient? Will you
Learn before you are quite old
How suddenly comes the betraying kiss of the cold?
And will you try, as your delicate dreams creep back into the
            sod,
To believe—still—in God?

JOHN GILLAND BRUNINI

For a Young Idealist: "Godspeed!"

Embark as joyfully you may; be gay
With breakers, laugh against the vortex wind
And mock with barely clearing hull the cay—
No perils real in sight or sound may find
Your courage less their master, sure, bold, strong.

Embark intrepidly, for so you must
To spread or reef these sails, and raise your song
Of hope to drown wise tales of others' trust,
Of others' faith dismayed—but know the chart
You midnight marked may save your body harm
But not your heart, alas, but not your heart.

Oh, none will warning sound the calm's alarm,
Oh, none will name the loneliness aright—
Few sights of land and funnel's smoke, no crew,
(But these foresworn you knew were short delight),
Oh, none will say no port shall welcome you
Or call you citizen who speak in language lost
And new and known of scattered lonely kin.

Count carefully the underweighing cost
And scorn such care a minor useless sin
For one who sees his secret star aflame
In constancy to guide, compel, reward

239

On whatsoever day. "Fool, fool!" may shame
The weak but not the heart of blameless guard
Which pleads in charity to follow sure
And, braving seas' so meagre worst, endure.

Thus spurred to seek a higher nature's need,
Sail, sail, oh lonely, needless bade "Godspeed!"

Descent of the Holy Ghost

Of what avail these willing finite minds
That now, bewildered, ponder prophecy
And parable?

        Hark, hark, the rushing winds!
All sound is poised upon their mighty beat,
The rhythm of their flight suspends all thought,
The very air astounds this cenacle retreat
And, lo! on Mary and the apostolic twelve
The cloven Tongues of Fire flame.

        All, all
The shackles of the senses fall, they see the Light,
These children of the Light, they know the call—
"Go forth and teach all nations."

        This new rite
Of confirmation sanctifies the Truth, the fruits
The Vine has borne are purged—lift up your hearts,
O orphans now no longer!

        Love confutes
The wicked, justice is the girdle of your loins
And faith the girdle of your wills. O be
Wise as the serpent, simple as the dove,
The wolves will flee your fortitude and piety,
The sheep will shelter in your words of love,
And in the ends of earth your divers tongues
Will praise the mercies of the Cross.

        Let down your net—
The fish will close its many meshes cast
In waters known and distant seas that fret
Strange hidden coasts more dangerous than these.

Behold! He is with you all days—the keys
That loose and bind are in the rock nor shall the gates
Of hell prevail against these mysteries.

240

ERIC BRUNO, O.F.M.

Libera Nos a Malo

Free us, safe God,
from the bright dangers
our eyes have seen in blindness,
from the grassy world of serpent sounds
that glide across the door-drums of our hearing,
from the crackling page and charcoal ink
that would sear our minds and boil our veins
with their worded pyres,
from the shifting treachery of waterways
that gnarl our toes and gash our fallen knees
against the jagged rocks of detoured bends. . . .

These are not new hurdles for our feet
(scrape the layered crusts of time
to find old Adam sitting in a thorny field
biting on this bitter bread),
yet they age as modern as do we:
They chant their challenge
in the vacant ears of an undiscovered morrow,
while wombs today are not delivered yet
of their already burdened heirs!

But saints will come—
they were always more
than just more of us—
to stand gazing at our traffic lights,
walk on superhighways, ride our elevators;
who will see them stretch their arms
above the clouds, pull down on us
the aftermath of warring prayer
our hearts were dumb to speak?

They will be the ones whose hearts
will telegraph our urgent code
on rusty wounds from some alvernian height,
the sweet-faced children sowing roses
in their cloister fields,
kneelers in a city dump,
new messengers of our Lady trimmed in oak.

Will we *then* cease slaying prophets
between the Altar and our fleshy temples,
cease turning our red anger
upon a judging Christ?

241

While sight has eyes, speech a throat,
scan these numbered skies
send new sounds afloat:
the parched gaspings of stout penitence!
for our precision clocks cannot exact
one extra tick of time
when death the needle comes,
touches the disc of cold wax tongues
and blares our modern
scratched recordings of delivery
deep into the ear-halls of eternity!

JOHN BUNKER

Serenade

Sometimes you seem a star,
  Sometimes a wind-swayed flower,
Sometimes a lovely princess
  High in a lonely tower.

The phases of the moon
  In her white innocence
Give no such pure delight
  Or joy in difference.

Yet to me who love you
  No aspect strange you wear—
Familiar as my beating pulse,
  Vital as breathed air.

Oh, once the starry sky,
  Oh, once the moon-bright sea,
Oh, once this blossomy earth
  Held bound my heart and me.

But now beneath your window
  Lost in a dream I stand,
And I've forgotten the singing stars
  And sky and sea and land.

Remembrance

How is it, when death comes, the simple things
Flash to remembrance? Not on the resolute deed
Performed in the breach does eager memory feed,
Nor wisest words nor mastered sufferings;
But some stray kindness, laughter that yet rings,
A trick of gait, a word given passing heed,
A smile, a gesture—these shall fill our need,
Bringing a flood of light, a glint of wings.

And that is why, my friend, now you are gone,
I do not think of your heroic stand
Against pain's long-drawn siege and your strange fate
Of dark neglect, but rather recall that one
Swift generous act when you first reached a hand
In aid to me, a stranger at your gate.

HENRIETTA A. BURKE

Transaction on the Roman Exchange

They offered barter—love.
And from the throng that jostled round
    There stepped
Rome's comeliest youth rose-crowned,
    Proud-born.
    And Agnes wept.
(Remembering other Eyes, wreathed by a braided thorn.)

They sought foul mart—to have
The white, the virgin fleece, her fame,
    Defiled
In crawling mire of shame
    Slime-trod.
    And Agnes smiled.
(Knowing a Shepherd's care for small ewe-lambs of God.)

Their closing bid—the sword!
The serpent-hiss of steel drawn fine
    Whose fang
Would strike at soft throat line
    Of dove.
    And Agnes sang.
(Seeing the blade a wing, to bear her to her Love.)

243

KATHERINE BURTON

The Exile

He was put out of Eden
One bright day—
Said boastfully how glad he was
To get away—
Sneered at the angel
Who wouldn't let him stay.

The world made him welcome,
But he felt a lack:
Something made him restless,
Something drew him back.
In Eden's wall
He found a crack.

Eden looked neglected
Without his care;
Weeds and animals
Running everywhere:
He kept the place right
When he was there.

If he could rush the angel
With the gleaming sword,
If he could once get in there
And talk to the Lord—
Show Him little things wrong
That only he saw—

Not mix up this time
With Everlasting Law.
If only he could get
Inside that gate—
And do again the little things
He used to hate.

GERTRUDE CALLAGHAN

Who Goes By Lightly

I shall go by lightly,
Grasses, do not fear;
I shall step so softly
You will scarcely hear.

I shall touch you gently,
Fern and moss and leaf;
Cedars dark and silent
Shall not look on grief.

Birch and ash and alder,
Pine against the sky,
There is none so frightened,
None so small as I,

Who ventured here undaunted,
Thinking not to stay,
Who came to look on beauty
And cannot go away.

New England Fog

The fog rolls in across the fields of heather
That yesterday lay underneath the sun,
And things familiar in this shrouded weather
Take on an eerieness, and one by one
Accept a new identity. The ships
Offshore are lost to sight. A ghostly curtain
Enfolds them in a world unreal, uncertain,
Of clammy hands and chill and sculptured lips.
The foghorn lifts a gray voice hoarse with ire
To boom out danger's secret mysteries.
A proud-backed woman lights her evening fire
And tries to keep her thoughts from fog-bound seas,
And lays out courage from her pent-up store,
With all her hearing straining toward the shore.

245

Native Son

Swift in his step and careless of his speech,
A child of canyons and deflected light,
Neighbor to skyscrapers, within eye's reach
Of wonder, it becomes his second sight.
Undaunted where the curious come to stand
And blindly stare, confusion in the mind,
He goes a jaunty boy, his pockets lined
With vision that is plastic to his hand.

Bound by no grim tradition, narrowed in
By no harsh creed, this city child walks free.
His meadow is a paving stone worn thin
With hurrying feet, each corner light his tree.
A traffic lane his Eden, he is shod
Against alarm, a favored child of God.

Award

Had you been strong I would have dared
To lay my weakness at your feet.
Had you been brave I would have bared
Each beat of my heart's beat.

But you were white and you were spent,
And you had failed, and how could I,
Who cared, have seen you body-bent
When our fears rode by.

And so I buckled on the sword
And breastplate—now you love me less;
And veins of steel are the award
Of my defenselessness.

JOSEPH CAMPBELL

I Am the Mountainy Singer

I am the mountainy singer,
And I would sing of the Christ
Who followed the paths thro' the mountains
To eat at the people's tryst.

246

He loved the sun-dark people
As the young man loves his bride,
And He moved among their thatches,
And for them was crucified.

And the people loved Him, also,
More than their houses or lands,
For they had known His pity
And felt the touch of His hands.

And they dreamed with Him in the mountains,
And they walked with Him on the sea,
And they prayed with Him in the garden,
And bled with Him on the tree.

Not ever by longing and dreaming
May they come to Him now,
But by the thorns of sorrow
That bruised His kingly brow.

I Will Go with My Father A-Ploughing

I will go with my father a-ploughing
To the green field by the sea,
And the rooks and the crows and the seagulls
Will come flocking after me.
I will sing to the patient horses
With the lark in the white of the air,
And my father will sing the plough-song
That blesses the cleaving share.

I will go with my father a-sowing
To the red field by the sea,
And the rooks and the gulls and the starlings
Will come flocking after me.
I will sing to the striding sowers
With the finch on the greening sloe,
And my father will sing the seed-song
That only the wise men know.

I will go with my father a-reaping
To the brown field by the sea,
And the geese and the crows and the children
Will come flocking after me.
I will sing to the tan-faced reapers
With the wren in the heat of the sun,
And my father will sing the scythe-song
That joys for the harvest done.

247

The Shining Spaces of the South

The shining spaces of the south,
The circle of the year, the sea,
The blowing rose, the maiden's mouth,
The love, the hate, the ecstasy,
The golden wood, the shadowed stream,
The dew, the light, the wind, the rain,
The man's desire, the woman's dream,
The bed embrace, the childing pain,
The sound of music heard afar,
The breathing grass, the broken sod,
The sun, the moon, the twilight star—
Do all proclaim the mind of God.

Then why should I, who am but clay,
Think otherwise, or answer nay?

ROY CAMPBELL

Autumn

I love to see, when leaves depart,
The clear anatomy arrive,
Winter, the paragon of art,
That kills all forms of life and feeling
Save what is pure and will survive.

Already now the clanging chains
Of geese are harnessed to the moon:
Stripped are the great sun-clouding planes:
And the dark pines, their own revealing,
Let in the needles of the noon.

Strained by the gale the olives whiten
Like hoary wrestlers bent with toil
And, with the vines, their branches lighten
To brim our vats where summer lingers
In the red froth and sun-gold oil.

Soon on our hearths' reviving pyre
Their rotted stems will crumble up:
And like a ruby, panting fire,
The grape will redden on your fingers
Through the lit crystal of the cup.

248

Familiar Daemon

Measuring out my life in flagons
(No coffee-spoon to skim the flood)
You were the prince of thirsty dragons,
The gay carouser of my blood:
We could not part, our love was such,
But gasconading, shared the fun
While every cripple's shouldered crutch
Was sighted at me like a gun.
What sport today? to swim or fly,
Or fish for thunder in the sky?
What laughter out of hell to fetch,
Or joy from peril, have you planned,
You hellward rider, that you stretch
The downswung stirrup of my hand?

A Good Resolution

Enough of those who study the oblique:
Inverted archaeologists who seek
The New, as if it were some quaint antique—

Nomads of Time, and pungent with its must,
Who took the latest crinolines on trust
As wigwams for their vagrant wanderlust;

Of jargons that a fuddled Celt will mix
By the blue light of jack-a'-lantern wicks
Fishing dead words like kippers from the Styx;

Sham Brownings, too, who'll cloud a shallow stream,
And in a haystack hide a needle theme
Till platitudes like propositions seem—

With *pontes asinorum* bridging ditches
That (fully armed, without the aid of witches)
Old Knights could hurdle in their cast-iron breeches.

Hide poverty beneath a chequered shirt
And trust from common eyesight to divert
The jagged ribs that corrugate the dirt.

I will go stark: and let my meanings show
Clear as a milk-white feather in a crow
Or a black stallion on a field of snow.

The Zulu Girl

When in the sun the hot red acres smoulder,
Down where the sweating gang its labour plies,
A girl flings down her hoe, and from her shoulder
Unslings her child tormented by the flies.

She takes him to a ring of shadow pooled
By thorn-trees: purpled with the blood of ticks,
While her sharp nails, in slow caresses ruled,
Prowl through his hair with sharp electric clicks.

His sleepy mouth, plugged by the heavy nipple,
Tugs like a puppy, grunting as he feeds:
Through his frail nerves her own deep languors ripple
Like a broad river sighing through its reeds.

Yet in that drowsy stream his flesh imbibes
An old unquenched unsmotherable heat—
The curbed ferocity of beaten tribes,
The sullen dignity of their defeat.

Her body looms above him like a hill
Within whose shade a village lies at rest,
Or the first cloud so terrible and still
That bears the coming harvest in its breast.

FRANCIS CARLIN

Vessels

He strangely gazes up
Who peers within the cup
Of tulip, self, or Christ:
Three chalices unpriced.

One holds the imaged flower;
And one, our vesseled power;
And One, unimagedly,
Both dust and Deity.

So they peer upward who
Gaze down beyond the dew,
The tears, the Blood, to reach
Through depth to height in each.

250

The Solar Road

From the start of Life
To the end of its strife
    There is many a weary league,
But the Road that runs
Among the Suns
    Shall cause us no fatigue.

Alchemy

Because of the light of the moon,
    Silver is found on the moor;
And because of the light of the sun,
    There is gold on the walls of the poor.

Because of the light of the stars,
    Planets are found in the stream;
And because of the light of your eyes,
    There is love in the depths of my dream.

GEORGE CHAPMAN

Autumn Hour

Tree, sky and star my teachers,
What do I not learn.
Out of my heart a heart reaches
For a light that may burn!

High as God's brow this heaven,
Deep as His thought, this sea,
And all the earth a leaven
Working wonder in me.

Bright hues of the Fall, and over
The hues a red-shadow of sun;
Hyperion gone home like a lover
Proud of the loving done.

His fire in every changing leaf,
His blood on the brooding sea,
And his joy like a thing of grief
Rising in tears in me.

251

And to cry were a manly passion
When such beauty walks in power,
And things man cannot fashion
Fall to man for an hour.

ANGELICO CHAVEZ, O.F.M.

Lady of Lidice

From God's lofty City
my Lady looks down,
the remembering lover
of every small town,
looks down less with pity
than wistfulness over
the town that is not;
for gone are its people,
each household and cot,
the quaint Slavic steeple
that tendered them cover,
a smoldering plot.
From God's lofty City
my Lady looks down,
forever the lover
of every small town.

In Extremis

*St. James, hover near him
with God's flaming sword,
while he is annealed
In the Name of the Lord.*

Lay blaze to the evil
his gaze saw each day,
while Jesus is wiping
the hot tears away.

From ears sear the singing
of sirens there stored,
and soothe with a Name
as of oil being poured.

From nose smoke whatever
rank perfumes there were,

252

and waft in the freshness
of incense and myrrh.

As the lips of the prophet,
tip live-coals to his,
to utter and taste Him,
how sweet the Lord is.

Brand out all wrongdoing
his hands ever tried,
for Jesus to draw
to the wound in His side.

With heat clean the mire
from feet gone astray,
to feel the soft footprints
of Jesus the Way.

And light him through darkness
with God's sword of flame,
at peace and all-healed now
in good Jesus' Name.

Southwestern Night

The night had pitched her tar-dark tent
Which leaked with starlight everywhere,
When by the road on which I went
I came upon the firelit shapes
Of shepherds, lean and bent.

There was no wind to shake the flame
To which they drew me civilly,
Much less their voices when I came.
(My coming did not cut their words
To even ask my name.)

Their task was unaware of wars
And innocent of rapes and polls;
Each phrase fell in Gregorian bars,
And while their cadence skimmed the soil
They seemed to touch the stars.

Up to the ceiling's taut, dark crown
They flowed as one, the strand of smoke,
Their thread of thought; and as my own
Turned heavenward to follow them,
The dew of stars dripped down.

GILBERT KEITH CHESTERTON

Lepanto

White founts falling in the Courts of the sun,
And the Soldan of Byzantium is smiling as they run;
There is laughter like the fountains in that face of all men
    feared,
It stirs the forest darkness, the darkness of his beard,
It curls the blood-red crescent, the crescent of his lips,
For the inmost sea of all the earth is shaken with his ships.
They have dared the white republics up the capes of Italy,
They have dashed the Adriatic round the Lion of the Sea,
And the Pope has cast his arms abroad for agony and loss,
And called the kings of Christendom for swords about the
    Cross.
The cold queen of England is looking in the glass;
The shadow of the Valois is yawning at the Mass;
From evening isles fantastical rings faint the Spanish gun,
And the Lord upon the Golden Horn is laughing in the sun.

Dim drums throbbing, in the hills half heard,
Where only on a nameless throne a crownless prince has
    stirred,
Where, risen from a doubtful seat and half-attainted stall,
The last knight of Europe takes weapons from the wall,
The last and lingering troubadour to whom the bird has sung,
That once went singing southward when all the world was
    young.
In that enormous silence, tiny and unafraid,
Comes up along a winding road the noise of the Crusade.
Strong gongs groaning as the guns boom far,
Don John of Austria is going to the war,
Stiff flags straining in the night-blasts cold,
In the gloom black-purple, in the glint old-gold,
Torchlight crimson on the copper kettle-drums,
Then the tuckets, then the trumpets, then the cannon, and he
    comes.
Don John laughing in the brave beard curled,
Spurning of his stirrups like the thrones of all the world,
Holding his head up like a flag of all the free.
Love-light of Spain—hurrah!
Death-light of Africa!
Don John of Austria
Is riding to the sea.

Mahound is in his paradise above the evening star,
(*Don John of Austria is going to the war.*)

254

He moves a mighty turban on the timeless houri's knees,
His turban that is woven of the sunsets and the seas.
He shakes the peacock gardens as he rises from his ease,
And he strides among the tree-tops and is taller than the trees,
And his voice through all the garden is a thunder sent to bring
Black Azrael and Ariel and Ammon on the wing.
Giants and the Genii,
Multiplex of wing and eye,
Whose strong obedience broke the sky
When Solomon was king.

They rush in red and purple from the red clouds of the morn,
From temples where the yellow gods shut up their eyes in
    scorn;
They rise in green robes roaring from the green hells of the
    sea
Where fallen skies and evil hues and eyeless creatures be;
On them the sea-valves cluster and the grey sea-forests curl,
Splashed with a splendid sickness, the sickness of the pearl;
They swell in sapphire smoke out of the blue cracks of the
    ground—
They gather and they wonder and give worship to Mahound.
And he saith, "Break up the mountains where the hermit-folk
    can hide,
And sift the red and silver sands lest bone of saint abide,
And chase the Giaours flying night and day, not giving rest,
For that which was our trouble comes again out of the west.
We have set the seal of Solomon on all things under sun,
Of knowledge and of sorrow and endurance of things done,
But a noise in the mountains, in the mountains, and I know
The voice that shook our palaces—four hundred years ago;
It is he that saith not 'Kismet'; it is he that knows not Fate;
It is Richard, it is Raymond, it is Godfrey in the gate!
It is he whose loss is laughter when he counts the wager worth,
Put down your feet upon him, that our peace be on the earth."
For he heard drums groaning and he heard guns jar,
(*Don John of Austria is going to the war.*)
Sudden and still—hurrah!
Bolt from Iberia!
Don John of Austria
Is gone by Alcalar.

St. Michael's on his Mountain in the sea-roads of the north
(*Don John of Austria is girt and going forth.*)
Where the grey seas glitter and the sharp tides shift
And the sea-folk labour and the red sails lift.
He shakes his lance of iron and he claps his wings of stone;
The noise is gone through Normandy; the noise is gone alone;

255

The North is full of tangled things and texts and aching eyes,
And dead is all the innocence of anger and surprise,
And Christian killeth Christian in a narrow dusty room,
And Christian dreadeth Christ that hath a newer face of
    doom,
And Christian hateth Mary that God kissed in Galilee,
But Don John of Austria is riding to the sea.
Don John calling through the blast and the eclipse
Crying with the trumpet, the trumpet of his lips,
Trumpet that sayeth ha!
Domino gloria!
Don John of Austria
Is shouting to the ships.

King Philip's in his closet with the Fleece about his neck
(*Don John of Austria is armed upon the deck.*)
The walls are hung with velvet that is black and soft as sin,
And little dwarfs creep out of it and little dwarfs creep in.
He holds a crystal phial that has colours like the moon,
He touches, and it tingles, and he trembles very soon
And his face is as a fungus of a leprous white and grey
Like plants in the high houses that are shuttered from the day,
And death is in the phial and the end of noble work,
But Don John of Austria has fired upon the Turk.
Don John's hunting, and his hounds have bayed—
Booms away past Italy the rumour of his raid.
Gun upon gun, ha! ha!
Gun upon gun, hurrah!
Don John of Austria
Has loosed the cannonade.

The Pope was in his chapel before day or battle broke,
(*Don John of Austria is hidden in the smoke.*)
The hidden room in man's house where God sits all the year,
The secret window whence the world looks small and very
    dear.
He sees as in a mirror on the monstrous twilight sea
The crescent of his cruel ships whose name is mystery;
They fling great shadows foe-wards, making Cross and Castle
    dark,
They veil the plumed lions on the galleys of St. Mark;
And above the ships are palaces of brown, black-bearded
    chiefs,
And below the ships are prisons, where with multitudinous
    griefs,
Christian captives sick and sunless, all a labouring race repines
Like a race in sunken cities, like a nation in the mines.

They are lost like slaves that sweat, and in the skies of morn-
    ing hung
The stair-ways of the tallest gods when tyranny was young,
They are countless, voiceless, hopeless as those fallen or flee-
    ing on
Before the high Kings' horses in the granite of Babylon.
And many a one grows witless in his quiet room in hell
Where a yellow face looks inward through the lattice of his
    cell,
And he finds his God forgotten, and he seeks no more a sign—
(*But Don John of Austria has burst the battle-line!*)
Don John pounding from the slaughter-painted poop,
Purpling all the ocean like a bloody pirate's sloop,
Scarlet running over on the silvers and the golds,
Breaking of the hatches up and bursting of the holds,
Thronging of the thousands up that labour under sea
White for bliss and blind for sun and stunned for liberty.
Vivat Hispania!
Domino gloria!
Don John of Austria
Has set his people free!

Cervantes on his galley sets the sword back in the sheath
(*Don John of Austria rides homeward with a wreath.*)
And he sees across a weary land a straggling road in Spain,
Up which a lean and foolish knight for ever rides in vain,
And he smiles, but not as Sultans smile, and settles back the
    blade. . . .
(*But Don John of Austria rides home from the Crusade.*)

The Grave of Arthur

Down through the rocks where the dark roots dry,
The last long roots of the Glaston Thorn,
Dead is the King that never was born,
Dead is the King that never shall die.

They found him between the pyramids
In the subterranean land, men say,
And there was not rending nor rolling away
Of linen nor lifting of coffin-lids,

But the giant bones like the columns lie,
The far-flung towers of a flattened city
That is dead with a doom too old for pity
(Dead is the King who does not die).

Coiled on his left from neck to knee,
Huge and hollow the horn is curled,
White as the worm that devours the world,
Carved with the cold white snakes of the sea.

Flat on his right, in the dust grown grey
Is patterned the vast cross-hilted sword
Graven with the Coming of Christ the Lord,
Gold with the trumpets of Judgment Day.

Between the first and the last he lies
And between the false and the true dreams he:
Born without birth of a fabled sea
Armoured in death till the dead shall rise.

And back and forth as a tolling bell
And forth and backward the Roman rhyme
Rolls in a ring that mocks at time
Tolling the truth that none can tell.

In the high still hollow where time is not
Or all times turn and exchange and borrow
In the glass wherein God remembers tomorrow
And truth looks forward to times forgot.

Where God looks back on the days to be
And heaven is yet hoping for yesterday;
The light in which time shall be taken away
And the soul that faces all ways is free,

The rune shall be read though it twist and turn,
And the riddle be learnt that is past all learning,
Of the Man unborn who is ever returning
And ever delaying, till God return.

And for ever and ever till death discover
Why truth speaks double in dreams and day;
And the Myth and the Man that wandered away
Make tryst together as lover to lover,

A dream shall wail through the worm-shaped horn
"Dead is a King that never was born"
And a trumpet of truth from the Cross reply
"Dead is the King who shall not die."

Music

Sounding brass and tinkling cymbal,
He that made me sealed my ears,
And the pomp of gorgeous noises,
Waves of triumph, waves of tears,

Thundered empty round and past me,
Shattered, lost for evermore,
Ancient gold of pride and passion,
Wrecked like treasure on a shore.

But I saw her cheek and forehead
Change, as at a spoken word,
And I saw her head uplifted
Like a lily to the Lord.

Nought is lost, but all transmuted,
Ears are sealed, yet eyes have seen;
Saw her smiles (O soul be worthy!),
Saw her tears (O heart be clean!).

A Ballade of Suicide

The gallows in my garden, people say,
Is new and neat and adequately tall.
I tie the noose on in a knowing way
As one that knots his necktie for a ball;
But just as all the neighbors—on the wall—
Are drawing a long breath to shout "Hurray!"
The strangest whim has seized me. . . . After all
I think I will not hang myself today.

Tomorrow is the time I get my pay—
My uncle's sword is hanging in the hall—
I see a little cloud all pink and grey—
Perhaps the Rector's mother will *not* call—
I fancy that I heard from Mr. Gall
That mushrooms should be cooked another way—
I never read the works of Juvenal—
I think I will not hang myself today.

The world will have another washing day;
The decadents decay; the pedants pall;
And H. G. Wells has found that children play,
And Bernard Shaw discovered that they squall;
Rationalists are growing rational—

259

And through thick woods one finds a stream astray,
So secret that the very sky seems small—
I think I will not hang myself today.

Envoi

Prince, I can hear the trumpet of Germinal,
The tumbrils toiling up the terrible way;
Even today your royal head may fall—
I think I will not hang myself today.

FRANCIS D. CLARE

Sick Room

Yes, all your dutiful goodness I remember:
The grave inquiries, necessary thought.
Let some broad credits mark your careful kindness
Down on some page, but it escapes my heart
That holds, instead, your sweet, impractical presence,
The theoretic sympathy of eyes,
The quite unsterile warmth of sudden smiling,
Unantiseptic pressure of your hand.
The bones sag on, in prophylactic goodness;
But, oh! what brave strength surges to the heart
In ex officio moments love devises:
The slim cornflowers springing from your hand!

GERTRUDE JANE CODD

Strange Guest

Were pain a simple stab
That comes with severed nerve,
Except we prove we live
It would no purpose serve.

Even the cut of loss
That rips across our soul
But lifts us from the beasts
To play a higher role.

More delicate than these
There is a keener knife:
Companion of the hours
That have been best in life.

Oh hurt in fragrant rose,
Unspoken love in eyes,
Nostalgic peace in prayer
And heaven in sunset skies!

My strange and lovely guest,
Come closer still to me—
You are my surest proof
Of immortality.

FRANCIS X. CONNOLLY

For Having Thee

I thank Thee, Lord, for this good life,
For Water, Oil, Wine, Wafer, Wife,
For time to do a Penance in
And grace to half forget the sin,
For father's smile and mother's tears
And sister's salutary fears,
For friendships firm and friendships fleeting,
For adieus and happy meeting,
For laughter running like a boy,
For prick of pain foretelling joy,
For leaps the heart makes at the sense
Of sacramental innocence,
For having Thee to thank and praise,
Adore and hope for all our days.

MARGARET D. CONWAY

The Annunciation

That spring in Palestine when airs went forth
To rouse the turtle doves and fill with flame
Of flowers all the dun hills and the plains,
Sweet Mary, did you start to hear your name?

261

So lost in prayer, did Gabriel's gold shade
Astonish your profundity of peace,
Or did Life-in-you compensate your heart
With deep at-one-ment for the world's release?

Most surely so, for virginally wise,
You knew that love must root and bud and grow,
And feared not this strange spring nor future fruit,
But let the godly gift upon you glow.

In that one hour worlds were overturned
And peace restored to all of us amiss
As He in whom our final justice stands
Laid on your lips His convenanting kiss.

WINIFRED CORRIGAN, R.C.

I Turn the Key

"Omnipotence Divine," I pray in awe,
"By thy vast mercy, condescend to me."
As when the gate swung out, the Greeks surged in
To Troy and Helen shrank who turned the key

In awe; in awe as round a rippling pool
The self-forgotten one who cast the stone;
As Moses stood, come down the mount, in awe
To see in people's eyes his visage shone:

So am I lost in awe, when my turned will
Lets thee within me, round me casts thy sheen,
To see in people's eyes thy glory plead
I veil my face. Thy face I have not seen.

Since when I cry "Beloved" thou art gone,
All-beauty ebbed, all-splendor put to sea,
"Omnipotence Divine," I pray in awe,
Relying on thy mercy, "come to me."

JAMES F. COTTER, S.J.

Autumn Is a Season

Autumn and the elms unleaving.

                           "Come,
My Brother, the day is glassware
And the air is cider," into my room
You call with sudden laughter.
In my window I see brown leaves
Curtsy on the cemetery lawn,
Red leaves dancing in the hands of wind:
All the macabre ritual of Fall.

"I will go," I answer, "despite your cider."

Along the road the maple trees grope
For their lost loveliness.

                 "This path
Is too familiar and your air
Is, after all, plain beverage," I banter.

You retort, "If you want nectar, come,
I promise I will show you air
And ways you have never known before."

Autumn and the land disheveled.
Old stones that once told pastures
Wander aimlessly among the trees.

You stop, *"This* you have not seen.
It was years ago begun and never finished."

Through the ivy and laurel growth
Four stunted cement walls stand
In a hole cut like an open grave.

"Why show me this?" I ask,
"There is no meaning to a cellar;
It began and never grew to be.
The woods are littered with beginnings:
The ruins of many springs, of fields
And farms, and hopes of houses."

                      And I remember.
You laugh but without understanding.

263

How years have passed since I,
I too, began to build! Shovel and mattock
Sang in my hand; block, mortar and trowel
My daily hymn. And I laughed in my labor
As I watched the white walls rise
Like a choir around me. I walk
Among these beginnings and remember.
I feel the line and smoothness of the stone.
Prodding the loose gravel I watch
The chips clatter like bones
In the black spaces below.

Up above the elms unleaving.

JAMES J. DALY, S.J.

Nox Ignatiana

His vigil was the stars; his eyes were bright
With radiance of them. Mystically slow
Was their processional, while far below
Rome's quick and dead slept—fellows in the night.
These very stars had marched in cryptic rite
For Vergil in clear evenings long ago,
Gliding, like motes, athwart the overflow
Of splendor from immortal tides of Light.

"What is this ant-life on a sphere of sand
That it must drive, with ant-like cares, my soul
Than all the stars together more sublime?"
So in the spacious night Ignatius planned
His spacious morrows—centuries his scroll—
Upon a background of Eternal Time.

GEMMA D'AURIA

Subject for Prophecy

Let us turn, now, from the rigid clocks,
Turn from the heart-strung coils contrived
To hold the moment captive. They confine
Too small a present from the unbounded whole.
Look out upon the vast
And open thoroughfares of time to where
The instant's exclamation speeds,
A fugitive, and free.
For there, upon a distant sun,
The light that shone on Pericles,
Or shattered into darkness on Christ crucified,
Is only now arriving.
At this immediate hour of striking bells,
A far-off eye, upon a far-off star,
Might see the pyramids in building, or observe
That stubborn Genoese
Dare the sea-horizon's false finality,
And, on another Indies, still
His caravels.

Let us turn, then, from the narrow moment,
Turn from tensions of the moment's fear,
Remembering
That this, our anxious now
(That holds us fixed upon its little stroke),
For some dim world among the nebulae,
Has not yet come,
Is still the uncreated future, the unknown—
Subject for prophecy.

JOSEPH DEVER

Queen of Horizons

O Lord, give me a plane,
And waft me high again,
To where the Mary-hue
Is one pure, vasty blue.
Oh, I will romp the airy ocean,
Make sun-winks with my mothy motion.

265

Below, chameleon clouds obscure
My ethered glee, make sure
Men cannot see my suit
Of her, although the brute-
Blotch-steel may rend her gown,
And from her mantle claw me down
The blurring avenue of space.

Yet, richly have I known her face,
For sweet, abounding purity
Was bluely clad and smiled on me;
And every crimson blob of death
Becomes a lambent, crystal breath.

Howl-spatter-demons, have your riot,
You will be azured and be quiet.
Yankee, Jap and German, too,
Blue, my Lady, fold in blue.

Fold them warmly in your arms,
Where the flung steel never harms,
Where the blinding wedge of dawning
Dazzles, yet is merely fawning
On the lady's world-embrace
Of azure. Do you know one place
In Heaven where there is no Mary?

You, with pinions, be not wary
Of the blood-fleck and the flame,
For blue can clean and blue can tame
The hotly spiked, infuriated sky
Blue-silently; and only death will die
Therefore, Lord, give me a plane,
And waft me Mary-high again.

KEVIN F. DOHERTY, S.J.

The Astronomer

To wonder, Plato told, revealed the wise:
some childhood night perhaps his prison bars
were starlit when he felt his first surmise
of wonder at world beyond the stars.

Forever to become and never be,
was this the heartbeat of the night and day?
he grappled with a cosmic mystery
and spanned an aeon-embered Milky Way.

The eyes of Alexandria were keen
to center all the universe in man:
the heartbeat of the Ptolomaic scene
was dawning witness to a cosmic plan.

For other eyes Chaldean skies once shone
in darkness pregnant with a wonderlight:
their winding caravans discovered dawn
within an Infant's eyes and swaddling white.

O world's expanding in the womb of space
now flash within the sweep of Palomars
and wildfire galaxies have left a trace
of wonder in the eyes that pierce the stars!

WILLIAM A. DONAGHY, S.J.

Stations of the Cross: III. He Falls

The crowd is thrilled to see a fighter downed,
Battered and bloody, sprawled upon the floor,
Like multitudinous surfs upon the shore
Its shout arises; so the sickening sound
Of splintering wood upon the flinty ground
Brings from this mob a swelling, bestial roar.
What though the fall renewed the wounds and tore
His flesh, and jarred His head so crudely crowned.

These worthy citizens are men of name,
Respectable, judicious, just, discreet;
I cannot bear to have them know my shame—
My brother dying in a public street—
And though I hear our mother's choking sob,
I turn and shout "My brothers!" to the mob.

267

XIV: He is Buried

The mourners slowly bring Him through the gloom,
The valiant women, and three faithful men;
Her shoulders shaking, stormy Magdalen
Is weeping as in Simon's dining room;
But she who felt Him stirring in her womb,
Who wrapped and laid Him in a manger then
Is still His handmaid, ready once again
To wrap Him up and lay Him in His tomb.

Once Delphi was the navel of the earth,
But now this sepulchre, which blackly yawns,
Becomes the point and center of all worth,
The focus of all sunsets and all dawns;
Within this cavern, could the world but see,
Mythology yields place to mystery.

Ancestry

Old Sam was black and long of limb,
And when the sweat stood out on him,
Behind the whirring lawn-mower, he
Glistened like oiled mahogany.

"Happy as a hive where the fat bees hum,
Happy as a trout in a river of rum;
Happy as the desert beneath the rain,
Happy as a whale in a sea of champagne.
For I opened my heart and I chased out sin
And I let the good Lord Jesus in."

Rich and ripe was his mellow bass,
Touched with rapture were his eyes and face;
And the soft, blurred accent of his lazy tongue
Around the hymn like a halo hung.

Behind him lay the burning plains
Of Africa; and whips and chains;
And Noe, Japheth, Cham, and Sem,
Claver, Augustine, and Ephraem.

JAMES J. DONOHUE

Hymn

Eternal Founder of the sky,
  The suns are numbered where they swing;
The very star-dust is not free
  To fall without Thy reckoning.

Carefully leaning long ago
  Among the labyrinth of night,
Thy questing finger found and kept
  One track secure, one planet bright.

Blind to the pattern earth described
  Pre-natal on the loom of space,
We only know we woke at dawn
  And felt Thy breath upon our face.

We know the garden of our prime
  Darkly in dreams and whisperings,
Remembering one boyhood hour
  Of wiser laughter, better things.

We know at noon the garden gone,
  The portal coldly crossed with bars:
Darkness is never far from day,
  And earth an exile in the stars.

Carefully bend as long ago
  Among Thy truer points of fire
And turn our outcast planet square
  Upon the land of our desire.

Father and Founder of the sky,
  Only-begotten Truth and Light,
Spirit and kindly Beacon-Ray,
  Bring us to Eden in the night.

God Said: Let There Be Sky

This is for poets . . . Reasoner and empiric,
Measure this vault deep as the suns aspire,
Broaden conclusions coldly in your pyrrhic
Conquest of compass at the price of fire.
Which of you dare proclaim what bitter waters
This shell divides from the sweet nether rain,

269

What suction tenses or what deluge batters
The limits that you fix or ascertain?
Not only where the Bear remotely raises
His vaguest nebula, but here upon
Earth-rind and sea-film, cell-wall, skin of faces,
Shingle, and shroud, the firmament is drawn.
Wisdom will tell where surface bends and why,
But only poets see behind the sky.

Praise of Engineers

I sometimes think that mountains are not worth
The singing. Yes, I know how long the world
Smoldered at heart, I know the sudden surge
Squandering sunshine hoarded from the spume
Of seething galaxies, irreparable
Heartbreak of shrieking atoms, rigid jars
Wringing the iron veins and ecstasy
Grinding complaining bones of stony deeps,
Hot thrust and thaw of granite-smothered fires,
And stiff earth-stirrings—till the tortured land
Writhed into hills. Mountains do this: they shout
Above their silence brute omnipotence,
And men unwilling suddenly see God.

JAMES L. DUFF

Dies Irae

There were no footprints left upon the waters
When Jesus walked on Lake Genesareth,
The unrecorded words His finger penciled
In dust upon the road are gone like breath.

Yet when the charts and books are all discarded,
And, dreadful in the dawn, the horn is heard
Above the ended roads, the canceled phrases,
Behold! the endless Way, the deathless Word!

Upon This Rock

"Simon Bar-Jona, lovest thou Me?"
Three times the question, and three times I
Made the Master the same reply—
    And that was true.

"Thou wast with him, wast thou not?"
Three times the question, and three times I
Answered it with the selfsame lie—
    Then the cock crew.

"Simon Bar-Jona, lovest thou Me?"
This is the answer of Peter, the Rock:
Out of my love I shall feed Thy flock—
    Each sheep and each lamb.

JOHN DUFFY, C.SS.R.

Domine Jesu!

Up from my golden saucer in the dawn
Flows without fleck, in streak of utmost glow,
The Floodlight of my Savior Jesus Christ,
Ascending soundless, like an upward snow.

More than the rainbow's last invisible hues—
Intangible yet scorching bolt of Grace,
Probing the poles of space and all the stars,
It finds and floods with joy the Father's face.

Lo, from my mirror, lacquered like a lake,
Lo, from my dish, as from a focused arc,
God from the shallow bottom of the world
Streams upward unto God through all the dark.

And I, with *Domine Jesu!* on my lips,
Bend and look softly over in the blaze,
Bend and look downward in the blinding beam,
My lips, my eyes, caught betwixt Gaze and Gaze.

By Thine effulgence breaking on my brow,
Domine, bear mine image on with Thee
To cast my shadow on Thy Father's face,
That in Thy look He may remember me.

271

The Thrush

The brooks that flush
The windpipe of the thrush
Water our winds today.
I find him on the branch he loved last May.

What passionate direction sloped aright
His straight-as-lighting flight
Up from the south? Oh, what compelling good
Has called him there,
Out of a billion boughs to fix on the elect,
Its shape and feel in this explicit wood?
What imprint in the land or definite cast of air?
I know, I know, and I will say:

There's One who throws the thrush our way,
As cleanly traveling as a javelin,
And has it in His heart to see
The thrush's little ache of melody
From spring to spring will never kink or carp,
Will never shift its silvers by the slenderest sharp.

EILEEN DUGGAN

Plea

A song? What goes to make a poet's song?
Such longing as a dumb child hostage has
Among the watchful women for his home,
Lost in a great green jeopardy of sea;
Such will as bees have when they fly by night,
Foreseeing a sour summer for the comb,
When pelts of rain shall pit the wizened rose;
Such pride as hunchbacks hold in martial sons
With wonder that a dream begat a deed;
Such hope as lanes that count in buttercups
And feel their dips break burning from the sod;
Such agony as ewes that hear their young
Moaning and lagging in the dusty drove;
Such awe as hemispheres when in their vasts
Night, the slow dragon, ruffs its lambent scales.
Give us all these, not even for our land,
Though she may walk her islands in the spring,

272

Upon a little floss of grass and flowers,
And all our songs, made flesh, may ring her head,
Nimbus on nimbus of crosswoven birds,
But for song's sake that has no latitude
And needs no other nation than the heart,
Though it be written in a script of stars,
The countrymen of beauty never die.

Twilight

I was driving the cows and the frogs were soothsaying,
"Woe, land and water! All, all is lost!"
It was winter full grown and my bones were black in me.
The tussocks were brittling from dew into frost.

The earth looked at me, ears up in a stillness.
I was nine at the time and a coward by fate:
The willow trees humped into cringing old swaggers,
And the cows lunged up unicorns, passing the gate.

A sudden wind clouted the nose of our chimney,
It rumbled and bellowsed its sparks in a spray;
I took to my heels in the terrible twilight,
For I thought that the sky was blowing away.

The Bushfeller

Lord, mind your trees today!
My man is out there clearing.
God send the chips fly safe.
My heart is always fearing.

And let the axehead hold!
My dreams are all of felling.
He earns our bread far back.
And then there is no telling.

If he came home at nights,
We'd know, but it is only—
We might not even hear—
A man could lie there lonely.

God, let the trunks fall clear,
He did not choose his calling;
He's young and full of life—
A tree is heavy, falling.

273

Aspiration

Oh never call it waste of wishing,
Although too wild it seem.
In any sky there is from moon to Saturn,
From tale to fable,
The distance of a dream.

But the between is never idle.
The learned will lay it's true,
By some great mystery beyond our knowing,
The blue is able,
The gap is nimble, too.

Distance is power, of its own birthright,
And space is toil like star.
Dream on—desire itself is working for you,
The goal is stable,
Merely by being far.

The Discipline of Consequences

The last wild element is mastered now
But its revenge has taken our old world,
And man must face with awe upon his brow
Life underground, an Adam twice out-hurled.
Distance and time are words that speed can craze.
Sky is the ear and land is but the lobe.

The molten fox, flame-eared and brush ablaze,
Runs raging round the body of the globe,
Setting the air alight, the sea a-boil,
Such heat flies from him as he plunges past.
To find an earth he rips to rock the soil,
Destroying all, before the hounds at last,
Blistered and blown, can rally for the kill,
The hopeless kill, for, though the mask be won,
Sparks from its rush will fly or smoulder still
And countries catch as they go roaring on.

Sky is no longer neutral—to our shame.
Once failed the burning fox where all is ire.
Blizzards of embers and monsoons of flame!
Tropic and pole have now one climate: fire!

Didymus

I wonder that the grot was bare of birds
Though it was night when even sparrows roost;
I marvel that the moon's dry water-sheds
Did not uprear like chargers at a joust.

I ponder that the run-a-gate, small ass
Who would not weep such tears for goad or thong
Was not transported to lark-level there
So that his bray was silvered to a song.

I would have thought the oxen's noded knees
Would wear the while they lived a dust of gold
As though that stable brimmed with buttercups,
Bright, wilful flowers waylaying winter's cold.

I wonder thus and yet had I been there
I would have stood aloof as one who deems
The shepherds were but simple, loreless souls,
All lightning-dazed and duped by common dreams.

And had I followed when the Magi came,
Clinking with gold and smelling like a pine,
I would have said a cud of stars could be
More heady than their daisy-stems to kine.

For any native in the air of faith,
Where will to instinct yields the empery,
Believes as quickly as an ant can breathe,
But aliens need the thirty years and three.

It takes an Easter to convince my kind;
I am like him who till his hand explored
The gaping spike-holes in His offered feet
Still shook his head against a risen Lord.

275

VIRGINIA EARLE

Night Concert

We come to music for defense
who come in guilt and need,
imploring through the stricken sense
atonement for old violence—
for blood we shed and bleed.

No stars, no incarnations rise,
no kings or shepherds pass,
no tree is notched for sacrifice;
the night lies, and the music lies
over our sprawl on grass

mourning the helpless sword, the shut
gate, and the ruined ground . . .
but high the ripe unbitten fruit
hangs in an otherwise of flute,
in pure unfallen sound.

Receive, Beloved

Below this music, grave and slow,
The under-climbing shadows go,
And over deed of brass and string
Drifts unperceived the pure intent;
The ear hears only the lament
For the uncaptured perfect thing.

The deed is here. But who can tell
The heights from which it failed and fell,
The dark lost shining which it trails?
Receive, beloved, not my love
Alone, but under and above,
The height, the depth in which it fails.

RICHARD LINN EDSALL

Resurgent

I had almost grown grey before my time
With solemnness and dark-browed meditation;
A sleigh-bell was a monastery chime,
A peal of laughter was a profanation.
Now that I know your love, I have thrown away
Old age's ragged garments in the breeze;
I kick bare heels up, through the shouting day,
Far from the shade of immemorial trees.

For we are young, and youth is rich with laughter:
Above the fading of the crimson flowers,
Above the shroud of snow that follows after,
We ring forever through the deathless hours
Till we reach God, and look Him in the face,
Laughing all three at man and time and place.

NORBERT ENGELS

For an Old Man

Here is the rose you planted long ago,
And here the maple and the creeping vine,
The flowered arbor where your children played,
Your brown-eyed laughing children. Here you made
A bed of purple iris, where the slow
Dull drip of summer rain turns into wine.

And we who walk these friendly ways today,
Who, hand in hand, breathe of an old romance,
Pause for a moment at the half-closed door
Where you're asleep, and wonder how the score
Of love shall be returned with memory
When death's dark angel holds you at her lance.

JOHN FANDEL

The Pulse of Darkness

At first I feared the color of the dark.
The midnight spectrum sealed the open eye.
The zero vision trembled to remark
Nothing at all but nothing in the sky.

Nothing but nothing starred the density.
I stood perhaps upon the world. Perhaps.
I held my hand like hope in front of me.
I could not see my hand. Dark lay the maps

Of darkness. Whether I looked ahead, or turned
To look at every direction of the place,
Only a similar pulse of darkness burned,
Blurred the usual features of my face.

Time was an endless weather. Dark. I thought
I must be standing on the time of rock,
The wrecks of time. The air, a timeless taut
Stillness, was darkness, darkness air. So stock

Stern turned nothing but a motion of
My breath; my least of breathing testified
In core and center of that darkness: Love.
The darkness was the light where darkness died.

A Synonym for God

My flesh is out of fashion for eternity,
Beggar of limited time, for coffin fit;
An anxious soul strives in an image of dust:
The prayer of God's breath must rescue it.

As patiently as life stirs in myself,
Dresses the ultimate skeleton I am,
More beautiful with impatience the soul beats
Double-beats to my heart's dithyramb.

The soul would flee to light as my shadow flies
To a haven of darkness, wonderfully convulse
With the sudden Forever, deep as far as skies,
As lost as shine in fire, as pulse in pulse.

278

ROBERT FARREN

What I Have

Another might have spared your pride
the parasite of indigence,
the living on your eyes' light
upon your fingers' diligence:

And so made practical your rare
wit for apparelling a house
in a disposed and patterned grace.
Now, lacking purse, your gift lacks use.

But I, being born inheritor
of wit no pinchèd purse can bind
unto high ghosts one servitor,
perpetuate engendering mind.

In one more flesh enchalicèd
it spends the purse of living breath
and only such high-habited
house as your heart conspires to deck.

From rooms that lack the barest lath
I will attract your taunted glance,
house in your rich-appointed heart
my wit's poor sticks of elegance.

The Mason

Nothing older than stone but the soil and the sea and the sky.
Nothing stronger than stone but water and air and fire.
Nothing worthier than stone but the harpstring, the word and
    the tree.
Nothing humbler or stubborner than stone—whatever it be!

Stone is the bone of the world, under moor, under loam,
under ocean and churchyard-corruption of buried bone;
floor of the mountain, pound of the ocean, the world's cord.
God's creature, stone, that once was the vault of its Lord.
God gave me stone to know for a womb with child,
the time of delivery come but waiting the knife:

279

I free the stone-born glory into the air,
rounded and grooved and edged and grained and rare.
I have mastered the grain, the make, the temper of stone,
fingering it and considering, touching with hand and with soul,
quarrying it out of the course, piercing and severing it,
with a chirp of meeting metals like a bird's chirp.

Basalt I know—bottle-green still pools of stone
harder than hawk's beak, shark's tooth or tusk of the boar;
basalt—the glass-stone, stone without pore or wart;
causeway stone stepped across Moyle-fjord in the north.

Granite I know—dust-pearl with silver eyes—
that moulds domed hills, with snow, rain, wind and time.
Marble—the multiple-tinted—the satin-flesh—
daughter of the King of white Greece in the lands of the west.

Dark flint I know with the feel of a fox's tongue,
the unconsumed cold carrier of fire its young,
stone of hairedges and thornpoints, the dagger stone,
spearstone, swordstone, hatchet-stone, hearth-gilly stone.

O Christ, the stone which the builders rejected
and which is become the head of the corner,
part me from them the stone shall grind when it fall;
leave me not a stone in thine enemies' hand!

Una Bhan

[Adapted from the Gaelic]

'Tis Una has hair looped and twisty like horns of the kine;
Her two eyes cup quiet like dew and drown fire like wine;
Her arms sweep out white, as the salmon leap light in the sun.
O my salt sea of grief! That her life and my life were one.

In what summer bloomed whin that could dim the gold floss of
    her hair?
What wave, what swan-pinion laved wan as her white throat
    bare?
What strings upon streams ever tingled blood more than the
    breath
Of her mouth that has troubled, will trouble my birth and my
    death?

I sought west to Erris, and east to the bawns of Meath;
I never saw maid for my love like my maid of the heath;

I never saw star without fault and alone in its light
But her beauty outstarred, putting glory on roads of night.

O Una, 'tis you made my mind like a trembling sod:
'Tis you that have leaped between my spirit and God:
O Una, *a rún*, looped, twisty maze-head of curls
Had my eyes but lacked light when we met where the water
  whirls.

MAURICE C. FIELDS

How Long till April?

How long till April? I have asked my heart;
endlessly grim winter triumphs here;
no crocus blossom springs, no songsters start
re-echoed melody through wine-bright air.
Yearningly my gaze has searched the sky,
reaving the gleaming hieroglyphs of stars,
and found the chill-blue palimpsest to lie
shattered by signs of planetary wars . . .

Heart—we must magic springtime of our own,
kindling love's silver flame within the breast—
in phoenix-wise consumed; yet gain a crown
nimbused in fragrance as from roses pressed:
magical flame, in which all Aprils dwell—
fountain to Heaven with its source in hell!

FRANCES FRIESEKE

Armor the Bud

Shy as the April weather,
I have unfolded this petal and this—
Slowly, gently, halting my breath,
Sheathing my touch, halting my eagerness
To see the bud closed tight around his manhood.
Here have I tugged a little at the leaf, trembling;
Blunted the thorn, fear in my hands
That I might break his guard—
Brittle his steel. His arms against the gathered years.

281

Around her womanhood the flower furls
The many, many petals of these hours,
And I must open one by one their silk,
Let the sun shine, and shade blow against time,
Let the rain fall and mellowness come in
Opening wide and wider near her heart,
The leaves that blush, the perfume shy and sweet.
But in the night, walking where moonbeams fall
Across white gardens of their childish sleep,
I think how soon, how soon the hour will shine
When I shall seize their blossoms to my heart
And desperately try to furl the time,
To close the flower, bud the opened breast,
Armor the bud with my own bones, my flesh,
And guard them from the searing of the frost.

You Need Not Fear

When your lips have turned to dust, and your hands
Rest in the quietude of death,
Light as a petal in the sun and still
As moonbeams in the summer's breath,
You will not need me any more.
You will not need a word or listening smile
To wing your words and make them soar
As swift and high as birds that breast the dawn.
You will not need me any more.

You must not fear the loneliness of sleep;
No, nor the ending of the years,
For, robed in peace, your soul may come to me,
Joyous, yet pitying my tears.
There is no solitude in death;
Only the living know dark loneliness—
The living, to whom years bequeath
Remembered happiness, in winter dusk.
There is no solitude in death.

JAMES GALLAGHER

As Always

Honor invoked, no man may save his hide
By love's most territorial embrace;
Flesh is too frail to ever circumscribe
One castle from the utter human race.
Though he may tense to her with quickening breath
Swearing his love enough, where there is love,
No wall of rosy skin can wall out death
Striking without, within, below, above.

As armored knights and legendary gods
Time's citizen must kiss his love and go,
Newly embattled against scientific odds,
Himself inadequate to stop the blow.
Yet as in other wars, where each man falls
A weeping woman crumbles with the walls.

Love's Growing Pains

He wears a tattered coat of dreams
   With very careless art,
Threadbare and bursting at the seams
   From largeness of the heart.

He patches up each ragged hole
   Before it's seen by men;
But soon the growing of his soul
   Is pushing through again.

JAMES J. GALVIN, C. SS. R.

Spanish Alleluja

Sweet Risen Christ! They shall not gag our song,
They shall not, though their rifles crackle halt
In every cloister-yard—though every vault
Be charred with smouldering altars, still our song
Shall gaily rise above each strident wrong
Poising triumphant over their vilest fault.

283

Nor shall we blench before their foul assault
For Thou art with us—dying with our throng!

Lord, though our squares with bleeding rivers flow
Choicer than casks of Spain's ancestral wine,
Sweet Christ, since here Thy wounds so fiercely glow
Somewhere Thy mystic limbs must whiter shine.
In far Wyoming tulips shall untwine
And drifts of daisies stir in Tokyo.

Photograph

Click, click! like an elfin musket
A camera flickered . . . and puff!
The clock was halted forever
With a pinch of enchanted stuff;
And the fields surrendered to magic,
And the surf hushed under the bluff.

And a charm was cast over Mother
Between the sea and the sky,
Sitting apron-deep in the daisies
Watching the clouds go by;
For now she shall never grow older a breath
And the daisies never shall die.

WILLIAM J. GRACE

Suspense

As tapering pines, still stately watchers
fall against the sombre moon's simplicity,
or as a leaf that, flatly graceful, frilled and pointed,
trembles in the air,
so we are poised in life—
save that in us a hope trembles unsatisfied
an aspiration that holds us quivering;
and in our virtue and nobility
we are most like to nature's vigor
held taut, tense, in carpeted lawn.

RICHARD F. GRADY, S.J.

God Wills It

Bohemond and Tancred and Raymond St. Giles
Went to the Holy Wars and saw the Greeks and Crocodiles;
They fought the Sultan's Turkomans and quarrelled on the
    spoils,
But minstrel bards, when they came home, sang legends of
    their toils.

Now, Robert of Flanders went crusading with the first,
And fought amain, but quarrelled not; and suffered wound
    and thirst:
But he was such a modest man, sans jealousy, sans pride,
That he, the bravest of them all, sans bard, sans legend, died.

LOUIS HASLEY

On Her Twenty-fifth Birthday

This is your loveliest moment; now the song
That bore your heart through all the lightsome days
And took you to this hilltop, stills along
The fringe of woodland in the distant haze.

Here as you settle for a while to rest
Girlhood has come to its bright journey's end;
Now you must fill the longings in your breast—
Your heart will bear your song as you descend.

There would be beauty too and quiet laughter
Bound in the singing strands of Love's glad tether!
Oh, brand this moment with a kiss, and, after,
Let us go lightly down the hill together.

285

DOYLE HENNESSY

And Left Me Stranded on a Hush

Once, as a lad, alone in bed,
Holding a story book I'd read,
I knew a moment of golden awe;
But I can not tell what it was I saw.

I remember only the sudden hush,
  The exultation and the glow,
Upon a wintry, windy night—
  How long ago!

But yet though I am now beyond
The touch of any fairy wand,
At times, I know not when or where,
A wind of wonder stirs my hair,

And I'm alone on unknown seas
That wash the shores of mysteries;
Or I am facing pagan hordes
With knights who fight with broken swords . . .

But soon, too soon, the vision fades,
  And Roland's sobbing horn
Quavers faintly—then is still—
  And I am left forlorn.

M. WHITCOMB HESS

First Grandchild

Our hearth has been lighted!
The new fire laid there
Waited only the sound
Of your step on the stair:

The table stands ready
Drawn up to the grate,
The wine in the jar
And the bread on the plate.

286

As the match to the firewood
So, knowing you're come,
My heart catches fire too:
O, Child, welcome home!

The vine's vintaged sweetness,
The bread of Love's yeast
And a fire freshly kindled
Are ours at the feast.

The Mirror

O not by Phidias' art alone
Was shaped the unresisting stone!
When marble or the poet's word
Gives a dream birth, lets song be heard,
Be sure the image is but part
Of beauty mirrored in the heart . . .

Within blind Homer's Odyssey
Shine cities he could never see.

DANIEL WHITEHEAD HICKY

Escape

Some day there would be an escape, she knew;
Escape from endless toil of sun to sun,
Escape from lonely twilights cold and blue,
From pain and strife and hunger . . . every one!
And so her fingers moved unceasingly
About the old, old house, and candles' gleam
Fell golden on her aging brow, as she
Moved lightly as the shadow of a dream.

And neighbors now can hear outside their door
When nights are silent, and they lie awake,
Familiar feet, a voice stilled long before,
And they can hear the limbs of poplars shake
With falling leaves that bear the summer's rust . . .
Remembering the freedom of the dust.

HELEN WALKER [HOMAN]

Rain at Night

Tears, long-stayed, that well
    From silent, ceaseless pain,
Slow and heavy drops—
    Are like the midnight rain.

Is it that the stars
    Have bent their heads to weep,
Now that wounded earth
    Is deaf and blind in sleep?

DANIEL J. HONAN

Dostoievsky to a Young Communist

I know. You cannot keep your passion hid;
Nor fuel of it, no, nor whither bent;
Impatience, passion; object, to be rid
Of every pain; and fuel, discontent.
Some simply call you schemer, but I say
No schemer anywhere but out of dreamer.
Fantastical compassioner of clay,
Too passionate to be a simple schemer,
This lesson for you: God has other ways;
Jerusalem you shall not build below;
And suffering is good, and crazy days
Await Jehosophat's revolving show.
You strain in vain back to the sentried sill:
The angel stirs: the sword is flaming still.

Apocalyptic visionary, you
Who stand with dreadful dreaming in your eyes,
You, fed on fume of phantasy and lies,
Shouldering off the terrible and true;
I know your secret. There are not a few
Whose impudent impatience would despise
Slow excellence of Providence; whom skies
Have sullen-fretted. And they must break, make new.
Oh, Babel's bump is beaten down, and all
Man's lowliness, and penury, and rue
Are purposeful, nay good. And all the gall

With vinegar inmixed which you outspew
You'll drink at length. And the rod's stinging fall
You will not kiss, at last shall stab you through.

JOSEPH G. E. HOPKINS

Variations on a Theme

Little Jack Horner
Sat in a corner
Eating a Christmas pie;
He put in his thumb
And pulled out a plum
And said, "What a good boy am I!"

T. S. ELIOT:

Horner, aroused, looks up again,
But it is quiet in the street;
Only the dripping of the rain
Like treading of agnostic feet

Intrudes upon his sallow mood.
He bares his teeth and bends his head
And gets to work upon the food.
But where are the unanswering dead?

The Yuletide pie he rends apart
And finds a plum within the crust,
Dark, dead and rotten to the heart.
Such is the price of simple trust.

Horner has risen from his place
As did Achilles, bold and young,
To meet the heroes, face to face.
Horner goes out, unwept, unsung.

WILLIAM WORDSWORTH:

I marvelled how a little child
So hardly drew its breath
And did not speak and never smiled
But looked as if on Death.

289

I closer looked and then espied
A pie, or what remained;
The most of it was stowed inside.
The child and I were pained.

"Alas, my child," I said, "a shame
"It is to gorge and stuff.
"And have you parents and a name,
"And don't you eat enough?"

The suffering child looked up and said,
"My name is Jackie Horner,
"My mother washes for our bread;
"I live around the corner.

"Granted I gorged upon this pie:
"I see but little food.
"The system is to blame, not I;
"At bottom I am good."

Just as my mind had clarified
This deeply moral question,
He fell upon the stones and died,
Happy, of indigestion.

JOHN DRYDEN:

Horner it was who sought the corner's nook
And conned a pie as closely as a book;
No common pie that kitchen-clowns might bake
Or scullions discourse on or boors partake,
But pie of Yule contrived in cunning mould
By men of art with execution bold:
Such pie as did the proud Dardanian taste
When first he glittered at the Punic feast,
Such princely pie as might a king inspire
To eat with joy and graciously admire.
Horner it was whose short, plebeian thumb
Excised the crust and plundered out a plum;
Horner, whose boast of his own excellence
Rang hollow and was void of evidence;
Horner, whose slow, ambiguous smile betrayed
Inner contention and a mind dismayed.

SOI DISANT LIBERAL:

Watch
the slow, curling agony, the abysm
of the exploited stomach, the pain
of instinct deprived. Now comes
the passionate surge, the surfeit,
the stomach pump, too late, too late,
and then Death.

Horner, you were my brother!
You too knew the snickering lash of the oppressor,
the great want, the unfulfillment.
How many times have we shared the limp herring
in the dark evening after a day of suffering?
You were strong with me when we marched on May day . . .
Now you are gone, Horner,
victim of appetite, slain by a pie at Christmas.

Rise up, comrades, to fill the shoes of our brother, Horner.
He is dead now. He will not need them any more.

For a Child Who Died

High on a shelf we keep the books you had,
Their pages bright with princesses forlorn,
Bold knights, unsuccoured Roland and his horn,
Things afar off and exquisitely sad.

But in these days the dragons all are dead,
No more they menace princesses, no more
Does romance wait, all shining, at the door,
To crown with high desire a young boy's head.

Far better, then, you went before you found
The world so wan, the childish dream a lie,
And men, not paladins, but dull of eye,
Heavily stumbling on a barren round.

Death has a hollow vaunt when such as you,
Hailed homeward early, hurrying to be
A child in heaven's fields immortally,
Smile in his face and pass his portals through.

CARYLL HOUSELANDER

Mediocracy

All the young men
and all the young women
hope for serenity,
a mild prosperity,
respectability,
and a dull old-age.

They want the Sunday smell—
beef in a dead street—
six days to be bored
and one to overeat.

Poor little birds in a cage,
sitting behind the bars!
It isn't life:
it's the living wage
and the night without the stars.

JOSEPHINE JACOBSEN

Listen, David!

Listen, David! brighter than a leopard,
Brighter than a dandelion, whistling through a stem,
Moving through the morning—harper, fighter, shepherd—
With the silly, woolly sheep, a-crop at Bethlehem.

You were a singer, David; listen!
You stood up at morning when the day blew fair
And the light south wind made the wet grass glisten,
Tooth-torn grass in the great bright air.

Spattered by advice, you burned like a rebel
And you ripped off your armor, unused to such;
Fighter, listen—you found a pebble
In the cold brook water, smooth to your touch.

David! We have fighters, but the body left dying
Is our tiny twin, not the hulk the heart dreads.
We have singers, David! sighing, sighing,
On puce-colored sofas they shake their heads.

David, David, kindle our thin fingers
To snare the giant and wake the golden string,
Quick, before we lose you—quick, while still lingers
The echo of you, David, harper, fighter, king!

SEAN JENNETT

The Island

This island is the world's end. Beyond
the wide Atlantic drives its thunderous tides
backwards and forwards, beating on the land
time out of mind, a hammer on the heart,
and the storms of the west race from the huge
infinity of sea, gathering anger,
and split their bellies and their fists of rage
against the island's shattered, silent mountain.

The puffins and the rabbits own the land
and the gull and the circling ravenous eagle
and the seals bark on the edge of the sound
between the black rocks where the sea beats.
Where man trod once and wore the hard earth bare
the green illimitable grass
creeps back, over the garden and the gear
that fished the sea and farmed the ungenerous soil.

A lizard by a loosened door
peers into an abandoned room,
twisting his nostrils to the mummied air
that bore the shape of words, a cradle tale,
or some young girl's fresh, careless, idle song:
the sea wind and the subtle rain
break down all things at last, even the strong
stone of the wall, and the stubborn heart.

And yet they loved this island. Its hard rock
became their bone, its meagre earth their flesh,
the sea their tide of blood; and in the black
night they turned its sullenness to song.
The dancing foot that stirred the scattered sand
is quiet now or heavy overseas
and the singing voice has only songs that wound
with bitterness. The land is dead.

293

A. E. JOHNSON

Return of the Prodigal

Now he was coming voluntary home
Before the padfoot Death could run him in;
And this, to his happy heart, was the whole tome
Of comedy, and in itself divine:
Miraculously his drink-illumined eyes
Had seen the blessed wafer in the husk,
And he had been God-readied in the sties,
Had lit the love-star by his self-made dusk.

There was a tuneful chuckle in his breast
Carilloning his heart. Now any time,
Even when his soul was most distrest,
He need but listen to this merry chime—
That God employed (He has quaint deputies)
O Lord!—a pig to grunt where Heaven lies!

GEOFFREY JOHNSON

The Appian Way

It seems that Rome through the long roars of war
Climbed to her culmination like a wave
And broke to greatest purpose, unaware,
On the still country of the Catacombs.

It seems it was divine pre-ordinance
That let her boast through centuried certitude,
"The stars alone are limits of my power,"
Just to bequeath a narrow road that runs
Under its grave-browed heavens and on forever
Between these monumental cypresses,
Umbrella pines and fragments of hewn stone
Inscribed with legends of departed glories.

This was her ultimate conquest, and undreamed,
This abdication of her sovereignty
For self-effacement, the most dominant
Of all dominion, and most hard to learn:
This narrow road, the map says, runs to Naples;
This narrow road, the heart knows, runs unbroken
Through every age and kingdom and beyond,

With its own silence wonderfully woven
Neither of chariot echoes nor ghostly footfalls
Of mercenary legionaries, but the slow
Tired and triumphant sounds of martyr-sandals,
Murmurs of master-spirits catching their breath
At the far towers that crowned the seven hills,
And towers beyond them in the sunset fire.

HERBERT A. KENNY

Pleasure Is Too Surely Found

Pleasure is too surely found today.
My radio crouches in silence among my books
Waiting to pass me symphonies my father never heard.
And I can cast a ballet on the glass
Or watch a war by touching dials.
In the mnemonic network of the soul,
In the metallic miasma of the mind,
In the intangible treachery of time,
Are there no dials. For love has none. Remember
Love has none . . . but comes
Unbidden from the soil of understanding,
Is suddenly there, scented, frail and fair,
Full-possessing and irreducible,
Fast in color, frozen beyond time.
Love is a way through time, a path through woods,
A passage through the crags, a sandbar under tides,
A corridor, a channel, an eternity.
Yes, love is time's dial. But love has no dials.
And pleasure is too surely found today.

THOMAS MICHAEL KETTLE

To My Daughter Betty

In wiser days, my darling rosebud, blown
To beauty proud as was your mother's prime,
In that desired, delayed, incredible time,
You'll ask why I abandoned you, my own,
And the dear heart that was your baby throne,

295

To dice with death. And, oh! they'll give you rhyme
And reason: some will call the thing sublime,
And some decry it in a knowing tone.
So here, while the mad guns curse overhead,
And tired men sigh with mud for couch and floor,
Know that we fools, now with the foolish dead,
Died not for flag, nor king, nor emperor—
But for a dream, born in a herdsman's shed,
And for the secret Scripture of the poor.

ALINE KILMER

Olim Meminisse Juvabit

Sometime it may be pleasing to remember
  The curls about your brow,
To talk about your eyes, your smile, your dearness,
  But it is anguish now.

Often I feel that I must speak and tell them
  Of all your golden ways,
How all the words you ever spoke were happy,
  Joy-filled your laughing days.

But though I miss you every empty moment
  Of all my longing years,
How can I speak about your thrilling beauty
  When all my thoughts are tears?

Sometime it may be pleasing to remember
  The curls about your brow,
The way you turned your head, your hands, your laughter,
  But oh, not now, not now!

I Shall Not Be Afraid

I shall not be afraid any more,
  Either by night or day;
What would it profit me to be afraid
  With you away?

Now I am brave. In the dark night alone,
  All through the house I go,
Locking the doors and making windows fast
  When sharp winds blow.

For there is only sorrow in my heart,
  There is no room for fear.
But how I wish I were afraid again,
  My dear, my dear!

JOYCE KILMER

Main Street

I like to look at the blossomy track of the moon upon the sea,
But it isn't half so fine a sight as Main Street used to be
When it all was covered over with a couple of feet of snow,
And over the crisp and radiant road the ringing sleighs would
    go.

Now, Main Street bordered with autumn leaves, it was a
    pleasant thing,
And its gutters were gay with dandelions early in the Spring;
I like to think of it white with frost or dusty in the heat,
Because I think it is humaner than any other street.

A city street that is busy and wide is ground by a thousand
    wheels,
And a burden of traffic on its breast is all it ever feels:
It is dully conscious of weight and speed and of work that
    never ends,
But it cannot be human like Main Street, and recognize its
    friends.

There were only about a hundred teams on Main Street in a
    day,
And twenty or thirty people, I guess, and some children out
    to play.
And there wasn't a wagon or buggy, or a man or a girl or boy
That Main Street didn't remember, and somehow seem to
    enjoy.

The truck and the motor and trolley car and the elevated train
They make the weary city street reverberate with pain:
But there is yet an echo left deep down within my heart
Of the music the Main Street cobblestones made beneath a
    butcher's cart.

God be thanked for the Milky Way that runs across the sky,
That's the path that my feet would tread whenever I have to
    die.

297

Some folks call it a Silver Sword, and some a Pearly Crown,
But the only thing I think it is, is Main Street, Heaven-
town.

A Blue Valentine

[For Aline]

Monsignore,
Right Reverend Bishop Valentinus,
Sometime of Interamna, which is called Ferni,
Now of the delightful Court of Heaven,
I respectfully salute you,
I genuflect
And I kiss your episcopal ring.
It is not, Monsignore,
The fragrant memory of your holy life,
Nor that of your shining and joyous martyrdom,
Which causes me now to address you.
But since this is your august festival, Monsignore,
It seems appropriate to me to state
According to a venerable and agreeable custom,
That I love a beautiful lady.
Her eyes, Monsignore,
Are so blue that they put lovely little blue reflections
On everything that she looks at,
Such as a wall
Or the moon
Or my heart.

It is like the light coming through blue stained glass,
Yet not quite like it,
For the blueness is not transparent,
Only translucent.
Her soul's light shines through,
But her soul cannot be seen.
It is something elusive, whimsical, tender, wanton, infantile,
   wise
And noble.
She wears, Monsignore, a blue garment,
Made in the manner of the Japanese.
It is very blue—
I think that her eyes have made it more blue,
Sweetly staining it
As the pressure of her body has graciously given it form.
Loving her, Monsignore,
I love all her attributes;

But I believe
That even if I did not love her
I would love the blueness of her eyes,
And her blue garment, made in the manner of the Japanese.

Monsignore,
I have never before troubled you with a request.
The saints whose ears I chiefly worry with my pleas are the
    most exquisite and maternal Brigid,
Gallant Saint Stephen, who puts fire in my blood,
    and your brother bishop, my patron,
The generous and jovial Saint Nicholas of Bari.
But, of your courtesy, Monsignore,
Do me this favor:
When you this morning make your way
To the Ivory Throne that bursts into bloom with roses because
    of her who sits upon it,
When you come to pay your devoir to Our Lady,
I beg you, say to her:
"Madame, a poor poet, one of your singing servants yet on
    earth,
Has asked me to say that at this moment he is especially grate-
    ful to you
For wearing a blue gown."

The Singing Girl

There was a little maiden
    In blue and silver drest,
She sang to God in Heaven
    And God within her breast.

It flooded me with pleasure,
    It pierced me like a sword,
When this young maiden sang: "My soul
    Doth magnify the Lord."

The stars sing all together
    And hear the angels sing,
But they said they had never heard
    So beautiful a thing.

Saint Mary and Saint Joseph,
    And Saint Elizabeth,
Pray for us poets now
    And at the hour of death.

Trees

I think that I shall never see
A poem lovely as a tree.

A tree whose hungry mouth is prest
Against the earth's sweet flowing breast;

A tree that looks at God all day,
And lifts her leafy arms to pray;

A tree that may in Summer wear
A nest of robins in her hair;

Upon whose bosom snow has lain;
Who intimately lives with rain.

Poems are made by fools like me,
But only God can make a tree.

KENTON KILMER

Dawn

Come and smile into my eyes—
    I can ask no more.
Let me, while the starlight dies,
    Silently adore.

I can speak no word today;
    Ask no word of you—
Silently we go our way
    Through the sparkling dew.

Though your silence be as cold
    And as sad as mine,
Place it in the sunlight's gold;
    Let me see it shine.

CLAUDE F. KOCH

Words for Artificers

Friends of my heart: O worker at the frieze,
Meticulous carver in rare ivories,
Painter of barren bays and smoky lone
Last bitten fences in the swamp's gray teeth—
Commemorate our losses in your peace.
Though spirit flow like water over stone
And wear the flesh and bone it plays upon,
Conspire to hold it as a coastwise light
Is held intransigent against the night
And strangely fashion on your groping part
The bright and flowing elegy of art
For eyes that follow still the druid white
Into the brooding shadows of cold stone;
Though art is elegy and comes to breath
When time has settled action into death—
But mirror what the ages brood upon
And death shall stand denied while you alone
Transfigure the fleet spirit's dwelling place
Whose tenant plots too soon his scarred release;
Inform the wayward breath with certain speech—
Commemorate our losses in your peace.

MARY KOLARS

If This Old Place

If this old place had held no grief before
No wild, unchildish woe wept out alone,
Where dirt turns into sand here by the shore
And bushes droop above the marking stone;
If memory were not made of things untender,
Could memory call the heart out of my breast?
O sorrow of a child, O dark befriender
By whom my lost comes back, my repossessed!

My far-off golden laughter has no reaping,
My far-off joy has not held these in keeping—
The rock, the road beside the sandy shore;
But grief, once sown, can split the granite portal;
Youth's moment, incorruptible, immortal,
Is rendered back to me forevermore.

301

PAULA KURTH

Association Copy

To think that Keats once held this volume dear,
And pondered it on many a lonely night.
Perhaps, beside Tom's bed with lowered light,
It made his vigil not so hard to bear,
The while he read with half-averted ear
And head a little toward the piteous sight
Of his young brother sleeping, lest he might
Lift weary eyelids and not find him near.

Ah, Keats, who loved to summon a remote
And favorite poet back to life, and took
Delight in things he used, would understand
This sudden pain, this catching at the throat,
And know the reason, as I hold this book,
Why warm, unbidden tears fall on my hand.

RAYMOND E. F. LARSSON

Antique Carved Figures

I do not know what
dance:
the swirled
ribbons and the scarves of marble,
the spent, upraised carved hands
curved to say "Birds
upsprung and flying";
heads
bent, as ones' who say:
"This way
the flowers
went."
I do not know what
dance. What step
follows?
(What follows this leaf
drift and this
grief?)
"Dancers: what step
follows
for lead feet?"

CLIFFORD J. LAUBE

Dream across the Dark

Man rives the granite from its ledge
    And wakes the marble from its sleep
Because there is an ancient pledge
    That he is bound to keep.

Some word more subtle than his will,
    Some dream across a dark abyss,
Bids him to make of every hill
    A cold acropolis.

Where cypresses outshade the dark
    With secrets they will never tell,
Agate and alabaster mark
    His hope beyond farewell.

He hears the living plea, and yet
    Upon a stone his tears are shed.
Hearts pulsing warm he may forget
    But not the silent dead.

Last Rally

Be rootfast. Never yield
    What rightly is your own:
Your altar, home and field,
    Your fruit of blood and bone.

Ever the vandal crew
    Waits, ready to despoil
Your founded dream, your due,
    The treasure of your toil.

Nor have the Caesars died.
    Their brutal lictor-rods
Menace on every side
    Your equity—and God's.

So freedom's final claim
    Can only be appealed
To you who guard her flame
    And die, but never yield.

The Bees of Christ

There is a honey none shall taste
Save those upon whose brow is traced
In living script the seal and sign
Of Christ, the Victim, Rose and Vine.

This is the honey nectared clear
From Rose-leaves by a Roman spear
Laid open, and from Rosebuds more
On that same stem, red nail-marks four.

Thither the Christ-bees early came.
Hardly the Resurrection-flame
Had paled when, power-girt and flushed
With Pentecost, they Roseward rushed.

There such a concentrate they cupped
As that on which the Twelve had supped;
And later, on the pagan stone,
Left scarlet honey of their own.

Ages! Another Nero strives
To filch the honey from these hives;
But here and elsewhere there is stored
Safely the honey of the Lord.

FRANCIS LEDWIDGE

Had I a Golden Pound

Had I a golden pound to spend,
My love should mend and sew no more.
And I would buy her a little quern,
Easy to turn on the kitchen floor.

And for her windows curtains white,
With birds in flight and flowers in bloom,
To face with pride the road to town,
And mellow down her sunlit room.

And with the silver change we'd prove
The Truth of Love to life's own end,
With hearts the years could but embolden,
Had I a golden pound to spend.

DOMINIC BEVAN WYNDHAM LEWIS

Ballade of the Harrowing of Hell

Saint Michael of the Flaming Sword,
Provost of Paradise, dear Knight,
High Seneschal of Heaven, Lord
Of legions massing for the Fight—
Monseigneur, on its way last night
Aspersing terror like a dew
There passed in strong decisive flight
The soul of Lady Barbecue.

Where now is Lucifer, who soared
So high for pride in Hell's despite?
And swaggering Moloch, and the horde
Of Belial? O the dismal plight!
Firm, but quite freezingly polite,
What Voice observes that This Is New?
With disapproving lips pressed tight . . .
The soul of Lady Barbecue.

Array! Array! The Call is roared,
In vain the Enemy, as white
As goat's milk curdling in a gourd,
Strives to conceal his deathly fright;
The Voice that brusquely sets him right
Is known and feared from Staines to Kew!
Who told the Devil he was trite?
The soul of Lady Barbecue.

ENVOI

Prince, in your golden armour dight,
What rumblings roll Hell's arches through?
Cordite? T.N.T.? Dynamite? . . .
The soul of Lady Barbecue.

305

JOHN W. LYNCH

The Crucifixion

He is alive with pain: His body lifts
And turns and quivers as the lightning streaks
Again, and iron thunder cracks and breaks
And shatters in the dark beneath His blood
Until the tremors in His flesh are stopped,
And breathing, He discovers He is vised.
His body forms a frame to hold a frame;
He is a Man made one with blunted beams! . . .
Their voices rise to Him from distant pits.
They are like echoes of an ended world
He once had known where men with hands and feet
Could move among contentions and be brave
With gesture. He could hear them, feel their stride
And strut along the ground, receive their scorn,
Their laughter, know that they were tall and bold
And beckoning to Him that He come down,
Come down and be a Man again in whole,
Unfastened body that will need a robe
And pathway to the pardons of the world.

"Father, forgive them, for they know not what they do."

The blood swelled sickly in His mouth, and breath
Was ended, and His heart was all he heard.
Somewhere, as a bird might sing to Him,
Above Him, level to His hair, so near
He need not search, nor move, nor seek for space
Of quiet in the sounding of His blood,
He hears a voice that begs last royal gift
Of brief remembering. He cannot see,
And wrenching now athwart the rigid wood,
His head uplifted, pulling at the nails,
He cannot reach least moment of relief
That He may bring to eyes that seek His own.
They are two faces in the sun, so fixed
Against the posts they must stare outward only,
Separate, and must declare their loves
In quick companionship of lonely words.

306

"This day thou shalt be with me in Paradise."

The light is bronze against Him in a sheet
Of stilled, unblinking time that does not move,
Nor yield, nor cease until a shimmering
Like golden curtains comes, and looking down,
He finds that time has folded to a long,
Bright, gleaming coronal, and she is there.
He does not look away, He watches her,
And the light that was a crown about her, breaks,
Increases, brightens, and becomes a path
Where she is mounting, mounting up to Him,
Not for comfort, not for any kiss
Of soothing, not to lessen Him nor ask
His hands refuse these nails for Infancy:
Not to soften, not unloose the years!
He seeks her here and in her heart He finds
Too deep a silence for the need of tears,
For new Announcement bleeds in her, so old
It is Gethsemani, and Nazareth,
Fused and sealed within a single will
That still is crying: *"This be done to me."*

"Woman, behold thy Son."

The dark was like a thin, descending shroud
Of cold that closed around the world and left
Him shivering beneath an ashen sun.

The wind was chill upon Him, stirred His hair
In faint and lonely movement, and the dust
That lay along the barren rocks had raised
And sifted softly when the wind had gone.
He was alone: and in His hands the nails
Were cinders of a fire once had flamed
And reddened in His blood, but now had dulled
To crusting of a spread, accustomed pain,
Without a plan. He had wearied of His crown;
His head that had been bowed upon His breast
Tossed upward in a search for any friend,
To find around Him blackness and the deep,
Unstarred abysses where creation's Word
Has hung no light or mercy to the blank
Rejections of a worse than primal dark.

The wind that knifed across His shivered soul
Came cutting from the frozen lids of Hell. . . .

"My God, my God, why hast Thou forsaken me?"

Thereafter, time on Him became a slow,
Eventless draining and His body sagged
And ebbed and whitened in the drip of long,
Increasing silences that breathed and soaked
And mingled on His limbs until the flow
Pulled down from Him all semblance to a Man,
To make Him but a Wound that hung from nails.

He does not move nor murmur to the dark,
And now is gone beyond His search or hope
For friends who might, in grieving, come to Him;
His eyes lie closed, but when His hand had strained
Against the stake, and helpless, tried to brush
The dried and stiffened cavern of His mouth,
He whispered, and they heard His human need.

"I thirst."

A sponge upon a reed was thrust to Him,
And He who gave good wine had tasted sharp,
Astringent vinegars that were the last
Of favors that the earth could give to Him.

He wakened; He was tall again and taut
Against the throning of His cross; His head
Was crowned, and on Him majesty returned.
He drank the air and as a Man who sees
Far kingdoms over continents beyond
The sun, He traces with His eyes the dim
Receding circles of the world. He feels
The freedom of His hands, the swing, the lope
And striding of His feet; He feels His heart
Within Him beating to the endless stroke
Of Infinite, and swelling to subdue
The vast dimensions of forgotten time.
He stands, He towers, He is Adam come
Again to the ancient garden: He is man
And woman, He is Paul and Magdalen,
The martyrs, housewives, sinners, and the saints.

And then His love is falling on the hills,
The roads, the little sea that had been dear.
He touches to the mountains where He spoke
His prayer, and He remembers Bread. His hands
Enclose again the smiling of a child.

They test the tumult of the fish in nets.
He hears the echoed word He said to John
And Martha: Peter keeps command against
The years. The cot and table that He knew
At Nazareth are not afar from Him.
And He remembers Joseph and the straw.

Then breath is great within Him. He is tall
And upward from His cross His voice ascends
To break confining spaces of the stars
And thrust His triumph past the end of stars.

"It is finished!"

His head is sinking: peace is on His brow.

"Father, into Thy hands I commend my spirit."

This sterile wood He carried to the hill
Has burgeoned with His meaning, and the Tree
Of good and evil, standing in all storm
And contradiction, waits the endless Spring.

JAMES H. McCABE

On the Reported New Outbreak of Christianity

Here's Christianity again!
And vouched for by the foremost men!
That comical, gimcrack, haunted roost,
Where even a child could scare the ghost,
Now haunted by the truly great,
Booming like oil and armor-plate!
(The poor are always two years late.)

Where have we come? And isn't this
Reaction? Back to Genesis?
What can we trust, who saw it plain
That Abel's spite invented Cain,
And cheered the laboratory table
Where nitrogen disposed of Abel?

Revise we must; somehow unlearn
The factual bent, the liberal turn.
Farewell the run-down universe
(O splendid dream) for good or worse!
Behold who come to Christianize
With one-armed texts and homilies:
The reconditioned Atheist,
The second-sighted Bigamist,
The royally bred Adulteress,
The never really doubting Press,
The Skeptic, cleansed of all his grief,
The Banker, radiant with belief.
The Gun-maker and the Second Thief!

O hark the strong regenerate choir,
Tangled these years amidst the briar,
They'll kill with prayer, who never prayed
Before the all-murdering guns were laid,
And cheer on to a rich increase
The inheritors of Final Peace.
Swift now, and rush to Grace ahead!
Sweet mystery of the anointing lead!
Salute our Phoenix, from the dead!

LEONARD McCARTHY, S.J.

Holy Thursday

Spelling with love the Word among the flowers
I think how soon the Repository topples down;
And then where will we wander, whose the towers
To be watchmen of, and where the town?
Think a little; though it's three o'clock
All is not well tonight, something is loose;
Behind the candelabra struts the cock.
He screams. The lilies twist, become our noose.

No one is here. The door is blowing wide
Yet no Elias comes to trim the lamp,
Set right the flowers, call the hurrying bride;
Now the cross falls down, decayed and damp,
A lonely bauble from the Thursday fete;
I hold the sweetening wood, the sweeter weight.

Breviary on the Subway

More out of dearest duty now than joy
I sing the psalms of David on the train;
"Do not remember us when we were boys"—
What monstrous Arks we dance before again,

Crying, This false and cooling air will heal;
Crying, Here is the subway to the moon.
"As the hart does pant for living waters' feel"—
Our rush-hour hearts bleed even now at noon.

One of the tunnel children squirms and squeals,
Asking her mother do I read or pray;
Her answer lost amid the pins and wheels
Of station-lights. All out, all out, we say
And rush for asphalt pasture, Park St., Park.

Saul or David, hold us from the dark.

GEORGE A. McCAULIFF

The Quiet Place

I have come to the quiet place.
Dawn's slow fire washing over skies,
Warm winds circling,
Lift of air over the lake,
Leaf on leaf pushed to falling
And suddenly thy image everywhere,
In the one tideless time of peace.

Let leaves fall, grow, fall again,
Skies change in changing dawns,
Nights lonely of stars, days burned in brightness,
Water, earth and air, all things elemental,
Let them change, dissolve,
The world recede
To the edge of genesis.
Only thou, beloved, thou
Forever more fast, close as my heart.

311

DONAGH MacDONAGH

The Veterans

Strict hairshirt of circumstance wears the flesh
On delicate bones;
Years of counter and office, the warped mesh
Of social living, dropping on stones,
Wear down all that was rough and worthy
To a common denominator of dull tones.

So these, who in the sixteenth year of the century
Saw their city, a Phoenix upturned,
Settle under her ashes and bury
Hearts and brains that more frantically burned
Than the town they destroyed, have with the corrosion of time
Spent more than they earned;
And with their youth has shrunk their singular mystery
Which for one week set them in the pulse of their age,
Their spring adventure petrified in history,
A line on a page,
Betrayed into the hands of students who question
Oppressed and oppressor's rage.

Only the dead beneath their granite signatures
Are untroubled by the touch of day and day,
Only in them the first rich vision endures;
Those over clay
Retouch in memory, with sentiment relive,
April and May.

THOMAS P. McDONNELL

The Next Voice You Hear

On the porch of the three-storied flat
(And less than half of seven mountains),
Having feasted on various Heinz,
I sit alone after supper,
Idling the dial of the fingertip world.

Palaver of politicians
Thickens the purchased air,
And news flashes flock like ominous pigeons
On the roof of my unrest;

312

And I am told that life would be ruined
Without this kingly cigarette,
Or that I can find my salvation
In scented soap
And the green flowered breath of chlorophyll.

Gyrations of the dial
Spin towers and babble of words,
As vast as the piled-up thunderheads
In the sky, in the west—
Where now, just now, some light breaks through
And a bird flies far away.

And I turn down the dial
And ask: Yes? Is that You, Lord?
Is there something *You* wanted to say?

A Psalm for Moderns

I walked along the cedar grove
soft in the sacred dawn
and there beside the crystal pool
I saw the sleeping fawn;

O why do you sleep, my soul,
in the land of honey and spice,
nor drink from this clear spring
as cold as glacial ice;

I glanced upon the brimming stream
and far beyond the hills
and light went running after
and down the sparkling rills;

O why do you wait, my soul;
O come to the mountain-side;
the Hart appears across the land
in great majestic stride;

I stood alone in Lebanon
amidst the fragrant fir
and soft beside the crystal pool
I saw the fawn bestir;

Awake, rise up, my languid soul
(O fawn that seemed but sleeping);
across the hills I see the Hart
And O how lovely leaping!

313

JEAN McDOUGALL

Quarrel

I might have touched you where you lay
   Counting the long night hours away
In silence, pillowed hot and deep,
   Lying too quietly for sleep.

My tongue that struggles and is slow
   Was swift before to deal the blow,
But sudden pain could not disguise
   The sober judgment of your eyes.

I might have reached to take your hand—
   The gesture you would understand—
And failing utterance, to seek
   Your lips, the shelter of your cheek.

But dawn came up while the only talk
   In the room was made by the noisy clock
Stabbing, accusing, chattering, loud:
   Too proud, too proud, too proud, too proud.

ARTHUR MacGILLIVRAY, S.J.

Madonna of the Dons

Before the stirring of the notes at the lecture
There is the time for learning,
Bread years and water and the single lamp,
Tracing the maze of a long thread through the hemmed mind.
We find this lonely going.

Not all are twelve-year-old instructors, Lady,
Giving graduate courses on the Father.

Has the desk a future and have the vacant chairs
Voices that we hear in the evening?
Are facts like flowers, pressed dead between the pages,
And can we run our business without the blossoming vase?
We want a blackboard answer.

The snakes beneath the flowered fact, Lady,
Need the finding and the crushing out.

314

The pencilling hands we talk to this young hour
Will hold other ammunition:
Fingering a throw-flame, grasp-knife, throttle-neck, drop-
    bomb.
The copyright of birds has elapsed. Air is man's road,
And that is where you come in:

Lady, breathe down the air you dress yourself with,
Cover the words we form with flesh.

Death

The hare has only the hound to fear
    At a rustling in the brake,
But ready he is, the hare, the hare,
    When the wind strikes on the lake.

The winds are keeping the hare alert
    And the world is filled with sound,
But ready he is, the hare, the hare,
    For the hunter and the hound.

PERCY MacKAYE

Look Inland Now

                                    Look inland
Now, where the engulfing sea-mists swallow the hollies
In yonder burst of sun-glow, crimsoning
Their green thorns berry-bright—and listen, listen
From high the lark's epistle, chanting his lauds
Of heaven, to shame us sodden underlings
To emulate his trances, and pierce through
This grey veil to the blueness, ever beckoning
Above us. Hark! His vow hath no abatement
In God-forgetfulness. That word of a bird is grooved
In His great signet ring, to press in our souls
The seal of certitude, that this indeed
Is He, the living God, who cannot lie,
Uttering His love of all.

315

GLADYS McKEE

First Reader (Fifth Reading)

The final, finger-printed page is flipped,
The simple sentences at last are done,
No more need she restore a hard word skipped
By restless readers. One by growing one
Read as she listened. Now, like homing birds
Straight to her heart the little stories go,
About the dog, the cat, the ball, the words
All laced with memories that will ever flow
Whenever there is need. Time stretches tall
And years are shod in wind, but nothing pricks
This book's illusion, seven inches small,
That can restore them to quicksilver six.

First Geography

Today the world is bound in blue,
Its pages smooth, its ink is new.
It swings in this September air
Without a heartache or a care
In the schoolbag of my nine-year-old
Who soon will seek its ancient gold.
As you and I, he will explore
From the sunlit square of Grade-A Four,
The continents, the wide, wide seas
And as usual bring to these
Enough of heart and mind and scheme
To shape the things a man must dream.

Legacy

A West road for my father,
    His banjo and his pride,
His eyes as cold as blue steel,
    His heart that knew he lied.

An East road for my mother,
    Who could not bear to wait
Until a candle sputtered
    Or steps turned in the gate.

316

For me the lonely cross-road,
   The stifled song and sigh,
And a heart that never will know
   One road to travel by.

FRANCIS MAGUIRE

Sweet Land

In loving you, sweet land, we love a thing
Dearer than any acre dreamed of now.
Oh, some of us are sick for hills in spring,
And others yearn for fields they used to plow;
But, knowing these, we knew an atmosphere
Of sunlight streaming through a blossoming tree,
Of winds between the oceans, vast and clear,
That sang: sweet land, sweet land of liberty.

For what they sang is your excuse for being,
The element, my land, in which you live.
It is a climate found but ever fleeing,
A fragrant empire love nor lease can give
But subjects everywhere may serve and share.
And look: the world around us! Sniff the air!

The Bull

Beauty is gull,
And goodness hind;
But truth is a bull
Gone wild in the mind.

He tramples the corn,
The fruit, the flowers.
His eyes burn
As your heart cowers.

He murders your swan,
Your goat, your tup—
But woe to the man
Who shuts him up.

The Sin: A Definition

I saw a terrible river
Sweep from eternal space:—
Birds, the sweet trees,
Men, hills, the face
Of firmament, stars
Tumbling, and row on row
Rolled constellations
In tempest-flow.
Suns, saints, and even
My body rushed by,
Awful, silent.
And further, I
Sensed in the vision
That what seemed so
Vast merely imaged
A Fearfuller Flow.

I saw a small figure
I knew for my soul
Peer at the river,
Measure the roll,
Step importantly
Into the flood
And walk against it.
Marvel: no blood;
But the river parted
For a soul that said
"I give no glory.
No glory," it said.

Oh the flow was full
Of earth and sky
And thick with archangels
Floating by.
But against it traveled
A little head.
"I give no glory.
No glory," it said.

And Rest in a Flame

How shall we answer?
What skill, what art
Can cool to reason
This flaming heart

When all of our logic
And all our words
Are a clock's dull ticking,
The cry of birds?

What can we do
But pray, but pray?
That only. And if
It is true, as we say,

That the heart has its logic,
Then it must lead,
How rough the highway,
How slow the speed,

To the town where desire
And reason, the same,
Shall blaze in a Silence
And rest in a Flame.

People as Flowers

If for a moment only, and then ineptly,
Let us consider the people we chance to encounter
As neither lovers nor rivals. Let us consider
People as flowers,
Rare and bud-like, each with his proper fragrance,
Each with a pattern, a hue unshared by the others.
The daisies we know, of course, and then the blossoms
Of darksome powers.

But in between are the thousands and thousands of species,
The men as well as the women, the stem and stamen
Of body, surely, but also the succulent, tender
Poise of the mind,
And the spirit too, the scented not sighted. Truly

319

It is not these but the whole, the integral being
That makes the flower. And those who cannot perceive it . . .
Are they not blind?

Address to the Body

Body, if age or uppish soul
Should ever cast you down,
Know that I once was warm at home
In this my bony town.

I like my flesh. I like the singing
Girders of the bone.
I like a finger's hinges moving
Silently, alone.

I stand and reverence the heart,
The blood's long train,
The zooming of sensations flying
Up toward the brain.

Body breathing, there are times
One scarce prefers the day
When glory filters out the flesh,
Electrifies the clay.

JOSEPH R. N. MAXWELL, S.J.

The Old Bard Speaks

Like autumn winds that rustle in the leaves,
I bind my mellowed fancies into sheaves
Of studied rhymes. My happiness and fears
Strike like the muffled gongs of dying years.

Here are the dreams of vanished yesterdays
Swept down the lonely, heart-deep valley ways,
Like tumbleweed along the desert blown
By winds that keen with melancholy moan.

Here in the timid songs that I have sung,
The sounds of silenced bells that have been rung
Echo in measures sadly out of tune.
My lute is old and cracked. I must release it soon.

320

FRANCIS X. MAYNARD, O.F.M.

The Chiseler

Rebellious, he studied
  His cross of pain,
Decided at last
  It was much too plain.

With his will for a knife
  He whittled and cut,
Concessions for ease,
  Concessions for smut.

A little chip here
  That fitted too tight;
A little bit there
  To compromise right.

With a smirk on his face
  And a twist in his soul,
He found he had made
  A totem-pole!

THOMAS MERTON

Like Ilium

Is this the night the world must burn like Troy?
Is there no wise Aeneas
To look the Greek gift in its wooden teeth
Or fly the lovers of the hollow horse,
Loading his cross and sorrows
(With old Anchises) on his contrite shoulder?

Is there no priestly king
To crack the wooden wonder with his prophecy:
Does no one see the crowded sabres
Behind the lancets of those eyes?
The peace that sings like a muezzin
Upon that crenellated brow
Calls Troy to love a loaded citadel!

You who receive this idol full of pitch and matches
Yet curse Cross-branch and Calvary
Because you hate the nails and Blood,

Refuse the peace price of that saving Wood,
Go, then, be deafened by the bonzes of your animal
Jumping and barking in the marble ruin
Too loud for you to hear the unborn armor
The steel heart bumping in that great
White horse's wooden drum.

Is this the night the world must burn like Ilium?

Two States of Prayer

In wild October when the low hills lie
With open eye
And own the land like lions,
Our prayer is like the thousands in the far, forgotten stadiums,
Building its exultation like a tower of fire,
Until the marvelous woods spring to their feet
And raid the skies with their red-headed shout:
This is the way our hearts take flame
And burn us down, on pyres of prayer, with too much glory.

But when the trees have torn up all their programs,
Scattering the pathos of immense migrations to the open-
    handed winds,
Clouding and saddening the dusky valley,
Sorrow begins to bully the bare bars
Of those forsaken cages
As thought lies slaughtered in the broken doors.

But by the light of our December mornings,
Though words stand frozen in the voice's well
And all the country pumps are dumb,
Look where the landscape, like a white Cistercian,
Puts on the ample winter like a cowl
And so conceals, beneath the drifts as deep as quietude,
The ragged fences and the ravaged field.

The hills lie still, the woods their Sabbath keep.
The farms, half buried in their winter coats
Are warm as sheep.
When was there ever greater than this penitential peace
Outshining all the songs of June with radiant silences?

November analyzed our bankruptcies, but now
His observations lie knee-deep beneath our Christmas mercies,
While folded in the buried seed
The virtual summer lives and sleeps;
And every acre keeps its treasures like a kingly secret.

322

Ode to the Present Century

What heartbeats, lisping like a lizard in a broken cistern,
Tell you, my prudent citizen, that you are nearly dead?
We heard your pains revolving on the axis of a shout:
The cops and doctors view the winter of your knifelong blood.

They chart the reeling of your clockwise reason
Flying in spirals to escape philosophy,
While life's ecliptic drives you like an arrow
To the pit of pain.
And one by one your wars break up the arctic
Of your faultless logic,
And wills retreat upon themselves until the final seizure:
Your frozen understanding separates
And dies in floes.

Oh how you plot the crowflight of that cunning thief, your
    appetite,
But never see what fortunes
Turn to poison in your blood.
How have you hammered all your senses into curses,
Forever twisting in your memory
The nails of sensuality and death.
Have we not seen you stand, full-armed,
And miss the heavens with the aimless rifles of your fear?
When are you going to unclench
The whited nerve of your rapacity, you cannibal:
Or draw one breath of truth and faith,
You son of Cain?

But if you are in love with fortunes, or with forgery,
Oh, learn to mint you golden courage
With the image of all Mercy's Sovereign,
Turn all your hunger to humility and to forgiveness,
Forsake your deserts of centrifugal desire:
Then ride in peaceful circles to the depths of life,
And hide you from your burning noon-day devil
Where clean rock-water dropwise spends, and dies in rings.

Messias

Stranger, the world expected You for long days.
We were all looking at the wrong horizon.
We came out and stood with our flags
In the gates of the wrong year.

323

We wanted to believe You with banners:
Our cannons prove us wrong.

God dwelt in our town without parades,
Stood with the poor men on the river bank,
Went down into the water before the blistered Baptist.

He came out of the river without armies and without money
But walked the red roads like a conqueror.
No man starved when thousands
Sat down around Him on the land.
But His miracles were without sin,
Without demonstration, without shame.

He did not despise the wild jasmine
Or turn His eyes away
From the young almond tree,
Yet He has refused the crumpled roses
You offered Him for your own pleasure.
And by that act I'll swear that He is true.

If He had been born of our sorrow
He would have bombed the Samaritans with thunder,
Made of Jerusalem a solfatare.

Without revenge He blessed our country.
But we have praised the chastity of God
With our own rotting lilies:

Those dirty trumpets turning brown
Those wide, white mouths, painted with golden meal!
The musicians have sighed at His picture with the noise
Of circus angels.
Painters have praised Him with heresy.
We have not known You, Virgin's Son!

He is the one clean King
With weapons in His hands
Rising in the night of our defeat
Armed with a heart more burning than the sun.

Having ignored our ways, our gates,
He entered by the center of the ruined capital,
Stood like a giant in the smashed buildings,
And burned the long converging streets with the gentleness
    of His expression.

The children praised Him with the voice of orchards
And clung to Him like vines and surrounded Him like birds
While death was being destroyed.

O Emperor! When will You come again?
When will we all sit down in thousands underneath the trees?
Some who have washed their hands with their own tears
Have said: "How shall we know Him when He comes?"

He is the light by which all truth is understood,
The light inside us,
Knowing His own truth in the true world, the mountains and
   the stars.
He has locked the moon and stars in His treasury,
Can my eyes see my own eyes?
How can I seize the light that knows me from within?

But we shall trace Him by the track of His own immortal
   music,
Not count His wisdom by our own candlepower,
Yet find Him in our own mansions,
Catch Him in His own joy, and find Him in the echoes of
   His Father's feast.

J. CORSON MILLER

St. Thomas Aquinas

You said the lodestar of the mind,
Fired with energy from above,
Seeking the Triune God, will find
Him centered in the core of love.

Yes, as of old the olives bloom
In blest Ovieto this fair spring;
But you, in love's celestial room,
Forever banquet with your King.

Song for Love's Coming of Age

Sound me brass trumpets of the sun!
Unlock me moons with silver keys!
Down ways of childish ecstasies
Dear, shining ghosts of beauty run.

Beyond blue seas of sweet desire
The ruby tower of morning stands,
Where windows stir with elfin hands,
And faces touched by fairy-fire.

Far off the gongs of wonder chime,
Old, starry woodbines stir in sleep;
There souls immortal taste the deep,
Full joy of youth's green summertime.

Shake down the ripened hours,
Blow bubbled joy on wings of song!
Let Love lead in his dancing throng—
My heart's a carpet strewn with flowers.

Mad Poll

Poor mad Poll, pretty Poll
Is a girl with glass-green eyes,
Who flirts with the frogs in the village pond
And answers their croaking cries.

Had Poll been nurtured a lady—
Rigged out in a lacy dress—
The villagers all would raise their brows
And purr: "What loveliness!"

But Poll goes about in her brown, bare feet,
With her skin burned berry-brown;
So she is the butt of the village jokes,
And the talk of the town.

They say Poll's dad was a fiddler,
Stabbed dead in a sailors' brawl—
Oh what is the music in a bull-frog's throat
When the moon-drunk willows call?

For the bull-frogs are her only friends,
And they sing, as if bent on a prize,
To poor, mad Poll, to pretty Poll,
The girl with the glass-green eyes.

JOHN MAHER MURPHY

Family History

My father's father's father and he who fathered him
Were men whose last horizon was drawn forever down
A furlong in the distance where homely hills grow dim
And roads run on, disdaining a little market town.

Their hearts and heads were harnessed to acres always known,
And even death was kindly and sowed them close at hand,
Till resurrection morning asleep among their own,
Beneath the loved in living—the deep, the loamy land.

But one of them one morning just after milking-time
Saw curlews flying over beyond the boreen's bend,
And took the white road after, a long and lonely road
Past Aran and the ocean; and no one knows the end.

It's tenderly I'm folding live earth in my two fists
The way one warms a linnet struck down from winter skies.
The kinks of timeless plowing are rigid in my wrists—
Yet he, the lost, the drowned one, goes seaward in my eyes.

JOHN FREDERICK NIMS

To the Rulers

You will die and your friends with you and be forgotten.
Some day you will not matter much any more.
Only the old will remember the stormbird sweeping,
And a rumor of guns on the shore.

Only the old will remember how love was herded
Afloat dim waters sharked with the glint of death,
To learn how lead divulges the vein's warm secret
And the intimate breath.

But the young who never knew fire nor a strange bird lifting,
Her wing set snowy and cruel in a whistling sky,
The young will away to the hills for an august evening
When the pleiades fly.

The hands and the night-bright lips and more will be meeting
Till dream takes flesh and the moon is drowned in a whirl.

She will stand where we and a wasp of iron are sleeping,
Will the moon-graced girl.

And you dead and your friends with you and dim forgotten,
The world secure from hawk and the sky's hot clutch.
And still two shapes in a whirling moon on the hillside
Never you can touch.

Barrier

Out of midnight smile on me
Faces I shall never see.
Out of dreams are reaching still
Arms that I may never fill.

Should the phantom fair and white
Step into the living light,
Mind and heart and spirit's core,
I were lost forever more:

Straightway unto duty dead
I would stumble where it led,
Down the ruin of the years,
Drought of longing, rain of tears.

Thanks to God within the sky
That the walls of sleep are high,
That the rusted bolts are shot,
And the countersign forgot.

JESSIE CORRIGAN PEGIS

Stay Little Always

Stay little always, do not ever grow
Beyond the loving measure of my hand.
Already you have lost that soft pink glow
Which you brought with you to this strange new land.

Stay little always, do not turn your wide
Blue eyes on this tall world beyond your reach.
Learn not our language, it is harsh beside
The little ripples of your wordless speech.

328

This was a moment's thought, idle and fleet;
There where the bud is, soon the flower appears,
But oh, you are so little and so sweet,
Where can I hide you from the rush of years?

The Eyes of Wonder

All things are wonderful to him
    Who is but lately three;
Still guided by the seraphim,
He steps upon the earth's bright rim,
    Nor parts with heaven's key.

He walks among created things
    With unperverted sight;
And all the birds have golden wings,
And sticks and stones are made for kings
    To handle with delight.

And I, who shall see ten times three
    No longer and no more,
Am sometimes privileged to see,
To look where I shall never be,
    Behind that hidden door.

PATRICK MARY PLUNKETT

Vale

Beauty is but a passenger: she will not
Inhabit long in anybody's face.
You cannot seal her up in any case,
Or ornamental jar, or colored pot.
A little villa's cultivated plot,
The city's tailored houses, or the grace
Of trim parterre and sundial are a space
Too tight for Beauty, who will not be caught.

Goodbye Beauty! Fly away, away
To your abiding kingdom in the south.
Drink will I not, nor eat, until the day
Those ample parks I enter, and my mouth,
In the wide courts where many fountains play,
Close on abundant waters after death.

329

JESSICA POWERS

I Would Define My Love

Here on the flyleaf of the garish day,
Here at the noonday of the long despair
I write the grave inconsequence of words.
When men stampede in panic-stricken herds
Down tangled roads of thought,
Speech dies without the seal of action there,
And even song, cast forth, must come to naught,
Lost in the blowing pockets of the air.

Shall I then sit apart in a sun stupor
Out of the rush of the bewildered feet
And fan my heart to keep it fresh and cool
And say "O beautiful . . . " and say "O sweet . . . "
Watching the butterflies that try to settle
On wet leaves in a water lily pool?

No, for my heart is on the road with these
Spiritual refugees,
And I would flee the grim inaction of words
And the paralysis of wish and dream.
How can a man in love sit still and stare?
O people of earth, if I am not with you, running and crying,
It is that I am paging hurriedly
Through wordless volumes of reality
To find what love has indicated there.
I would define my love in some incredible penance
Of which no impotent language is aware.

If You Have Nothing

The gesture of a gift is adequate.
If you have nothing: laurel leaf or bay,
No flower, no seed, no apple gathered late,
Do not in desperation lay
The beauty of your tears upon the clay.

No gift is proper to a Deity.
No fruit is worthy for such power to bless.
If you have nothing, gather back your sigh,
And with your hands held high, your heart held high,
Lift up your emptiness!

330

Boundaries

The heart can set its boundaries
On mortal acres without fear.
Descent of skies, cascade of seas
Are not to be expected here.

The heart can take a human love
To feed and shelter, if it will,
Nor think to see its cities move
In avalanches down a hill.

Only when God is passing by
And is invited in to stay
Is there a split of earth and sky.
Boundaries leap and rush away.

And wound and chaos come to be
Where once a world lay, still and small,
But how else could Infinity
Enter what is dimensional?

Beauty, Too, Seeks Surrender

Love writes surrender as its due,
But how is beauty actor?
The heart remembers wound and loss
While mind sings benefactor.

God takes by love what yields to love,
Then pours a glowing allness
Past the demolished walls and towers
Into the spirit's smallness.

God's beauty, too, surrender seeks,
And takes, in the will's lull,
Whatever lets itself be changed
Into the beautiful.

And so, as Michelangelo
Has marked it out to be,
Since beauty is the purging of
All superfluity,

The yielded soul that lifts its gaze
To charms past nature's claim
Expects to have experience
Of blade and file and flame.

331

Celestial Bird

O sweet and luminous Bird,
Having once heard Your call, lovely and shy,
I shall be hungry for the finished word.
Across the windy sky

Of all voiced longing and all music heard
I spread my net for Your bewildering wings,
But wings are wiser than the swiftest hands.
Where a bird sings,

I held my heart, in fear that it would break.
I called You through the grief of whip-poor-wills,
I watched You on the avenues that make
A radiant city on the western hills.

Yet since I knew You not, I sought in vain,
I called You Beauty for its fleet white sound.
But now in my illuminated heart
I can release the hound

Of love upon whose bruising leash I strain.
Oh, he will grasp You where You skim the sod,
Nor wound Your breast, for love is soft as death,
Swifter than beauty is, and strong as God.

Obscurity

Obscurity becomes the final peace.
The hidden then are the elect, the free.
They leave our garish noon and find release
In evening's gift of anonymity.
Lost, not in loneness but in multitude,
They serve unseen without the noise of name.
Should you disdain them, ponder for your good:
This was the way our guests the angels came.

Doxology

God fills my being to the brim
With floods of His immensity.
I drown within a drop of Him
Whose sea-bed is infinity.

332

The Father's Will is everywhere
For chart and chance His precept keep.
There are no beaches to His care
Nor cliffs to pluck me from His deep.

The Son is never far from me
For presence is what love compels.
Divinely and incarnately
He draws me where His mercy dwells.

And lo, myself am the abode
Of Love, the Third of the Triune,
The primal Sweep and Surge of God
And my eternal Claimant soon!

Praise to the Father and the Son
And to Their Spirit! May I be,
O Water, Wave and Tide in One,
Thine animate doxology.

LOUISE CRENSHAW RAY

Steel Mills after Midnight

Unresting as the pulse of arteries
Hidden in darkness, mighty dynamos
Fan flames to silhouette the spires and trees
Upon a sky where sunset-color glows
Awhile, to flicker, die, then flare again.
Symbolical as heart-beat is your sound
From hour to changeful hour; for toiling men
Have daily bread so long as engines pound.
Throb on, great heart of Steel! A million ears
Have sunk in slumber to your lullaby,
Giant yet rhythmical, subduing fears
The while your hand illuminates the sky.
At dawn a million men will wake in wonder
And thankfulness, for your recurring thunder.

Middle-Aged Quixote

From gossamer illusion
There has grown
A coat of armor
Harder than a stone.

333

No longer does a windmill
Tempt my lance,
A creature fortified
By circumstance.

HENRY MORTON ROBINSON

Heaven Tree

Were I a painter I'd paint only skies:
Skies whipped and bare, skies cumulate with cloud,
Skies sinister with stormy auguries,
Skies mutely starred or brazening thunder-loud;
The peach-blown sky of dawn, thin blue of noon,
Stallion-of-lightning skies with orange mane,
The zinc sky of November, pearl of June,
Skies panting clotted blood, or gray with pain.

Nothing so changeless as the changing sky;
Nothing so lonely as its purple arc;
Nothing but man so propped by mystery;
Nothing but life as swift from bright to dark;
Nothing so vast as this great heaven tree
Housing the whirlwind and the tremendous lark.

FRANCIS J. ROCK, S.S.

"Tell Ye the Faint of Heart"

Master Artisan, make me over
From feckless clay to thrifty clover,
Bee, lizard, sparrow, anything
That sings or can lift us to sing.

Made man with awe full destiny
To hymn rich attributes of Thee
Profoundly more than other creatures
I've failed . . . so modulate these features
To simpler but assured scale
Of bloom, chirrup, buzz, or hitch of tail. . . .

Unless . . . unless . . . miraculous leaven
Quicken this tuneless clod with heaven!

334

RAYMOND ROSELIEP

Youth Autumnal

Here in a garden sung for two,
hawthorns bleed;
but flesh walls off the cry of your
inner need.

Your note and the last bird note
have been blown,
and to the dark south the last bird
has flown.

A winter claw already hooks
the heart.
October can be desolate
with two apart.

Wait, youth. The garden will again
know birds—
a rustle not of feather—music:
and your words.

LOUIS J. SANKER

Honey for the Heart

These are the wells of incredible wonder:
Petals that thrive on the thrust of the thunder,
Nest of a swift in a flue's smoky throat,
And letters you wrote.

These are the riddles that fathom delight:
Shape of the wind on a forest-fogged height,
Cool of a spring in the parch of a drouth,
Your lips on my mouth.

335

Trumpet for Yuletide

Gabriel, Gabriel, come blow your horn!
The moon's in her meadow, constellations in corn.
The clouds are in fold—a woolly-white throng—
But where are the shepherds to hearken the Song?
And where is a cock with arrogant crest
To herald a Star, nugget-new on the nest?
All the lanes with snow-lovely linen are spread—
But where is a robe for a manger-rude bed?

Gabriel, Gabriel, sky-candles tower;
The moon wears a halo, and holy the hour.
The ox and the ass are astir in the dark—
But when shall the stable emblaze with the spark?
And when shall the stubborn, who star in the door,
Grow humble and kneel on the earth-beaten floor?
Gabriel, Gabriel, come blow your horn!
The moon's in her meadow . . . a Saviour is born!

Boy at the Door

He knocks upon your door,
And worried waits an answer.
His eyes are troubled doves;
His trust a stumbling dancer.

He bears a crumpled rose
In penitent submission.
And at your soul-touched tears
Breathes humbly in contrition:

The rose was mostly thorn—
He only had a penny.
Where are your ramparts now?
Or could a heart have any?

DANIEL SARGENT

A Change of Subject

Let's talk about some unpretentious things:
A sea-shell which a mile of waves sweeps over,
Or one small star which over the sunset's wings
Chooses to play the part of silver rover.

Or things almost invisible like the swift
Furrow that Gabriel made through silken air,
Down to our Lady. Few could see the rift,
And first it was, and then it was not there.

Or things that are still more delicate like the hand
Which deft, adroitly unrolled the winding sheet
From an inconspicuous man in a far land
And set a dead man, Lazarus, on his feet.

Or things that are spare and slender. Take the gold
And tapering horn of Saint Michael. All it can do
Is bring the world's end, shake from heaven's stronghold
Ten million stars, and split the earth in two.

ELIZABETH SEWELL

Image Imagination

Image Imagination!
    Try if you can;
Uncover weedgrown pathways,
    Unreason's plan,
Some recondite relation
    Of God to man.

Image Imagination?
    Perhaps one should;
But will you, from a planet,
    A darkening wood,
Preceive the integration
    Of bad and good?

Image Imagination!
    You must divine
Man-Woman star-encrusted,

337

Love's androgyne,
Cloud-brimmed intoxication
    In skies of wine.

Image Imagination?
    How can one so?
In these angelic spaces
    Fierce sun and snow
Shrivel black lips' narration
    Of what they know.

Image Imagination!
    Bodies must turn
To force of naked water
    Through intellectual fern
In whose gesticulation
    Cold rainbows burn.

Image Imagination—
    Then bind my wrists,
And, bound, with pain and blindness
    For catalysts,
I hymn the consummation
    Of all that exists.

JOHN D. SHERIDAN

Each in His Inmost Heart

We are so lonely—all of us—
Each in his inmost heart seven times prisoner;

Neither can leave nor ever entrance grant
To those we love and would have share our being.
They only stand without and try to grasp
The meaning of our signs—who cannot sign!
For who can know the full portent
Of those eternal things that echo chill
Within the cloistered spirit?
In that deep place there is a sanctuary,
A sacred shrine where no man ever comes,
A secret dwelling single-tenanted.

We are so lonely—all of us—
Each in his inmost heart seven times prisoner.

338

GEORGE N. SHUSTER

What Highway?

What highway, dear, shall our true loving climb?
Up cold-browed peaks? Or on the gypsy plain,
Merry with rainbow caravans that stain
The road from Ithamar to Hagersheim?
Maybe a path, hedged tidily with thyme
And maples, where the thrushes mingle rain
With tears. There softly whispers day's refrain;
All noons are cool and movement calmest rhyme.

What matter where our living's lanes go through
If bright or dim, or swift to cross or long,
So my heart be a mantle for your shoe
And that most gentle! Then the morning's strong
Brown eyes shall find earth beautiful in you
And evening echo as with evensong.

JOHN W. SIMONS

The Broadcast

Surely the toothpaste magnate who controls
The crooner's voice and spot time on the air
Deserves some counter syllable of praise
From the indentured servants whose paroles
In Arcady would otherwise be rare.
Besides, it's said that advertising pays.
Why risk to have Prometheus unbound
Now that all his teeth are sound?

On Sunday evenings the ethereal clowns
Ascend the pulpit to divulge the news
That all is well in Gotham, that the Lord
(An old semantic ghost!) approves our towns,
Admires our politics and merchant crews,
And will send other favors, freight on board.
See? The deity who dwells beyond the moon
Is really an American tycoon.

The airways dance with purchased molecules,
The crowd awaits its sabbath harlequin,
All mammon maunders at the microphone.

339

O African Augustine, were they fools
Who watched the juggler to forget their sin
And left you preaching in the streets alone?
The crooner sings, "You Left Me in a Lurch."
On Mother's Day perhaps we'll go to church.

Simeon's Light Remembered

Today is Candlemas, and by the light
Of feast and symbol I survey the night
Of this most tenebrous city of the dead,
Wherefrom all vision and all hope have fled.
I hold the shimmering candle in my hand,
And gaze on it, and seek to understand.

I, through the fetid city, see disease
Mistily rise from dead philosophies.
I see the dogmas shaken one by one
And hear the madmen cry in unison,
"Truth is truth, but truth is relative
And plastic to the age in which you live."

The danse macabre of brittle-phosphor bones,
Nocturnal revel on the graveyard thrones:
Here in the drunken polis of the blind
They celebrate the obsequies of Mind,
I hear the corpses of the city shout,
"We've gouged the eyes of reason out."

Perplexed, and scarcely knowing what to do,
I look on Simeon to seek a clue.
The candle never wavered in his hand;
His eyes are fixed upon another land.
And through the luminous air the Spirit stirred,
Carrying the advent rumor of the Word.

Today is Candlemas. O holy Feast!
I hold my shimmering candle to the east,
And there I see the overthrow of night,
And there I see epiphany of light.
A City, like a bride adorned, descends.
Her tent is pitched. The reign of darkness ends.

The Whale and the Tiger

When Ahab saw his white leviathan
And Blake his burning tiger in the night,
They conjured metaphor from fevered sight
For that old sin which shadows everyman.

When Ahab wrestled with the monstrous whale
In the surging theater of liquid hell
He traveled evil fathoms and he fell,
Opposing the white mirage to no avail.

When Blake endured his forest interlude
And eyed with dread God's blazing antonym,
No answer to his question came to him
Save echoes of subliminal solitude.

Dual projections of a self-disease
Contracted in the primal garden where
The search for good and evil shook despair
From that most blighted of all blighted trees.

Forest dilemma or marine defeat,
Shaper of tiger or leviathan,
Are crossed and canceled symbols to the man
Cleansed in the Lamb, purged by the Paraclete.

SISTER AGNES, C.S.J.

Our Lady's Assumption

It was the Sun that drew her up from the earth
As lilies lift at His light, as daisies rise
Fresh in His morning out of the dark ground,
As irises open from gaze of His warm eyes.

It was the Sun whose light lay curled so long
Under the folded petals of this Rose
That now drew her with strong, invisible fingers
Up from the grassy mound of her repose.

It was the Sun took root and leaf and petal
Straight into Heaven where no other grew,
Drawing her wholly by his radiant longing
Simply as sunlight lifting the morning dew.

341

More than the Moment

This is the measured moment
   more than the shadowed pall,
in but an instant
   even a shadow grows tall.

The sky is not spanned in seeing
   wide arches above,
white wanderings whisper
   caught in the wings of a dove.

This is the measured moment,
   more than the soul's swift flight,
where no candle gluts
   the ending dark of night.

Assuagement

The white wide wonder of a cloud
is loud in the lingering lull of noon,
and soon, too soon, the silence
splinters into futile fragments of words.

The birds glide on wings gold in the sun
and one trails his song, a streamer
along the edge of sound.

Pounding the shore is the crested wave,
white with the home-longing,
and heart-hunger and the lapping loneliness
for the far-away.

The day widens into an evening sky
and high is the last, long streak of light,
before the night covers the heart
with its hunger and its need.

Words in the Wilderness

Before the world was made
there is the Word,
heard on the aspen hill
leaf-quivering in Light.

God spoke
and broke the dark;
patens of white
high-starred the sky.

The mountain stillness
split into streams of song;
along and under the lightless hush
thronged the words: He is here.

God in the wilderness spoke
and the silence broke into speech,
reaching to heights unheard
in the far-flung world of the Word.

SISTER DAVIDA, I.H.M.

In Gusts of Music

Think it not idolatry
    That I am brought thus to my knees
    By melody.
See it caught among the flowers there,
    Blended with the gold leaf,
Tangled in the candles' flare.
How it quickens now the very stone
    As rumbling through the shadows
It climbs and climbs in tone on tone.
Nor pray I through this music;
    It is the music prays through me
    In gusts on gusts of melody.
Spirit of Prayer, speaking through flame and water,
    Working through wind and oil,
Pray now through harmony, their daughter.

343

MOTHER FRANCIS D'ASSISI, O.S.U.

Samaritan Woman

Here by this well at noon He sat
The day He said,
"Give me to drink. . . ."
And now, they tell me He is dead.

But still upon the tree, they say,
That dreadful day,
To all who thirst and crave
He water gave;
That from His open side
Gushed forth a tide—
Can living water come from one who died?

Then this is what He meant
That day He said: "Daughter, daughter,
You need but ask,
And I will give you water."

SISTER JULIE, O.P.

Zaccheus

Zaccheus, insignificant and mean,
Scrambled up into a tree to see
(He had no dignity).
And Jesus walking by
Looked up on high
And saw Zaccheus, eager-hearted, keen
With desire to see the Christ
(He had humility).
Ah! graciousness of God!
What blessed word
Zaccheus heard
Precariously perched high in a tree:
"Come down! This day I must abide with thee."

344

SISTER MARGARET TERESA

Matthew

Here at the wharves is payment for a loathing,
Lapping of clean sea for the spill of coin,
This Gentile-balm—Well, here sunlight and sea
For the Most High in finer gold conjoin,

And lavishly. I've had a deal of comfort
Looking past men that look their proudest down.
The gulls there, flinging up like psalms of David—
Making their count, sometimes, I've lost my own.

No matter now, let others look to Caesar;
Ended is all my tithing; for today
There hath stood One between me and the sunset,
Holding all seas and suns, who calleth me.

SISTER MARIA DEL REY, R.S.M.

"Haec Est Domus Dei et Porta Coeli"

[St. Anselm's Priory, Washington, D.C.]

House of God and Gate of Heaven . . .
Seven
Words weathered where buff bands the brick and wood.
Here once I stood,
Drowned
In the majesty of the liturgy in sound;
Here once I wept,
Swept
By waves of a gold and scarlet patterened sea
As color came crashing down on me.
Here now I pray,
Stay
Late where blazes of blue and purple, prism-rayed,
Darkle and fade,
And psalmody echoes in a thin, high, hovering hum—
But He does not come.

345

Blue Larkspur

The white flame of a candle,
   The green flame of a star,
The yellow flame of a young moon
   Beauteous are.

But the blue flame of a larkspur
   Torchwise on its stem
Burning along the garden wall
   Surpasses them.

Who has not seen blue larkspur
   May look where stars abide,
At moon and candle flame,
   Returning satisfied.

But who has seen will look at fire
   And in his heart will know
The pain of swift, unquenched desire
   For the flames blue larkspur grow.

The Jefferson Highway

By day
A ribbon of gray
From the arc at the east
To the arc at the west.
At night
Nothing at all.
Bubbles of light by two and two
Rise at the far horizon line
Bubbles of light by two and two,
Always more and always more
Rise from nowhere out of the night.
They float along where garish day
Has marked the earth with a strip of gray,
Always more and always more,
Out of the dark from east and west,
Bubbles of light, their end, their quest
No man knows and no man cares,
Bubbles of light the blue night wears.

346

SISTER MARIS STELLA, C.S.J.

Landscape with Children

Always waiting at the back of my mind
where old shapes are the familiar scenery,
hills lie beyond the water, and I find
cows there and crocuses, and three
children with tin lunch pails picking their way
along new grass cropped short by munching cows.
Three children gather silken crocuses. (They
call them wild flowers.) The warm wind blows
out of the past, ruffling the water still,
ruffling the children's hair, tossing the bob-white-
whistle, blackbird-meadowlark-mirth until
I am aware at last of how the light
fades out of that horizon. And I know
those hills are far away and filled with snow.

Out of Darkness

The light-winged wilding meadowlark—
his voice all joy, a fountain flung
out of the sky while yet the dark
over the nether valleys hung—
is singing still as the earth turns
these hills away from sun.

O more than bird, he is petals pelted
of apple bloom from orchard trees.
He is crocus cupped where snowdrifts melted.
He is violets and wild flaglilies
writing in light that spring returns
and the dark months are done.

But the other dark that lies deep-rifted
in valleys of the heart even now:
with what bird's song will it be lifted,
what yearning out of darkness, how
banished when the heart's earth turns
the hills again toward Sun.

347

SISTER MARY ADA, C.S.J.

Against Despair

You are a Treasure, Lord, beyond all price,
I needs must tell You as the pledge I lay
Against that bitter and regretful day
When I might well deny You more than thrice.

And lest I be as so much sifted wheat,
Oh, pray no grain by any wind shall blow
Beyond the magnet of Your eyes, or go
Outside the reach of pinioned hands and feet.

Or should I sell You, and the price be set
At thirty silver pieces, more or less,
Oh, let me not forget in my distress
The heart I bartered will receive me yet.

SISTER MARYANNA, O.P.

With One Swift Thought

Between us lie
The mountains and the plain,
White walls of snow, curtains of silver rain.

In this our life
Though never more we meet:
The rind is bitter but the fruit is sweet.

Prayer is a bridge
That spans the earth, the sea,
And flings its arches to eternity.

With one swift thought,
I reach God's listening heart
And there find yours, though we are leagues apart.

348

Meditations in a Museum Cloister

Mournful Madonnas with pathetic smiles
Hold out carved Babes to visitors with such
A wistful eagerness, a naive hope.
The printed placard says: *Please do not touch.*

Consummate skill, the guide remarks. It would behoove
The sightseer to note this item well. The Louvre
Contains the head. Where are the limbs? He does not know.
But here's the torso nailed tight to its cross. Still graceful,
     though.
The drapery has such finesse. The folds still keep
Their color. Tourists nod. Beneath, John and the Virgin weep.

SISTER MARY ATHANASIUS, B.V.M.

Meditation on Time

Yesterday has slipped the perimeter of perfection;
Its moments move as legends
On the page that feeds
The present worm.
Only the heart leans
To the fourth dimension for its needs
And grieves
Not knowing the passing moment achieves.

Tomorrow is held
In the other side of the glass
Until once shattered
At the grave's night
The scattered moments
Gather to a point of light.

SISTER MARY BERNETTA, O.S.F.

One Day at Rouen

"The Lord hath need of thee; do thou be good."
So preached the voices in Domremy wood,
And Jeanne the peasant child
Looked up, and smiled
More fairly than the harebells in the forest where she stood.

Not every crisis has its warning bell.
Among the things the angels did not tell
Was one day at Rouen
When holy Jeanne,
God's banner over Gallic troops, became His torch as well.

SISTER MARY BERTRAND, O.M.

Our Lady of the Apocalypse

I that am clothed with the sun
Have walked where the moonflowers are breaking
A fragrance like nard on the night,
Where wild things their small fears forsaking
Know peace without light.

I that am crowned with the stars
Have worn the white sea mists unfolding
Their soft veils to blindfold the land,
Have held the sure fingers all planets upholding
In the palm of my hand.

I that am sandaled with moonlight
Have seen it a white river spilling
Where cypress and cedar conspire,
Their high branches drenched in the silver sea filling
The world with its fire.

I that in pain
Have unraveled the ages to fair Paradise
Have felt in the darkness the swift winds unskein
To serry the skies.
I that in wonder
Drew light from the beauty of one human Face
Am clothed in the brilliance of infinite splendor
No dark can erase.

350

SISTER MARY CATHERINE, O.S.U.

Again for You

They named your name and suddenly
as snow from trees falls easily
embarrassed by the sun,
the pride I wore against the years,
the compromises and the fears
slipped from me: I was one
who stood with eager untried wings
poised for splendid, far-off things;
then with a child's quick choice and true,
I folded them again for you.

Who Know Thee Best

Who know her but as children do
   On lightly bended knee
And call her but the gentler names
   From her fair litany,

Who bring her likeness to their house
   By its soft lines beguiled,
Nor guess for all its innocence
   This child is not a child,

Who never wrestled with her will
   (New Israels) are slow
To learn no velvet syllable
   Her adamantine No.

There is no softness in her
   Though we call her for the snows
And name her name with a flower's name:
   She is more thorn than rose.

And who know thee best, O strong one!
   Of God thou hard echo,
Would chisel thee in granite, Lady!
   (Thank God that it is so!)

351

SISTER MARY CATHERINE, S.C.

Beside Lilia Dead

Of quiet things, of things at rest,
A dead child is the quietest.

Frozen rivers never stir,
But a little dead child is quieter.

No praying hands of fine clay molded
Are half so calm as her small hands, folded.

No ringlet chiseled by ancient Greek
Is still as the curl beside her cheek.

And nothing was ever so motionless
As the pale blue bows on her new white dress.

SISTER MARY DAVID, S.S.N.D.

Plain Chant of the Hill Country

It may have been a sunset such as this,
Flushed with expectancy, that saw her come
Unheralded along the dusty road.
You might have thought it just another day
Relapsing into quiet: glow withdrawn,
And birds and zephyrs nestling down together.
As was his custom, Zachary had gone
Before the lighting of the lamps, to see
That all the poppies and the lily plants
Were fortified with water for the night.
This way it chanced (or so you might have thought)
Elizabeth was left alone to spend
A moment dreaming on the western clouds
That were so like "the shadow of His wings."
Toward such a sunset did Elizabeth,
Whose name was "House of God," look down the lane.
From such a sunset, dear and unannounced,
Came forth the maiden Mary unto her.
Deep in the silent evening it happened:
Because her night had fashioned patient years,
Elizabeth knew Day-Star . . . felt the Dawn.

SISTER M. EDWARDINE, R.S.M.

At Palomar

One will be close beside you as you stare
That first and awful moment where no eye
Has been before. He will stand silent there
Who curves all planes to meet beyond the sky.
While you are focusing for galaxies
Beyond the milky way, He too will wait
In patience, having earlier seen these
And that new universe you contemplate.
All that your scales projected in that dark
Is there, orbits obedient to laws
You stammer over, tracing spark by spark
His way, who is the Light and Living Cause.
He is beside you, yearning to see you lift
Your eyes to Him, the Giver of the gift.

Disillusion

I shall not go to the autumn woods again
However brave they be;
Better it were to view them from afar
Than ever know
Their ghastly pageantry.

They lured me on,
Bright leaf and burning bough,
Until I stood beneath
Their flaming emptiness.

And now
I shall not go to autumn woods again;
Beauty is there,
But, ah,
Death under foot!

Candles

Dear, I have lit a candle for your birthday
Because a candle is so like to you.

What need is there of candles in the sunshine!
What need is there of love when life is gay!
But ah, a candle set within a window,
When twilight shadows come drearily gray,
Tells of a mother waiting with her dearness
To comfort hearts the day has touched with pain—
A little candle shining through the darkness,
How fearlessly it braves the wind and rain.

Dear, I have lit a candle for your birthday
Because in every grief I come to you.

The Lesson

I had not known what life might be
Until death came to talk with me.
But now I know the reason why
The brave, white stars are riding high.
I know why grass wants rain, and how
The eager twigs reach from the bough
To catch the sun, why April spills
Her bright, young laughter down the hills.
My ears are tuned to the strong whir
Of a bird's wings. I feel the stir
Of restless seeds within the earth.
The crying of a child at birth
Smites me to ecstasy. I know
The throb of water's undertow.
I love my pulse beats and swift breath
Since I have had my talk with death.

SISTER MARY ESTELLE, O.P.

From Desert to Metropolis

For years we live solitary in the soul's hermitage
With haircloth and locusts and wild honey
While the weapons of our asceticism
Lay waste the acres of our inheritance
(Not knowing that even in the kingdom of the spirit
Man lives not alone).

For years we are companioned only by the shadow
Walking beside us in the sun,
Until the day a chance word breaks as a voice of many waters
And the radiance from an upturned face
Emerging from a pool of pain
Blinds us like fresh snow on which the sun is shining.

The barriers of our surfeited self-sanctity
Are then shattered like crystal falling to the ground:
The desert is invaded by the multitude no man can number,
The sagebrush weighted down with canisters of grapes
As the cactus grows to fields upon fields of golden grain
Eager for His *hoc est enim corpus meum,*
And the mirage fills up with empurpled Wine
Overflowing into Harlem, Chicago, Los Angeles, Santa Fe.

Love is no longer a law thundered on Mount Sinai,
A voice crying in the wilderness;
It is now a symphony of joy in the metropolis of the heart.

SISTER M. EULALIA, R.S.M.

Denouement

With mask well fitted for your chosen role,
Intent upon your goal,
I saw you as one clothed in cap and bells
(Quicker than one tells
The story) stand at attention,
Awaiting words that you would mention
To let fall the royal robes of truth;
And I, in ruth,
Heard not a word you said
But tinkling of bells instead. . . .

Then you stood and kept on smiling
And said something about going,
And hoping I would keep well—
The exact words, now, I cannot tell. . . .
Strange how words cannot be retold,
When one grows old . . .
And the house seems colder than ever before. . . .

I rose and softly closed the door. . . .

To Archbishop Stepinac

Courage is a fabric
   So woven of the soul
It shrinks with fear, stretches
   When straining toward a goal.

But when in eyes it glows,
   Awaiting tyrants' rod,
It is of mystic birth,
   Holding a tryst with God.

SISTER MARY GILBERT

Meditation on a March Wind

Should man oppose a rash rigidity
Then may the mad March strip his proud, resisting limbs
And strew the green, incipient wonder
Of his May afar;
Or may the hailstones fall as loud as summer thunder
And blast his springtime promise to an ugly scar
Before white glory rims
The naked silhouette of undelivered tree.

What childless woe to kill the unborn flower!
To summon back a fruitless world of frost
Wherein no womb-life stirs, no leafy shoot.
Wed pliancy to wisdom: let the anchored root
Give leash to swaying branches, Spirit-tossed
To pinnacles of trust and quiet power.

SISTER MARY IMMACULATA, C.S.J.

Spring Comes to Our Garden

Spring comes to our garden
   Like the Holy Ghost;
And for one brief season
   It is Pentecost.

March winds had foretold Him,
   Mighty winds and high,
(Parted flames are portent
   As an April sky!)

Whispering His wisdom
   Where will lilac be,
Chalicing His counsel
   In anemone;

Stirring up the skylark
   Still bereft of song
(Winter wears a silence
   That is late and long!)

Giving to a poplar's
   Patient silhouette
Foliage for faith that
   Filled the fishers' net.

Who can know the courage
   That may Springtime teach,
Weighted low with color
   Multiple as speech?

Blessed be the bower
   Hallowed be the host
To whose garden Spring comes
   Like the Holy Ghost.

Joy

This is the secret love,
This is the tryst she keeps, clandestine,
Her flying feet echoing through the heart's deep caverns,
Driven to catacomb by the pagan suitors
Who hang their armor in her father's hallway,
Bringing pomegranates and quinces,
Offering her their arrogant carnelians,
Carved with their profiles, to bedeck her forehead.

This is the tryst she keeps, glad beyond laughter—
Lays out the linen and breathes forth the incense
Over the tombs of all her martyred wishes
Consecrated by fierce-shouldered lion,
By fire, by sword,
By Word.

Here, slaked of seeking,
White in the darkness as the marble table
Spread for her love's white Host,
Under the innocent surface where your speech rings hollow,
Deep, deep
Is the tryst.

The Young Dead Speak

We are the age predestined to lie fallow:
Out of our loins no radiant youth shall spring,
Nor our light craft, on waters glancing shallow,
Slip like bright birds on deft and lilting wing.
The light shall fall unheeded on our faces,
And song shall die on our new-parted lips,
As we go out to doomed, forgetful places,
Lit by illusion, in our fated ships.
But when new seasons stir another sowing,
Out of rich soil the goodly grain shall rise,
And crimson poppies in the wheat-fields blowing
Repeat the ardor of our lightless eyes;
Then thirsting men shall drink of glory lent,
Not by dark causes, but our high intent.

358

SISTER MARY JEREMY, O.P.

Desdemona

Old women do not know this piercing song
Nor show such alabaster in their dying.
It is the young who take their death of wrong.

Their elders mourn them the appointed day
And in the sun resume their grisly chat
Of heirloom ache and intricate decay.

But Death's a dancing angel with a crown
And not the snake-toothed summoner they know;
He calls his queens to music and renown,
And they will make a progress when they go.

Academy

The first meridian, new with light
For blue-serge girls in the amber air:
Secrets drowned by a copper bell,
The immaculate nun, intent and tall,
A vigil lamp by Gehenna-brink;
And under the incense suffusing all,
The smell of apples and books and ink.

We understudied the better part
And practiced vows in the corridor;
One of us, with Magdalen's hair,
Had a witty seraph for counselor.
We spoke with Christ in the snowy winds
And found His pearls in our quaking hands.

With *Ave Verum* and country songs
Our tempests melted to madrigals.
Fed at dawn upon angels' bread
We read of ardor and understood.
—Later, Hymettus and Dead Sea fruit;
But in that clement latitude
The herb of grace grew underfoot.

Such was the blessed land where we took root.

Legend

Lady up on yonder hill
   Underneath a cypress tree
Rang and rang her silver bell—
   All the children ran to see.

Like a queen she drew them in.
   "Tell me, children, all your names;
Here is shelter from the sun—
   I will teach you singing games:

"Shuffle Feather, Spaniards' Rout,
   Whigmaleerie, Rakes and Roans,
Hide All, Sally Turnabout,
   Great Marelle and Tumble Bones."

Sweet her look and who could fear?
   "Come and dance with me," she cried.
One and all they followed her
   When her green door opened wide.

Dance and dancers ended there
   Silent under mossy stones.
Hide all! mocks the chilly air—
   All they learned was Tumble Bones.

SISTER M. MADELEVA, C.S.C.

October Birthday

Were I immortal only I would proffer
Tokens tremendous as a god can give:
Planets in leash, an earth whereon to live
With all October's fugitive gold in coffer,
Its moon a sorceress, its wind a scoffer,
Oceans it carries in a sandy sieve,
And stars aloof and undemonstrative.
Gifts casually infinite I could offer.
But as a woman and your love I bring you
The simple, homely things a woman must:
A little, human-hearted song to sing you,
My arms to comfort and my lips to trust,
The tangled moods that, autumn-wise, I fling you,
The frail and faulty tenderness of dust.

Return

This is your home to which you are returning.
Because you have so hungered for the place,
Shall we not stop to say the simple grace
That you have spent a passionate lifetime learning?
Upon the hearth a brave, new fire is burning;
The flowers you hoped would greet you in the vase
You wished, are here; here that grave, tender face
You tell me is the sum of all your yearning.

The threshold's peace, impatient to possess you,
More lovely than, homesick, you clamored for;
Music at once to shatter and caress you;
The voice you dream, the hands that you adore;
All, all are here to welcome and to bless you.
Come to my waiting heart! What will you more?

Riddles

My lover is a fool more wise
Than Solomon;
My lover is a bird that flies
Into the sun.

He is a lighted lamp, my love,
A midnight cry,
A mortal worm that died to prove
He could not die.

My lover is a cedar tree
With branches spread;
A sweet and bitter fruit is he,
Alive and dead.

My lover is a quiet rain
Falling on fleece;
My lover is or endless pain
Or endless peace,

Or sometime an instinctive mole
Breaking the clod;
My lover is a thief who stole
The name of God.

361

At Winter's End

Buds are backward and winter lingers
But you, the eager, the quick, the wary,
Have found the first gold fritillary,
The clustered, rose-pink lady-fingers.

You have found, too, with cautious hunting,
That tricky one, the elusive towhee,
The tanager, splendidly shy and showy,
The summer-minded lazuli bunting.

I come not back with April weather;
Winds cannot woo nor sun unbind me.
Much as you seek, you cannot find me;
We shall not have this spring together.

But we warm our hearts at no dying ember.
Who can tell us how love is parted?
We are forever happy-hearted
Having one springtime to remember.

Design for a Stream-lined Sunrise

If you must draw mere beauty,
Subtend one third of the whole arc of heaven
With a gray chord of cloud
Stretched from the quick southeast to the still dubious west.
Edge all the chord with white, bright, mutable silver.
Draw it on cloudlessness at daybreak,
If you would draw mere beauty.
But you cannot do this
Because the artless air achieved this brief design for sunrise,
Once and forever,
Today, at dawn.
And then this long line, cutting with sheer simplicity of silver
The breathless, deep-blue arc of the south,
Became, because of my beholding,
Beyond potential beauty, beautiful.

362

As One Finding Peace

The secret of the King possesses me
Unutterably.
I am a child to sudden woman grown
Who never yet has known
Invasion so imperious, so complete,
Blindly and madly sweet.
I am a bud to sudden blossom blown,
Intoxicate, replete
With fragrance most divinely not its own.
I am dew thirstily drunk up
Out of dawn's lifted cup.
I am my own impotent, daring self, plunged in a sea
Ecstatically!

O God, encompass me!
Be infinitely mine to hold, to bound me;
Absorb, consume, encompass and confound me;
Be in me and beneath me and above me;
O Father, love me, love me!
Tremendously be,
Strong God, my sea.

In ultimate joy upon this Lover's breast
I come to rest.
Peace, like a song,
Envelops me;
Peace, like the night,
Folds me in conscious, beautiful delight.
Never has human love held me in tranquil thrall,
For not to human love does peace belong.
What if I be for the Lord God a wall,
Beauteous as cedar and as cedar strong;
What if I be a door, and sealed to all save Him,
Cunningly joined, guarded by flashing cherubim?
I am a door, a wall, tower of passionate strength
Around which multitudinously throng
Wild ecstasies, wild joys, unending blisses,
A God's caresses and a Father's kisses.

Presently let this rapture in profounder rapture cease;
A silver bulwark of wrought silence be,
My Father, since that I am come at length,
Captive and free,
Into Your presence as one finding peace.

363

SISTER MARY MAURA, S.S.N.D.

Professor of Medieval Balladry

Forty years he has pursued his love.
By dilettantes at once amazed, perplexed,
he peers beyond them, over, back again,
probing the footnote text.

Upon the minstrel his scholarship broods;
sluicing an intricacy of word, he stares
abstractedly around the graduate seminar
till everyone nods back, and smiles, and shares.

He reads the ballads like an unselfconscious lover.
Suddenly, with a "hey, nonny, nonny," his feet,
huge and forgotten underneath the desk,
pick up the ballad beat.

Once, long, long ago, fishing in the creek,
between his toes he oozed the sun-streaked mud;
no less warmly now there curls between his toes
Robin's greenwood, Edward's blood.

Data for Accreditation

Eighty-four acre campus . . .
outdoor swimming pool . . .
liberal arts (plus vocational skills)
a better-than-average-school.

Nodding, they swirl by the cloisters,
obviously hiding the suntan cream . . .
How make the stuff of martyrs
out of this lunch hour stream?

How teach that the flask is venomed
and flaking with rust?
the body chambered for children?
and pride more vicious than lust?

Modestly, past the cloisters,
the guileless sun-bathers stream;
how shall we suffer beatitudes
truncate this noon-day dream?

Eighty-four acre campus . . .
Out of our penance and pain
accredit us, God with mercy.
Grow, Thou, the grain.

Lucifer at Leisure

There are no hills for climbing;
day is meadow, night a plain;
sun glass shielded, lassitude frocked,
flicker no eye lash to the lever of pain.

Art and truth are relative;
in nothing be importunate;
flower the speech with counterfeits;
blessed are the comfortably fortunate.

With long and lacquered nails
tap the cocktail glasses lightly,
tinkling the ice, while certitude
sways oh so slightly.

Motif from the Second Shepherd's Play

[Stage directions: enter the shepherds who bring to the Child
cherries, a bird, and a tennis ball. They go out singing.]

Forever in Advent
harbor the bird,
splinter the bread crumbs,
promise the Word.

Forever in Advent
yoke the ball,
through winds of nothingness,
drop to All.

Forever in Advent
shield the flower,
that the fruit
may know this hour

when comes Christmas,
and the bird alight
on the finger,
cherries in right

365

hand, ball in left,
briefly the heart
comes home to God.
Salving the smart

of decades of sin,
joyously young,
taste the primal
carol on tongue.

SISTER MARY OF THE VISITATION

In Tenebris

This is the Darkness that they told us of
Where we would cry to You, and seek in vain
Your outstretched hand, Your omnipresent Love;
Here would Despair and ineluctable Pain

Come in upon us, press us to the ground
With weight of our own evil, and Your face
Would turn from us who go betrayed and bound
Into the terror of a darker place.

Yet, Darkness cannot hide You, for You stand
With us beneath the shadowing olive trees,
Facing the demon mob with Your command:
"If it be truly I ye seek, let these

Go on their way." Not ours the traitor's kiss,
The lonely agony, the bloody sweat;
But in the caves of our own sins' abyss
We share the darkness of Your Olivet.

Yet, how could we bear witness to the Light
Except our souls had sought You in the night?

SISTER M. PAULINUS, I.H.M.

Here at the Stable Door

Quick now—loose it—here at the stable door.
Let Christmas winds make sport of this most useless thing,
Tatter it blithesomely, blow it afar.
Be quick: You will not need it any more.

Not if you come inside: pride has no jot
Of relevancy here; it makes no sense
In terms of song or shed, angel or kine—
It has no truck with hay; fields loathe pretense.

Cast it away; lose it in depths of snow
Or in this night's munificence of stars:
You cannot find a single use for pride
Here where the Highest chooses to be low.

Canticle of Quietness

By David's mouth, God spoke, "Be still and see that I am
    God. . . ."
And when the searchers of the stars, schooled to the broad
Far quietness of night, followed upon the men of flocks,
Hill-bred to stillness as to grass and rocks,
The promise bloomed for them where she of David's line
(Ineffably hushed to the housing of God) held to her heart
    the Child Divine.

Barren to none of honest will who flee the trafficking within
The mind, quitting whatever market-place, whatever garish
    inn
The heart may hold, the promise blows to flower across all
    time.
And blessed is the quietness that gives it burgeoning clime.

SISTER M. PHILIP, C.S.C.

Air Mail, Special

Dear Saint Thomas,
                  Help me please,
With Medians and Frequencies,
Sham Credentials and Degrees.

Norms and Tendencies appear
To be less clutter-proof this year,
And Lesson-Plans are techni-clear.

Great Aquinas, hear my cry,
Nor let my laughter buried lie
Beneath Techniques and Syllabi!

And lest, perchance, you should conclude
That care-worn teachers *all* are rude,
Pardon, please, if I intrude.

Beside a glory-vibrant stall
We have met before. Recall?
Two dumb beasts who shared it all.

SISTER MARY ST. VIRGINIA, B.V.M.

This Sharpening Tension

Compounded out of nothingness and all,
Delivered from the void: thus always I
Away from vacuums crawl.

Non-being joined with being to design me,
Cried its own fiat. Shall the echoing cry
Finally undermine me?

Got with what seed, I feel my sire's dimension;
Yet, ripened in a womb empty and dark,
I know this sharpening tension,

This last and lonely stand of borrowed being
With nothingness ahead whose street-lamps mark
No avenue for seeing

368

The instinctive route down which non-being draws
(Till measurements reverse to the growing small—
Slowly), and slowly gnaws
Its way inside to Being which is All.

Great Silence

Almost emptied of sound and light,
The house is folding against the night
Whose silence and darkness traveled far
To fasten the hearing and shut the sight.

Yes, close the enclosure with bolt and bar,
Dismiss the final windowed star,
Erase the phrases that only were
Eddies where flowing waters are . . .

Out of the depths where outlines blur
Around a hearth which those deeps inter,
A glow, a gleam—like flame that clung
Under the ashes—begins to stir.

There in the hush which the house has wrung
Empty of echoes, love has hung
A word—that a listening house may learn
What God has heard since God was young.

To its own deep heart the house must yearn—
Must linger there and must discern
How hollows brim and shadows burn . . .

Edmund Campion

Quick hoof-beats down a moonless country highway—
A gentleman is riding to a tryst:
In some hushed room above a guarded byway
He must brand England with the Blood of Christ.
Take from the hiding-hole the massing chalice,
Gather the gallant at the godly post—
Quick! for they name him now in Whitehall Palace,
And Tyburn lies beyond his lifted Host. . . .
He was a sword that flashed in England's hand,
He was Saint George feeling the dragon's power,
A last proud true-born son of Alfred, and
A *verray knyght* defending Mary's Dower,
The laughter of England hushing over the land,
The soul of England soaring from the Tower.

369

SISTER MARY STEPHANIE, O.M.

That Far Lone Mountain

Matriarch of your chain and consort of the clouds,
White pinnacle of certainty and strength,
Your ultimate peak, snow-breasted blue, holds me in thrall.
Along your bold and ponderous cobalt length
Of slope—how far across this stretch of hazeless world—
Tracing your stark and unimpassioned swell,
My eyes, my heart, my very soul go vaultingly
Up to your alabaster citadel.
The heavens lie upon you like an old embrace,
That is most proudly tender, intimate still;
The wistful earth leans to you, hungry with the vale's
Deep and eternal hunger for the hill.
Far blue heart-shattering piercer of the spaces, God—
God did speak you mightily, aloud,
And crowned you utterly with this chaste dazzlement
Culled from the quiet bosom of a cloud.
Here is for me all pureness of white, shining glory
Baring a continent splendor to the sun.
Breath of the strong high beauty I, in my night, have quested,
Here is a gleam of God—Consummate One!

SISTER M. THÉRÈSE, S.D.S.

Moment in Ostia

[St. Augustine, Confessions, IX:23–26]

Spliced between Milan and Carthage this strip of days
In the port city, while the heart recruits
Quiet, aware that the trim ship tethered
At dockside crouches mad to spring
The foaming jungles to the tropic shore.

But where is argument for rest
When the precipitate spirit flays
Her wings in the sealed cage?

Unless that conjuring sirocco
That blows the window full of stars
Where Monica and Augustine lean into the night
Shall crack the aviary—

370

Parrying speech like lances
The birds escape and jet
Past moon and sun and every constellation,
The pedantry of matter, the linear plateaus
Of syllogism, the blaze of the analogies—
Out-distancing Plotinus infinitely—
Till with a last fine thrust of heart
They touch a little on that timeless moment
That lets them into Wisdom,
Beneath whose molten, syllableless text
The *Enneads* are ice.

An instant only—
Life in this stratosphere is execution
For birds still trapped in matter;
Lest sinew snap, bone melt, and blood unchannel
Love tricks them back into their hapless cages.

The night drops strict enclosure,
Leaving of this sharp flight
One visible sign:
A tired woman leaning on the sill,
Her son beside her watching the starlight sing
On the garden stones, loud as the light that played
Across his intellect, making new parables
Of the past months' presents:
A childvoice rising in a trifling rhyme;
The tears, the book, the stabbing word,
The irresolute resolution;
Monica wrestling with God till past her prayer
The invincible lightnings struck
The wincing cauldrons of Carthage to sifted snow,
The lions of Tagaste to their knees in the African sand.

The Bird

Against the rigors of an austere season
A bird flew into my garden one dark night;
Flung from some mew in the stars, this sweet unreason
Of song cut flaming through the chill and blight.
Such canticle might have leaped in Bernard's mellow
Matins, or shattered silences that stirred
In Juan's stark, mystic cell in Duruelo—
In all my woods there never was this bird.

371

What can I do to stay this plumed one winging
Into the lonely places where I hide?
I have no defence against his deathless singing
But to kneel at the sill and fling the shutter wide—
Praying that voice to flood each path and glen
That all my garden be made bright again.

Traveler

I have been searching for some metaphor
For the journeying of the mind toward eternal brightness:
Across two burning strips of desert floor
I know the will parched to an autumn lightness
That the wind could beat to a flame when the night is parted
On quiet acres sown with austerity,
Till love leaps like a young child April-hearted,
Who comes upon bright mountains suddenly.

Though you guard the season well, I still divine it
Through a snare of tensile branch and iron sky;
In futile, empty words I will define it—
The sure and changeless chart you travel by—
A bird winnows your heart with deathless wing,
Whose voice is your sun, your snows, your endless spring.

SISTER MIRIAM, R.S.M.

Give Me the Sun

Give me the sun, a bird, a flower,
   And I shall spin you a song
      That will last an hour.

Give me a heart, a joy, a tear,
   And I shall weave you a song
      That will last a year.

But give me a love death cannot sever,
   And I will build you a song
      To live forever.

Prometheus Unbound

You are, O Life, the strangest friend I know.
You hold together in me clay and cloud;
Marry the weed so high, the star so low,
Making the weed, till widowed, passing proud.

What quarrels thence arise to make the earth
A stage for tearful tragedies behind
The rose silk-curtained flesh, while mirth
Makes merry watching wars that mar mankind.

If both but knew how low the price of peace,
How they would bend to God and nature's law.
The weed would from her rash rebellions cease,
The star accept her servitude with awe.

Thus soul and body joined in love's embrace
Conceive anew the glory of the race.

SISTER MIRIAM TERESA, S.C.

To the Most Holy Crown of Thorns

Thrice-holy thorns, encircling with thy fire
The pain-racked Brow and agonizing Head
Of sin's redeeming Victim, anguish bled,
    Thou art my sole desire.

O blessed chaplet of mysterious woes,
Thou perfume bitter-sweet, a prayer unending
Of reparation to our God ascending,
    Thy beauty ever grows.

O sanctifying circlet, tight-compressed,
Thou boring band, thou sharp death-dealing vise,
Thou prodigy of mental sacrifice,
    With Thee I am caressed.

O once-opprobrious and shameful crown
Resplendent with a blood-red glory, now
Enshrined with priceless ruby-brilliants, Thou,
    Come weigh me sweetly down.

373

Thrice-holy thorns, encircling with thy fire
The pain-racked Brow and agonizing Head
Of sin's redeeming Victim, anguish-bled,
    Thou art my sole desire.

SISTER RITA AGNES

Limits

Man's spirit with spread wings
Would do ten million things,
But time does not expand;
And bilocation's feat,
Rare and divinely neat,
No saint would say he planned.

Externalizing thought
As fast as mind has wrought
Exceeds the power of verbs;
Succession of events,
Required by snail sense,
Inexorably curbs.

Yet all such limits will retire
From souls that win Faith's prime desire.
Oh, think of finding past Death's door
The freedom we were fashioned for!

SISTER ST. MIRIAM OF THE TEMPLE, C.N.D.

Mater Misericordiae

Our Lady walks the desolated lands
    To save them from the conquest of despair:
Her eyes are deep with comfort, and her hands
    Are eloquent of prayer.

With sacramental touch and healing lips
    She bends above each charred and lonely door

To lift the silence of the sad eclipse
  Where first-born sons have passed, to come no more.
She only brings to fruitfulness the seed
  That war has sown in tears and blasphemy
And startles to reality the deed
  Unborn in helplessness and agony.

Our Lady walks the sterile, darkened days,
  And mercy in her steps undesecrate
Floods the long shadow and the pathless ways
  Of unregenerate hate.

To acres bare of hope or of surprise,
  Deprived alone of vision and release,
She brings compassion and the glad surprise
  Of loveliness returning and of peace.
Spring is forever; roses still may bloom;
  Where she has passed no alien stars may glow
Deceptive, nor the cross distorted loom
  A clutching shadow where the fires burn low.

Our Lady walks the roads of hate and strife,
  Her veil upon a cleansing wind unfurled,
Herman the Cripple's dream of Hope and Life
  And Sweetness folding in a stricken world.

SISTER THOMAS AQUINAS, O.P.

Arbor Una Nobilis

When all our lovely words are blown away,
  Like petals from an apple-tree in spring;
When burnished leaves of wit have flashed their say,
  And fallen like bright chaff at harvesting;
This grief, a bare bough of reality,
  Holding the snows of heaven for an hour,
Shall be in bloom upon a single Tree
  Alive with Love, its rod, its root, its flower.

JOHN EDWARD SPEAR

If You Keep Faith with Me

If you keep faith with me, you need not weep
If I am killed, for I will not complain
Of any death if by it others gain
The things I think are worth my life to keep:
The right to have, to know, to love, to speak.
If all win these, I will endure my pain
And on the battle front where I have lain
Will find an honored place in which to sleep.

But if when peace returns to you once more
You break the word you gave humanity
By keeping not the pledge to which you swore,
Then carve in stone this epitaph for me:
"Here lies a fool who placed his hope in war
And gave his life to insincerity."

GLORIA T. STEIN

Heart's Poverty

Shattered, O Lord, is each enclosing wall.
Thou hast burst through this church on every side.
Demanding beams to part and rocks to fall,
Demanding entrance vaster, rooms more wide
Than eyes can offer or the mind contain.
How shall a low-roofed thought admit Thy height?
And how shall tongues announce Thee, who explainest
A guest whose radiance has lit the night?

At beggared hearts, why dost Thou stop and stay,
Stooping to enter that low wretchedness
Which owns no prideful furniture—display
Of its own wealth and wit and food and dress?
For now—as when a poor barn welcomed Thee—
Thou shalt be housed in each heart's poverty.

HENRY LONGAN STUART

Account Me Not

Account me not disgenuine that I wear
My Nessus-shirt of misery still bedeckt
With pitiful tinsel favors, still affect
Old fashions of flowers for the thorns I bear—
Nor, having made you confidant to my care,
Its worth to question and its shows suspect,
Bid me now change its utterance, now inflect
Anew its moods of passion or despair.

Friend, I have known you long—but sorrow longer.
She has no subtlety but my wit can reach.
Her arms my warders are, and surer—stronger
Their sweet compulsion grows than song could teach,
Since I must suffer and the art is mine,
To trick her torments and her pains refine.

A. M. SULLIVAN

Genesis

The light is music, and the first note breaks
The shuttered silence like a bird in flight;
This is not morning but the end of night,
The long night when the urge for being aches
In Time's slow womb, and a windy rhythm shakes
The shadows from the sun, and from the height
And breadth of Heaven fades the sullen blight
Of emptiness and God in joy awakes.

The layers of aeons crumble from the dark
Stirred by the anthem of angelic strings
And Order comes with a lordly whirr of wings
And worlds are made in the expanding arc
Of splendor till a last note finds its mark
And Man spits out the primal clay and sings.

377

Heritage

Where water folds across the stones
A kid glove over knuckle bones

And idles into pools, the trout
Lifts his speckled body out

Once, twice, and thrice he hurls
A whip of steel against the swirls,

Then leaps the rapids, and in air
Curves a note of music there

And with a swift contrary will
Climbs the staircase of the hill.

Villanelle of Light

Time is no measure, there is only light
To gauge the distance in the curve of dark.
Man blinks and holds the heavens in his sight.

The window's square describes the width and height
Of starry acres, never the chimes' long arc.
Time is no measure, there is only light.

Love gauges shelter in the gloom of night
By roof and wall, and with the sulphur spark.
Man blinks and holds the heavens in his sight.

Hate measures hatred by the steel in flight
But time will play her treason. Despots, hark:
Time is no measure, there is only light.

The tree of faith forever burning bright
Will brand the shadows with its golden bark.
Man blinks and holds the heavens in his sight.

We count the pulse beats with a secret fright
And watch space dwindle to a granite mark.
Time is no measure, there is only light;
Man blinks and holds the heavens in his sight.

Pilgrim

Grass is tougher than steel,
The sod outwears the spade,
The road outruns the wheel,
The task outlives the trade.

Here where I swing the scythe
And call the sudden clover,
Earth asks the season's tithe
Before the summer's over.

Earth's beauty I have found
Twice beautiful for change,
And my ear upon the ground
Hears music old and strange.

Life's answers are the same,
The questions vary only;
Man writes an ancient name
But men are new and lonely.

What little I have learned
Has added to my lack,
For the road has always turned
And never once led back.

Seismograph

The earth twitches its skin
Like a goaded elephant
And jars the electric pin
Which measures the irritant.

This is the pain recorder
Of the terrestrial ache
And sea disorder
By which men take
Heed of pressure points
By volcanic fountains,
And listen to creaking joints
In the fevered mountains.

It records earth's wounds
But never the patter
Of marching feet, nor sounds
Of iron throats that scatter
Hate on her crust.

Four horsemen who caper
In the horizon's red dust
Make no hoof prints on paper
Of the earth-geared drum,
No more than the deer
That plunges from
The scent of fear.

Jet Plane

Stung by the tail of a scorpion
Gravity loosens its grip
On the side of a hellion
Who scorches the sky
Through a curve of silence
While sound tumbles backward
In the tangled air.

The monster with open mouth
Sucks food from runnels of light
Washing blue space
Through a furious gut.

Tiptoe on the flattened world
The watchers are asking their eyes
If a dragon that swallows flame
Can burrow a hole
In the sagging roof of the morning.

Upon a ladder of smoke
The monster touches the zenith
But gravity roused from its spell
Reaches toward rafters of sunlight
And drags the scorpion down
To a crevice of earth.

RICHARD SULLIVAN

The Stranger

Once I knew for every rain
    the loving cloud: and knew
what way it came, by lake, plain,
    what way it swung and blew.

Intensest green of leaves, and smell
    of dew, bright sweeping beach
yellow beneath the blue-white swell
    of little waves—I knew each

and all: ached sometimes with thunder,
    burned and shrunk in sun:
with air about and earth under
    was one.

Once then I lived familiarly.
    I had put, I said, my seal
on my own world, presumptuously.
    But now, alarmed, I feel

a new wind; these stars are strange;
    this moon is not the same
as hung at home; that black range
    of hills has no name.

FRANCIS SWEENEY, S.J.

April

The fragile affirmations of the springtime
Glitter in the leaden darts of rain.
Shall I cut my coat this April to my cloth,
Bind the selvage with the cord of fear and antique grief?

Do not speak to me of the quick blades, oiled against the rust,
Or of the red caves of loneness, chasm on chasm under my
    feet,
Or the fire that burneth bitterly in the heart.
Though brow and nostril do not know the flame.

Your specious syllogisms tumble in my conscious throat,
Oh April, dear false Portia of my cause,
And though the notaries eat cakes upon my oaths,
And the priests have blessed to weariness my posture of
    contrition,
Speak, April, loveliest of liars,
And though I run and stop my ears I listen and *credo* I
    believe.

Tanglewood

Like buckskin and broadcloth and strange American shillings,
Like samplers and pistols and dry Plymouth mayflowers,
The lovely, various music of our people
Is gathered now and treasured here in Berkshire.
Shrill on the wind the fifes of Lexington,
The riot of the fiddles in a backwoods tavern,
The spinet's elocution in a Gramercy parlor,
Implicit in the sighing, wind-wroth trees.
Here where the clouds have room to cast their shadows
As wide as townships on the far, bright water,
In these sweet meadows tilted from the lakeside,
Where Hawthorne's daughters gathered ox-eyed daisies,
America has built a place of song.

In a Class of Moral Theology

This was the fire that ran in the wake of the promise
Like bird-prattle as morning stormed hill after hill.
We have learned too well the ultimate craft
Ten thousand times more ready than the crossbow or the
　　mace,
And torn up distance like a madman's letter.
But still the swallows nest as once in Ur and Ascalon
And still our hearts go the same road under the earth.

Cain bludgeoned down his brother in a field
Last week in Georgia,
(And Abel, being black, went unavenged).
The girl who saunters in the evening streets
Was booty to an Assyrian conqueror;
Came in a troop of yellow-haired German harlots
To Venice on a Renaissance April.

Far off the insensible hammers ring the noon's long chime,
Hammers rapping clear and small like the ticking of a watch,
Pounding together and then one insensible hammer beating
　　on.
And we are wise as gods and know not what we do.
Cry mercy on us, brother with the briar garland,
My mock laureate, my minstrel hanged for a thief,
My weary Christ deaddrooping on the nails.

382

JOHN L. SWEENEY

The Wind's Head

Wherever the wind's head walks
with its proud antlers bending
the weather, canting south and north
to toss a cornstalk cloud
into a corner of the torn sky, I
see the danger of talk, the swift
evaporation of will into a drift
of words, the condensation of thought
loosed like a toy balloon, soon
out of reach of all but the wind's head.

Only an artful calm
the guarded eye
the quiet ready arm
can serve. For
we have learned to fear
the livid nerve
that twitches near
the wounded tiger's heart.

ANNE TANSEY

There Must Be Silence

We must have silence where we go
Like the hush that follows snow.

There can be no leafy stir,
No sudden dash of sylvan fur.

No wind can blow delight away
Or mar the glory of our day.

Earth must lay its voices low;
There must be silence where we go,

So we can hear eternal bells
And echoes of a Voice that tells

In accents low and crystal clear
Things the heart is keyed to hear.

383

There must be silence where we go
Like the hush of falling snow.

Hearts are weary and afraid
Of the noises time has made.

Earth must quiet every sound
With warning fingers all around.

For messages to lessen fears,
For sounds that only Heaven hears,

For strains of Love's adagio,
There must be silence where we go.

SARAH WINGATE TAYLOR

The Master-Welder

Spirit is caged, they said, its prison flesh.
Aquin replied: No part of us
but serves! He welded whole
man's grip on body-and-soul.
They said: The ancients lied
their pagan light is dead. Thomas replied:
Reason was theirs, God-given!
And he reached, healing what time had riven,
purged dross, till all merged good;
no loss, sealing their sages
ours, blending one wealth of ages.

Wanly today: Man's mind and heart
(they say) are rent apart,
each in its alien distance kept
at war, crying our bitter need
somehow to find, bind, succor that shattered core.
St. Thomas stood intent
communing with Wisdom in the Sacrament,
till wholly suffused in Light, wholly in Love,
made one as God designed,
this titan man of mind
knew ecstasy, and wept.

Scholar and saint,
who forged great argument,
be it your way with us

384

no further to lighten mind
than love of humankind:
Oh, piteous,
let not our heart be blind!

Hope

Rash virtue, whose ambitious wing
too little heeding stress of storm
droops frayed on the gale, or plummeting
lies groveled with the lowliest worm;

vain mimic angel, plumage roiled
in giddy brashness, wan display,
what though the halcyon once beguiled
rude winds to calm, that's myth today.

Now fast to the haggard's roost until
some seasonal wisdom dawns; be shrewd,
submit to leash and jess, with skill
of vision chastening in your hood.

Mad innocent creature, battered sprite,
my pretty hope, poor fragile thing,
so wounded from your vaunted height,
gird next with steel that filmy wing.

Stancher my bird turned weatherwise,
come capable as the canny hawk,
lurk out the gales or gently rise;
circle, circle where you stalk.

Yet keep one sharper aim than all:
guard with most care that buttressed wing
whose sturdy lift makes my festival,
homing sweet quarry in songs you sing.

MARY DIXON THAYER

To Elizabeth

This I have read in some old book and wise,
Penned long ago by one who understood
The heart of man, and looked with seeing eyes
Upon the world, and evil things and good:

"Here where all changes and naught can endure,"
He wrote, "here where all beauty dwells with pain,
And love which at the first was deep and pure
By love of self is often rendered vain—
Here, when the many meet, they meet to turn
Back from the steep and toilsome upward way;
Few meet to rise together—few, to spurn
That which is base, to work, and climb, and pray.
Precious is friendship when friend calls to friend,
'Be strong! Here is my hand. Let us ascend!' "

FREDERIC THOMPSON

Plan for a Novel

Cut out the deep design of life,
Leave but the fancy edges,
The filigrees and minarets,
Gargoyles and spires,
High, narrow ledges,
And tendrils flung so far from solid centre
The ends attenuate to next to nothing,
And let the bulk seem pendulous
Through mists in a still dawn,
A miracle, afloat in the infinite.

FRANCIS BEAUCHESNE
THORNTON

Snow Meditation

There is no rest in falling, even so
The wind will drive the rain
In spatters, buffet the snow
In barbs of crystalline pain.

There is no rest in falling.
Lucifer, star of the morning,
When the void blazed
With your downward-quenching,
Air and angel-thought stood amazed,
Blenching.

Down, down you went
Into the clutching gloom
Whose icy depths freeze, torture
Love to lust,
Nobleness to creeping, crawling, weeping things;
Writhes to suspicion trust.

There is no rest in falling; rings,
Sings that sound!
(His voice has gone out into the earth!)
Sky and ground,
Sea and gaunt headlands
Shatter in a blaze of melody.

It is snow,
Falling snow, O Lucifer! . . .
He turns on his aching bars
Of twisted intellect,
Remembering stars.

JAMES EDWARD TOBIN

Song above Death

["Polish underground journal, *Culture of Tomorrow*, flooded
with entries for poetry contest; winners executed."]

Let the bright blood flow; starve and liquidate;
You cannot stop a river's source,
Trampling with boots of mad and mudded hate.
Scatter the bones with frenzied force:
A new-born race once sprang at Cadmus' feet.

Raze ruthlessly; a shard of wall still points
With witness fingers. Warsaw falls
But not Parnassus, for the Muse anoints
Her poets. Unslain song appalls
The murderer, burning with dragon heat.

Cut out a nation's tongue, it yet shall speak!
Maim, blind, lash, guillotine, and burn—
Yet shall the dying sing, their voices weak
But deathless. Even vultures turn:
The flesh of executioners is not sweet.

Conversation in Clichés

DEFOE:
The self-made hero, marked by virtue man
Defines—assiduous, assertive, bold—
Alert to occupy the Stuarts' place
Made vacant by extravagance, what can
He not attain, what good can not be sold
For honest profit, and what missing grace
Can not be purchased. This is true renown:
The triumph of the practical set down
And duly ledgered as a tradesman's gain.
Your man Lanier objects—

WHITMAN:
                                    An ugly stain
Upon the map of man's bright continent,
A misfit and a renegade, *outré,*
Who thinks that music, art-inspired, for strings
And reeds, can bring a true comrade-content:
And not what individuals can say
About intestine subtleties of things.
The free, untrammeled talk of men *en masse*
Is like the uprightness of trodden grass,
Each brother blade unique, and crying loud
That it disdains impress—

FRANKLIN:
                                    Land can be ploughed
And average man turned under. Find in each
The rebel, and equip him with a phrase;
An epigram, an adage, can confuse
The unenlightened who will never reach
To brush away the dusty spider's-maze
The past has spun. Then this elect will choose
To walk as destined, to accept no peer,
Control clouds, trap the elements, revere
No unheard voice; respect instead brave drum
And bugle words the printing presses hum.

Cradle Song of a Celtic Queen

I kneel beside you quietly, my son,
Born of a king, born of a kingly prayer;
I pray for you, long, long, my little one,
That you may rid your people's brow of care.

388

That you may be the courser of a spring
To free our weary, winter-bondaged land,
To oust the frost, and to an ending bring
The tyranny of the usurper's hand.

That you may be a dual stalk of corn:
A feast for us, tabled with golden gaiety,
But for our enemies the mark forlorn
Of famine, of a scarred and storm-slain tree.

That you may be a pale bloom, orchard-white,
Our fruit, but for our enemies a branch
Of barren wood, plague-pale, and pocked with blight,
Diseased by that before which all leaves blanch.

That you may be a plough to break the earth,
Turning warm waves of loam, but for them, stones;
For us, dawn's eye and a bright future's birth,
For them, night's crutch, and the past's bleaching bones.

That you may be a shower of slaking rain,
Our sweet well-treasure, but for them the drought;
A banner in our vanguard, the refrain
Of heroes shouting—and the wail of rout.

A burnished weapon: for your people's pride
A shield against the enemy, a face
Reflecting fear, but on the inner side
The mirrored picture of your princely grace.

That in your glory you be called a hound,
To bound across the moors pursuing game;
That every glen and hill may hail the sound
Of your swift feet, proud echo of your name.

GERVASE TOELLE, O. Carm.

Fra Carmelo's Morning Sacrifice

While he says Mass, Carmelo's sins
And he consort alone
Before the clement Father's bright
And most accessible throne.

389

Melkisadek, and Linus, Paul,
All went the lonesome way
That he repeats meticulously
At half-past-five each day.

He has no eyes: the angels on
The reredos all are lost
In love; the server on the step
Weighs premium and cost,

And wonders if his small prestige
Outscales the early hours;
A virgin in the foremost pew
Counts beads, and marks the flowers.

If ever love Carmelo knew,
Or ever any beauty priced,
Desired and got, returned or shared,
He kept his mind on Christ.

The ambiguity of love
Is jackstraws undecided where
To fall; is iron shavings spread
By chance, and torn between a pair

Of poles; a needle-point prepared
To turn beneath Carmelo's skin
If he should fall, or foil, or fail
To lose himself by entering in

This blessed, this ratified, this most
Acceptable round of bread
He blesses, breaks. He bows his high
With borrowed glory head

And mumbles "This is wine . . ." A fog
Of thick devotion lingers
As God is lifted up in stiff
And nicotine stained fingers.

ETTA MAY VAN TASSEL

A Joy as Old as Breathing

All lovely things: a bell across the snow,
The first faint star of evening shining pale;
The blue dusk gathered like an angel's veil;
The winter wind at sunset fallen low—
All these, my friend, as laughter lives in light,
Worship in wonder, joy in sweetest song,
Do in the thought of you by natural right
Most truly live and perfectly belong.
That this was true, an axiom too dear
For reason's careful question, I well knew;
For, in all years, when mystery drew near
Then I was comforted and close to you.
The thing I do not know is why, tonight,
A joy as old as breathing grows so bright.

The Splendid Flower

Now joy, the flower of heaven,
    Blossoms tonight,
Lifting, through earth's dark sorrows,
    Petals of light.

Joy fills the hearts of millions
    Heavy with dread;
Joy soothes the frightened children
    Crying for bread.

That other Child, the Outcast
    Of Bethlehem,
Enters their desolation
    To comfort them.

Takes in His arms the helpless,
    Shelters the lost;
Shares with the least, the weakest,
    War's bitter cost.

Now, in the earth and heaven,
    Serene and tall,
Opens the splendid flower
    Over us all.

391

J. PATRICK WALSH, S.J.

Now That You Are Gone

Now that you are gone I must stand to my arms,
because the whole world sees the new-made breach,
and the sky swoops down like a bombing attack,
and the worms move in like engineers.

Now that you are gone the walls are uneasy,
the traitors hiss in corners like cold snakes,
the crowds move restlessly in the streets,
and children lean from the windows with uncertain eyes.

We had made friends together of so many,
but now the mountains menace me alone.

I will not put you up for a dead hero,
nor instigate a purge to pay for you—
What could I kill?—nor seek alliances
to buttress my state with morning-trousered ministers.

I wait upon the event, shocked by the sniper-fire
of roads so friendly once upon a time,
sent staggering by rooms,
blasted by voices and a turn of words.

Mostly I dread the silent inner knives
that I, in the prevailing treachery, turn on myself.

The end belongs neither to you nor me,
as the whole rejoicing world shrinks to this—
I will keep faith: honor your name like a banner
and look upon your remembered face like a star.

For the Magi

In the end,
not valor, ecstasy of motion or of music,
high banners or the tricks with which
we spring the mine of passion in the breast
will take us home;
but in the mind,
the cold and wet-walled prison of the mind,
with fetters clanking and the high,
small single window to the light,
the prisoner the soul

will on the involuting, cold and fading trail
persist in searching,
till home he comes—
not like a traveler all stained and weary
whom air familiar bathes in blissfulness,
but like a stone
upon embattled walls from the blue air,
a catapulted stone kicked by the will,
shattering parapets, roofs and bearing terror,
drives through the hedge of spears, the lapping shields,
and striking the solid earth to make it tremble,
comes at the last to rest.

WILLIAM F. WALSH

Conversation

If I turn to the lady on my left, and say,
"The religious culture, although superior to the economic,
Is so intermingled with it,
That if we remove the economy, the religion falls,"
She will ask bright questions.

But if I say, "The moment I die
I expect to be catapulted
Into the presence of God,
And I hope to hear the word
'Always'
Uttered as human never spoke it,"
She will have a sudden headache,
And ask to be excused.

I am left with the live coal of knowledge.

WILLIAM THOMAS WALSH

Marriage Song

You are more beautiful than light
 That trips across a waking lawn,
To pour on jonquils washed with night
 The hoarded prism of the dawn.

393

You are more lovely than the ray
    That trembles on a new-born leaf
When dusk steals on the drowsy day
    To gloat on beauty like a thief.

Since that white flaming speechless hour
    When vast and overshadowed wings
Housed you with Joy itself, the Power
    To whom its own perfection sings,

O bride of uncreated light,
    Caressed by love's infinity,
There dwells no dark in any night,
    No danger lurks on land or sea.

Requiem

Out of the silence, the wind,
Out of the darkness, the stars,
Into the cold earth, the corpse, the corpse—
    Ah, never mind!

Out of my labor, my mirth,
Out of anxiety, peace;
Out of the cold grave my soul, my soul,
    Shedding his earth.

Out of my sinning, despairs,
Out of my penance, my hope,
And my new soul weaving, weaving
    A robe from your prayers.

LEO L. WARD, C.S.C.

Marginalia for Pentecost

I have heard song through the leaves
And the bird hidden,
In the shattered moment known
What is forgotten

To the heart insatiate, breaking
With sated yearning.
There are no letters that can spell
Our deepest learning.

No analysis can reveal this
To the mind's blindness.
No formula can explain ever
The bird's kindness.

Oh let the bird sing through the leaves
To the heart, broken,
The word that is forever silent,
Forever spoken.

JOHN WICKHAM

Song: To a Lady with Many Names

I will sing you a song full of quiet fire,
And ease my heart with your praises:
"Fair Maid, Summer Mead, Far-Mountain's Desire,
Warm Evening when firefly blazes,
Blue Sail on the lake, running-hill's Sudden Spire,
White Light, where the wild moth crazes."

I have seen green trees in the winter wood
And heard their soundful sighing;
And I loved them more when they horrid stood,
Summer elm and aspen defying:
But what if the leaves sooner fall than they should,
And the loon is no longer crying?

"Fair Maid, Summer Mead, Far-Mountain's Desire,
Warm Evening when firefly blazes,
Blue Sail on the lake, running-hill's Sudden Spire,
White Light, where the wild moth crazes,"
I will sing you a song full of quiet fire,
And ease my heart with your praises.

395

ROBERT WILBERFORCE

"Peace Is the Tranquillity of Order"

The splendours of this passing world
    Reflected in the mind
Offer a more imperial prize
    To those who seek and find.

When I have found the way of peace
    No king surpasses me.
My rule extends beyond the land,
    Beyond the distant sea.

My palaces are numberless;
    A throne in every town;
A scepter can be mine at will
    While memories form my crown.

But if above this kingdom
    I abdicate my sway,
Fierce warfare suddenly breaks out.
    My realm's in disarray.

To govern all these imaged things,
    The subjects of our thought,
The secret of an ordered peace
    Is in the rule Christ made.

JOHN HAZARD WILDMAN

To Pius X at Easter

Pius, the springtime rolls like a wave upon our land,
White-capped in bloom above the long-flung green,
With flame and rainbowed spray
Audacious, sudden, in the fierce engendering sun.

Strange wise men drone about the vast significance
Of all of this:
They draw on Tennyson and violets,
On hope resurgent and the brave atomic bomb;
And chorus girls in white samite
Put over the Resurrection in the city park.

The springtime spreads upon our land,
A splendid growth this time,
Seeking interpretation,
Knowing no answer for its roots within the tomb,
Finding no solution in the cold, unanswering ground.

We, feeling, too, the life within us stir—
The silver flower in the golden light—
Ask why, and will not take
The symbol for the reason,
Nor walk in blindness in the splendid dawn.

O holy man of God, wise pope,
Who spoke the bold, tremendous words of life
And blazoned Peter's promised strength
And Paul's bright sword against the night
And pointed newly to the minds of men
The clean, hard facts that gave the symbols truth
And cursed the sentimental lies
That lay upon us like the coddling hand of death—
Be strong for us in prayer
That in our dark, evasive days
We hold the simple truth
Of reclaimed flesh and broken tomb
And know the flame within
The glad, outrageous symbol of the spring.

MICHAEL WILLIAMS

Michael the Archangel

In white splendors and red terrors my thoughts
    Are like the lightnings of the Lord;
From abysmal vasts they spring in flame and
    Rush like wind—each one a sword,
That on the farthest frontiers of man's soul
    Maintains the Word.

Nuptial

There was a bride (the Gospel goes),
But whom she married no one knows;
Or if indeed she ever had
A likely lad.

Yet does it matter if she be
A shadow in antiquity?
That no man knows her height or weight
Or what she ate?

For of all brides who are, and were,
No one has ever equaled her—
That misty maid from out the East
Who gave a feast.

Who was so gracious that the Lord
Came down to grace her wedding board;
To wrest the wine from out the water
And woo a daughter.

Alas, that modern brides are girls
In satins and synthetic curls—
That no man dreams on Cana's child,
Who sipped . . . and smiled.